Foreword

This year we celebrate the 75th anniversary of the Battle of Britain. It is fitting that we mark this significant moment in our Nation's history; the ravages of time are gradually denying us the company of the 'Few'. We must also ensure future generations never forget the sacrifices made for their freedom.

During the summer of 1940 the UK faced the threat of invasion for the first time since 1805, when Napoleon assembled a fleet to carry his army to our shores. On that occasion the threat was defeated by naval action. In 1940 the threat was defeated in the first major campaign to be fought entirely by air forces.

Young men of many nationalities flew their Hurricanes and Spitfires at the spearhead of our defence. Then, as now, they were supported adeptly by the skilled work and dedication of ground crew, radar operators, fighter controllers and many others. Victory ultimately lay in the Royal Air Force's adaptability and capability, employing the latest in radar technologies and cutting edge fighter aircraft, and the quality of its people. These factors remain the cornerstone of the Royal Air Force today.

Several of the Battle of Britain squadrons remain operational today, not least Number 1 (Fighter) Squadron, which flew Hawker Hurricanes to secure the skies of the UK in 1940 and today operates the Eurofighter Typhoon in exactly the same role. This edition of *Salute* celebrates that remarkable history and examines aspects of our continuing capability in combat air, aerospace battle management and flying training, as well as the essential role played by the Reserves.

The primary focus of our public celebration and commemoration this year will naturally and rightfully be the Royal Air Force Battle of Britain Memorial Flight; its Spitfire Mk II is the world's oldest airworthy Spitfire and a Battle of Britain veteran. The Flight will also provide a Spitfire to fly alongside its 21st century equivalent, the Typhoon, in a spectacular 75th anniversary Synchro Display at several air shows and other events this summer.

I hope that *Salute* will entertain and educate, both helping to ensure that the work of the Royal Air Force in 1940 is never forgotten and illustrating how the capabilities and traditions vital to victory then are as relevant and crucial to our Nation's defence today and into the future.

Air Chief Marshal Sir Andrew Pulford
KCB CBE ADC, RAF

Contents

06 Timeline 1940
Although it was massively engaged in fending off the threat of invasion during the Battle of Britain, the RAF was also embroiled in desperate combat in the Mediterranean and North African theatres

14 Denmark to Dunkirk
Ill prepared to meet the rushing onslaught of Nazi supremacy, the RAF fought valiantly to stem the blitzkrieg sweeping Western Europe in the spring of 1940. Colonel Douglas C Dildy, USAF (Retd) explains

18 The Commanders
Air Commodore Graham Pitchfork (Retd) tells the stories of Dowding, Park and Leigh-Mallory, the key commanders at the head of the Battle of Britain defence

24 Battle Joined
Colonel Douglas C Dildy, USAF (Retd) charts the Battle's course

34 Air Defence: 2015
Flight Lieutenant Lucy Williams, an Aerospace Battle Manager at RAF Boulmer, describes today's UK air defence system

36 Air Defence: 1940
The Air Historical Branch's Seb Cox describes the Dowding System and its vital contribution to victory

44 Synchro 75
Flight Lieutenants Antony 'Parky' Parkinson and Ben Westoby-Brooks are flying a Typhoon/Spitfire Synchro display at venues up and down the UK to mark the 75th anniversary of the Battle. Paul E Eden talked to them about the routine, their motivation and a very special Typhoon

50 For Valour 1940
The desperate days of 1940 saw acts of tremendous courage. Air Commodore Graham Pitchfork (Retd) tells the stories of the RAF's five Victoria Cross recipients

56 Fighter Stations Old and New
Paul E Eden looks at RAF Lossiemouth, the UK's newest fighter station, and IWM Duxford, a typical Battle of Britain airfield that remains largely unaltered today

62 WAAFs at War
The Women's Auxiliary Air Force placed female personnel on the frontline for the first time in RAF history

68 The World of the Few
Geoff Simpson, a trustee of the Battle of Britain Memorial Trust, delves into the peculiar world of the 'Few'

Cover image: Royal Air Force Battle of Britain Memorial Flight Hurricane Mk II LF363, in 1 Sqn Battle of Britain colours, flies alongside the 75th anniversary Synchro Typhoon. Richard Paver

This image: Hurricanes from 615 Sqn return to their Northolt base. RAF (AHB)/© UK MoD Crown Copyright 2015

Published in association with Royal Air Force Media and Communications, Headquarters Air Command

EDITORIAL
Editor: Paul E Eden

DESIGN
Studio Manager: Steve Donovan
Design: Tracey Mumby

PRODUCTION
Production Manager:
Janet Watkins

ADVERTISING and MARKETING
Senior Advertisement Manager:
Alison Sanders
Advertising Group Manager:
Brodie Baxter
Advertising Production Manager:
Debi McGowan
Group Marketing Manager:
Martin Steele
Marketing:
Shaun Binnington, Debra Hagger, Amy Donkersley

COMMERCIAL DIRECTOR:
Ann Saundry
PUBLISHER and MANAGING DIRECTOR: Adrian Cox
EXECUTIVE CHAIRMAN:
Richard Cox

CONTACTS
Key Publishing Ltd
PO Box 100, Stamford,
Lincolnshire, PE9 1XQ, UK
Tel: 01780 755131
Fax: 01780 757261
E-mail: enquiries@keypublishing.com
www.keypublishing.com

DISTRIBUTION
Seymour Distribution Ltd
2 Poultry Avenue, London EC1A 9PP
020 7429 400

PRINTED BY
Warners (Midlands) plc, The Maltings, Bourne, Lincs PE10 9PH

The entire contents of RAF Salute 2015 is copyright © UK MoD Crown Copyright 2015. No part of this publication may be copied or reproduced without prior written consent of the UK Ministry of Defence.

PUBLISHER
Key Publishing Ltd
PRINTED IN ENGLAND

74 A Very Special Spitfire
Squadron Leader Clive Rowley MBE RAF (Retd) tells the story of the Battle of Britain Memorial Flight's Spitfire Mk IIA, the Battle's only airworthy Spitfire veteran

82 The Many Behind the Few
Ground crew and other personnel at RAF fighter stations found themselves under attack and well and truly on the frontline during the Battle of Britain, as Stuart Hadaway of the Air Historical Branch (RAF) explains

85 Spitfire Down!
Although it survived to fly again, the Battle of Britain Memorial Flight's Spitfire Mk IIA was shot down in the closing stages of the Battle of Britain, as Squadron Leader Clive Rowley MBE RAF (Retd) reveals

88 First In All Things
Very few of the Battle of Britain squadrons remain operational in the same role. As Paul E Eden discovered, 1 (Fighter) Squadron is a notable exception, continuing its air defence mission with the Eurofighter Typhoon

92 Reserves on the Frontline
Then as now, the RAF's Reserve strength was of critical importance to its success, as trustee of the Battle of Britain Memorial Trust, Geoff Simpson reports

94 Training to Fly, Then… and Now
Air Commodore Graham Pitchfork (Retd) and Wing Commander Chris Cartmell, Officer Commanding 72 (Reserve) Squadron, examine and describe RAF flying training in 1940 and today

January 11: No. 77 Sqn crews, in apparently ebullient mood, assemble prior to a leafleting sortie to Prague and Vienna from their Villeneuve-Vertus base in France. RAF (AHB)/© UK MoD Crown Copyright 2015

Timeline 1940

Royal Air Force Fighter Command's victory in the Battle of Britain was the Service's major action of 1940, but RAF Bomber and Coastal Commands were also in combat, while resources were committed to the war in North Africa and the Mediterranean

January

1   Identification friend or foe (IFF) coding was introduced on RAF Bomber Command, Coastal Command and Fighter Command aircraft, assisting in their automatic identification by radio interrogation. Very high frequency (VHF) radio transmitters (R/T) were completed in eight of Fighter Command's sectors
11   Armstrong Whitworth Whitleys from 77 Sqn leafleted Prague and Vienna
30   A 228 Sqn Short Sunderland shared the sinking of a German submarine with two Royal Navy ships. It was Coastal Command's first success against a U-boat

16   A 220 Sqn Lockheed Hudson located the auxiliary ship *Altmark* in Norwegian waters and carrying British prisoners of war picked up from the sea after their vessels were sunk by the pocket battleship *Admiral Graf Spee*. Royal Navy sailors subsequently boarded *Altmark* and released the captives
25   The first Royal Canadian Air Force (RCAF) unit deployed to fight alongside the RAF arrived in the UK

February

February 16: A 220 Sqn Hudson captured this image of *Altmark* moored in Jøssingfjord, Norway. RAF (AHB)/© UK MoD Crown Copyright 2015

6   No. 5 Operational Training Unit (OTU), the first Fighter Command OTU, formed at RAF Aston Down, Gloucestershire
7   Whitleys from 77 Sqn leafleted Poznan in the first such mission over Poland
11   Coastal Command scored its first solo success against a U-boat, when an 82 Sqn Bristol Blenheim sank *U-31*
12   The so-called Winter War between the Soviet Union and Finland ended. The Gloster Gladiators of 263 Sqn, ready to deploy in Finland's aid, stood down
16   Britain's civilian population suffered its first casualties of World War Two when Luftwaffe bombers attacked naval targets in Scapa Flow, Orkney Islands

March

TIMELINE

April 4: Number 75 'New Zealand' Squadron formed on the Vickers Wellington. RAF (AHB)/© UK MoD Crown Copyright 2015

May 29: The Defiant crews of 264 Sqn surprised the Luftwaffe with their unusually configured aircraft over Dunkirk, scoring the type's greatest combat success. RAF (AHB)/© UK MoD Crown Copyright 2015

April

1   The first Coastal Command OTU, No. 1, formed at RAF Silloth, Cumbria

3   Air Marshal Sir Charles Portal became Air Officer Commanding-in-Chief (AOC-in-C) RAF Bomber Command

4   Bomber Command's first Commonwealth unit, 75 'New Zealand' Squadron, formed

6   The first Bomber Command OTU, No. 10 OTU formed at RAF Abingdon, Oxfordshire

8   A 204 Sqn Sunderland spotted German ships steaming for Norway

9   Germany invaded Denmark and Norway

10   The Night Interception Unit formed at RAF Tangmere, Sussex for trials with airborne interception (AI) radar

11   The RAF attacked Norwegian targets for the first time. Six 115 Sqn Vickers Wellingtons escorted by two 254 Sqn Blenheims were despatched against the airfield at Stavanger/Sola

12   Having suffered grievous losses in its daylight-bombing operations, Bomber Command abandoned pre-war thinking for a revised policy of night bombing

13   Handley Page Hampden bombers from 44, 49, 50, 61 and 144 Sqns began mining waters off the German coast

15   Bomber Command attacked a non-coastal target for the first time, when Blenheim Mk IV bombers struck the airfield at Trondheim, Norway

24   The pilots of 263 Sqn flew 18 Gladiators off the carrier HMS *Glorious*, landing on Norway's frozen Lake Lesjaskog to set up base. Eleven of the aircraft were destroyed on the ground and two more damaged machines burned, before the survivors moved to Setnesmoen. Operations continued until April 28, when the surviving squadron personnel evacuated by ship. In the course of 49 sorties they engaged enemy aircraft 37 times and shot down two Heinkel He 111 bombers

May

10   Germany invaded Belgium, Luxembourg and the Netherlands under the code name Fall Gelb (Case Yellow). Belgian, British, Dutch and French aircraft rose in a poorly co-ordinated defensive effort. Of 32 RAF Fairey Battles committed to action with the Advanced Air Striking Force (AASF) in mainland Europe, 20 were lost. Nos 77 and 102 Sqns launched the first RAF attacks against German mainland targets

12   No. 12 Squadron's Flying Officer DE Garland and Sergeant T Gray were posthumously awarded the Victoria Cross for their actions during a Battle attack against the Maastricht bridges over the River Meuse. These were the RAF's first Victoria Cross awards of World War Two

14   Seventy-one AASF Battles and Blenheims attacked German forces breaking through French lines. Forty-one were lost

15/16   Bomber Command launched a force of 99 Whitley and Wellington bombers against targets in the industrial Ruhr area of Germany, after the war cabinet gave permission for bombing east of the Rhine. Little was achieved thanks to difficulties in navigation and poor bombing accuracy, although 12 aircraft also attacked Belgian targets, making this the first time that Bomber Command had committed more than 100 aircraft simultaneously

16   Air Chief Marshal Sir Hugh Dowding, C-in-C Fighter Command, protested to Harold Balfour, the Under-Secretary of State for Air, over orders to send more fighter squadrons to France. He said the action would cause: "…the final, complete and irredeemable defeat of this country"

RAF Training Command began preparations to install bomb racks on its de Havilland Tiger Moth and North American Harvard trainers, for attacks on incoming invasion barges

17   Eleven of a dozen 82 Sqn Blenheims sent to attack German troops in Belgium were shot down. The survivor returned, but was too badly damaged to fly again

21   No. 263 Sqn returned to Norway, again launching its Gladiators from *Glorious*

23   The Supermarine Spitfire met the Messerschmitt Bf 109 in combat for the first time

26   With German forces driving the Allies back across Belgium and through France to the Channel coast, the order was given to recover surviving troops at Dunkirk. The RAF provided fighter cover over the Operation Dynamo beachhead from stations in the UK

The Hawker Hurricanes of 46 Sqn flew off HMS *Glorious* to join 263 Sqn's Gladiators in setting up base around Narvik

29   No. 264 Sqn's Boulton Paul Defiant crews claimed 17 Messerschmitts, 18 Junkers Ju 87s and a Ju 88 shot down over Dunkirk

The RAF's first use of VHF radio-telephone to control fighter operations took place over Dunkirk

ROYAL AIR FORCE SALUTE 2015 | 7

TIMELINE

July 14: RAF reconnaissance images like this led to the first Bomber Command raids on invasion barges being readied for Operation Sea Lion, the German invasion of Great Britain. RAF (AHB)/© UK MoD Crown Copyright 2015

June

1   Several Royal Netherlands Navy seaplanes arrived in the UK. They became the nucleus of the RAF's first Dutch unit, No. 320 Sqn
4   The evacuation from Dunkirk was completed. Some 338,226 Allied soldiers were recovered
8   After losing five aircraft for two damaged and three destroyed, the remnants of 46 and 263 Sqns withdrew, landing back aboard *Glorious*. A combined attack by the battlecruisers *Gneisenau* and *Scharnhorst* sank the carrier later that day. There were only two RAF survivors
10 Italy declared war on Great Britain and France, immediately attacking targets in the South of France
11 Italian aircraft attacked targets on Malta for the first time
    A 24 (Communications) Squadron de Havilland Flamingo flew Prime Minister Churchill to France so that he "could see what the French are going to do"
    Whitleys from 10, 51, 77 and 102 Sqns raided Turin and Genoa, in the first attacks against Italy
    Blenheims from 45, 55 and 113 Sqns struck the Italian airfield at El Adem, Libya, in the first RAF attack of the North African campaign
13 Flg Off Haywood scored the RAF's first kill against an Italian aircraft, shooting down a Savoia-Marchetti SM.81 bomber in his 94 Sqn Gladiator
14 Jersey Airways began evacuating equipment and personnel from the Channel Islands, with the assistance of 24 Sqn
    German troops marched into Paris
    Flg Off Dean scored the RAF's first kill over North Africa, downing an Italian Fiat CR.42 fighter in his 33 Sqn Gladiator
15 AASF Battles made their final attacks before withdrawing to Britain
17 The last of the British Expeditionary Force's Hurricanes flew from Nantes, Western France, to Tangmere, Essex
18 The last Hurricane squadrons in France, 1 and 73, withdrew
21 France capitulated to Germany
    The first two of many Hawker Hurricanes arrived on Malta to bolster the island's air defence
    The RAF Parachute Training School was formed at Ringway, Manchester
    The first of the Canadian Hurricane squadrons to fight alongside RAF units, 1 Sqn, RCAF, arrived in the UK. It became operational on August 17
22 Flt Lt Burge claimed the first bomber shot down over Malta, flying a Sea Gladiator nicknamed 'Faith'
28 Flt Lt Campbell and crew claimed the first Italian submarine of the war sunk. They destroyed a second vessel the following day, on both occasions flying a 230 Sqn Sunderland. Campbell alighted to rescue survivors from the second attack and was awarded the DFC for the action

July

1   Germany completed its occupation of the Channel Islands
    Bomber Command struck targets in northern and western Germany
    The RAF's first Polish squadron – No. 300 – formed. Nine more had been constituted by mid-October
3   Bomber Command attacked invasion barges for the first time
10 The Battle of Britain began, RAF Fighter Command combating Luftwaffe raids against the south coast and Channel convoys
    The RAF's first Czechoslovak squadron – No. 310 – formed
14 RAF reconnaissance aircraft returned with photographs showing German supplies and barges massed in Channel ports ready for Operation Sea Lion, the invasion of the UK
16 Hitler issued *War Directive No. 16*, calling for the RAF to be rendered ineffective prior to invasion under Operation Seelowe (Sea Lion)
22 Flg Off Ashfield, flying a Fighter Interception Unit Bristol Blenheim, claimed a Dornier Do 17 shot down at night, the first aircraft found and destroyed by a fighter using onboard air interception radar

TIMELINE

July 24: Oberleutnant Werner Bartel's III./JG 26 Bf 109E-1 fell to the guns of a No. 65 Sqn Spitfire over Margate, Kent. RAF (AHB)/© UK MoD Crown Copyright 2015

August 16: Hurricanes P3059/SD-N and P3208/SD-T of 501 Sqn take-off from their base at Gravesend to intercept a raid. Both were lost on August 18. Bf 109s bounced P3059 over Canterbury, its pilot, Plt Off Kenneth Lee ending up in hospital. Barely five minutes later, at 1.35pm, P3208 crashed at Calcott Hill, killing Plt Off John Bland. RAF (AHB)/© UK MoD Crown Copyright 2015

August 31: Luftwaffe bombs hit this 222 Sqn Spitfire on the ground at Hornchurch. RAF (AHB)/© UK MoD Crown Copyright 2015

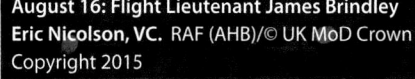

August 16: Flight Lieutenant James Brindley Eric Nicolson, VC. RAF (AHB)/© UK MoD Crown Copyright 2015

August 17: The memorial to US Plt Off William Fiske, who died of his wounds on August 18. RAF (AHB)/© UK MoD Crown Copyright 2015

1   Hitler issued *War Directive No. 17*, calling for the Luftwaffe to secure the RAF's destruction as quickly as possible while remaining fully prepared for Operation Seelowe

2   The Short Stirling, the RAF's first four-engined heavy bomber, entered service with 7 Sqn
    The first delivery of RAF Hurricanes by aircraft carrier to Malta was completed

8   The Battle of Britain entered its second phase, with fierce fighting over the Channel around Convoy CW9, while the Luftwaffe increasingly targeted radar stations and airfields

12 Luftwaffe attacks on radar sites and coastal airfields intensified
    Flight Lieutenant Roderick Learoyd pressed home his attack on the Dortmund-Elms canal, despite his Hampden being badly hit. He received the Victoria Cross for his actions

13 Known as Adlertag (Eagle Day) to the Luftwaffe, the 13th saw 1,500 sorties launched against Fighter Command airfields
    Eleven 82 Sqn Blenheims attacked the airfield at Aalborg, Denmark. All were lost, the second time in three months that the squadron had been forced out of existence

15 This day saw the heaviest fighting of the campaign. Three Luftflotten (air fleets) attacked the UK, flying from bases all along the European coast, from France to Norway

16 Flight Lieutenant James Nicolson's actions in remaining with his burning Hurricane to shoot down a Messerschmitt Bf 110 earned him Fighter Command's only Victoria Cross

17 Pilot Officer William Fiske, the first regular American pilot in RAF service, was seriously injured flying a 601 Sqn Hurricane. He died from his wounds next day
    Germany placed the UK under blockade, threatening to sink neutral vessels as soon as they were spotted
    Fighter pilot training was reduced so that student pilots could be transferred to Fighter Command to make good losses. New squadron pilots frequently had only 10 to 20 hours on the Hurricane or Spitfire

18 Known as 'the hardest day', the 18th saw the most ferocious attacks on airfields and radar units. Both sides took their heaviest losses of the campaign

21 The RAF formed its first unit to support the Special Operations Executive, No. 419 (Special Duties) Squadron

24 The Battle of Britain entered its third phase, with attacks on fighter stations near London and an increase in the Luftwaffe's night-time sortie rate

25/26 Bomber Command attacked Berlin for the first time, the War Cabinet having approved raids on the German capital after attacks on London the previous day. Fourteen Whitleys from 51 and 78 Sqns, 12 Hampdens from 61 and 144 Sqns, and eight Wellingtons from 99 and 149 Sqns flew the mission

27 Responsibility for disposing of unexploded bombs at RAF stations and near crashed aircraft was assigned to the RAF. Initially performed by armourers, the work passed to specialist Mobile Bomb Disposal Squads from September

August

September: Personnel at work inside the Sector 'G' Operations Room at Duxford, Cambridgeshire. The censor's pen has been at work removing information that was sensitive in this September 1940 photograph, including squadron identification details and maps. RAF (AHB)/© UK MoD Crown Copyright 2015

September 17: London was hit repeatedly through September. These Dornier Do 17Z bombers were over the India Rubber factory in the city's Canning Town area on the 17th. RAF (AHB)/© UK MoD Crown Copyright 2015

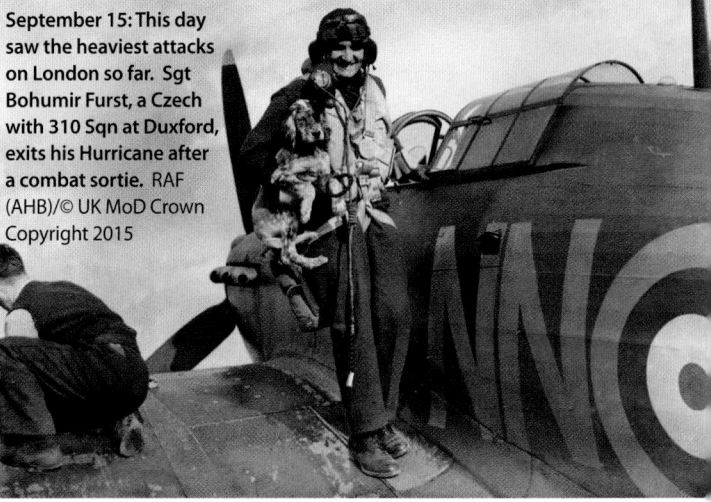

September 15: This day saw the heaviest attacks on London so far. Sgt Bohumir Furst, a Czech with 310 Sqn at Duxford, exits his Hurricane after a combat sortie. RAF (AHB)/© UK MoD Crown Copyright 2015

6   Based on photographs gathered by RAF reconnaissance aircraft showing barges and materiel continuing to concentrate at Channel ports, the UK was put on alert for imminent invasion

7   Commander-in-Chief of the Luftwaffe Reichsmarschall Hermann Göring took personal control of the offensive against the UK. In his frustration at Fighter Command's continued ability to counter Luftwaffe attacks, Göring halted raids on RAF airfields and instead tasked his bombers directly against London. The largest air combat ever, involving 1,200 aircraft and lasting 35 minutes, was fought as the capital came under direct attack for the first time

13   For the first time a balloon barrage accounted for an enemy aircraft. An He 111 crashed near Newport, South Wales after hitting a 966 Sqn balloon following a raid

15   Göring launched the heaviest strike yet against London, but the switch to attacking the city had allowed the RAF to remuster; it inflicted severe losses on the enemy

15/16   Wireless operator/air gunner Sergeant John Hannah fought a fierce blaze aboard his 83 Sqn Hampden caused by enemy fire over Antwerp. He was awarded the VC for his actions

17   A 29 Sqn Beaufighter flew the first operational night-fighter sortie using AI.Mk IV radar

19   US volunteer pilots flying with RAF squadrons were assembled at Church Fenton, in the West Riding of Yorkshire, to form 71 'Eagle' Squadron. The unit became operational, on the Hurricane, in December

       An initial convoy carrying Hurricanes for RAF units in the Middle East arrived at Takoradi in West Africa

September

TIMELINE

September 7: The Luftwaffe turned its attention to London, mounting massive raids on the capital. Here burning behind the backdrop of Tower Bridge, the Docklands area was a primary target. RAF (AHB)/© UK MoD Crown Copyright 2015

Squadrons Then and Now

Number	Established	Initial aircraft	Aircraft in 1940	2015 role	Aircraft
7	May 1, 1914	R.E.5, F.B.9 (from April 1915)	Hampden, Anson, Stirling	Support Helicopter	Chinook
10	January 1, 1915	B.E.2c	Whitely	Air Transport & Air-to-Air Refuelling	Voyager
12	February 4, 1915	B.E.2c	Battle, Wellington (from November)	Offensive Support	Tornado
24	September 21, 1915	DH.2	Hart (until March); Tiger Moth, Mentor and Envoy (until October); Rapide; Dominie; DH.86B; Magister; Vega Gull; Q.6; Electra; Flamingo; Hertfordshire (October); Hudson and Proctor (from June); Anson and Oxford (from July); Wellington (from August); Cleveland	Air Transport	Hercules
29	November 7, 1915	DH.2	Blenheim, Beaufighter (from September)	Operational Conversion	Typhoon
33	January 12, 1916	B.E.2, Scout	Gauntlet, Gladiator, Hurricane	Support Helicopter	Puma
45	March 1, 1916	1½ Strutter	Blenheim	Flying Training	King Air
51	May 15, 1916	B.E.2, B.E.12	Whitley	ISTAR	Rivet Joint
99	August 15, 1917	DH.9	Wellington	Air Transport	C-17
230	August 1918	Felixstowe F.2A	Sunderland	Support Helicopter	Puma

1 The Battle of Britain entered its final phase. The Luftwaffe offensive switched to daylight fighter-bomber attacks and heavy night-time raids on London
5 Air Chief Marshal Sir Richard Pierse became C-in-C RAF Bomber Command
12 Hitler ordered Operation Sea Lion postponed until spring 1941
19 A 419(SD) Sqn Westland Lysander completed the first successful extraction of an agent from France. Flt Lt Farley landed in a field to pick up Philippe Schneidau
25 Air Chief Marshal Sir Charles Portal became Chief of the Air Staff
28 Italy invaded Greece. By the end of the year, the RAF had responded by sending three Blenheim and two Gladiator squadrons to Greece
31 Although the Battle of Britain was officially considered to have ended on this date, Luftwaffe bombers continued to attack London. The Blitz had begun

October

October: The fighting through to October had been fierce, 303 (Polish) Squadron alone accounting for 126 enemy aircraft, as this Hurricane demonstrates. RAF (AHB)/© UK MoD Crown Copyright 2015

ROYAL AIR FORCE SALUTE 2015

TIMELINE

November 5: Blenheims and Gladiators began deploying to the Balkans as Greece came under attack from Italy. This 211 Sqn Blenheim IF was at Menidi/Tatoi, Greece, preparing for a sortie later in the year. RAF (AHB)/© UK MoD Crown Copyright 2015

November 13: Second of the four-engined heavy bombers into RAF service, the Handley Page Halifax was delivered to 35 Squadron. The unit flew its first raid with the type on March 11/12, 1941. RAF (AHB)/© UK MoD Crown Copyright 2015

November 12: This post-raid reconnaissance photograph shows the Italian fleet after the Taranto attack. RAF (AHB)/© UK MoD Crown Copyright 2015

December: Hornchurch Wing crews brief before a sweep over France, as Fighter Command turned onto an offensive footing. RAF (AHB)/© UK MoD Crown Copyright 2015

November

As the night Blitz intensified, Birmingham, Bristol, Liverpool, London and Southampton received heavy attacks. Bomber Command meanwhile struck at Berlin, Bremen, Essen, Hamburg and Cologne

5 RAF Blenheims and Gladiators were dispatched from operations in North Africa to assist Greece in repelling an Italian invasion from Albania

10 Regular ferry flights of US-built aircraft to the UK began with a number of Hudson patrol aircraft

11 In response to Bomber Command attacks on cities in Northern Italy, the Regia Aeronautica (Italian air force) launched a raid against the UK from Belgium. The aggressors suffered heavy losses and no further missions were attempted
Fg Off Warburton reconnoitred Taranto in a 431 Flight Martin Maryland. The intelligence gathered led to an audacious Fleet Air Arm Fairey Swordfish attack that night. Much of the Italian fleet was destroyed or damaged at anchor

13 The Handley Page Halifax four-engined bomber entered service with 35 Sqn

14/15 Some 437 Luftwaffe aircraft bombed Coventry in a devastating raid led for the first time by He 111 pathfinders using X-Gerät radio emissions for accurate navigation

25 Air Marshal Sir W. Sholto Douglas succeeded Dowding as C-in-C Fighter Command

December

The Blitz continued against London, Birmingham, Coventry, Liverpool and Manchester. Bomber Command attacked Düsseldorf and Mannheim

1 RAF Army Co-operation Command was established
No. 148 Sqn became the first bomber squadron based on Malta

16 Some 134 Bomber Command aircraft struck Mannheim in reprisal for raids on Coventry and Southampton. It was the largest force sent against a single objective to date and the Command's first area raid

20 UK-based RAF fighter units turned to the offensive over Europe, when 66 Sqn sent Spitfires on the first of many 'Rhubarb' fighter sweeps

29/30 London suffered a particularly heavy raid

ROYAL AIR FORCE 2015

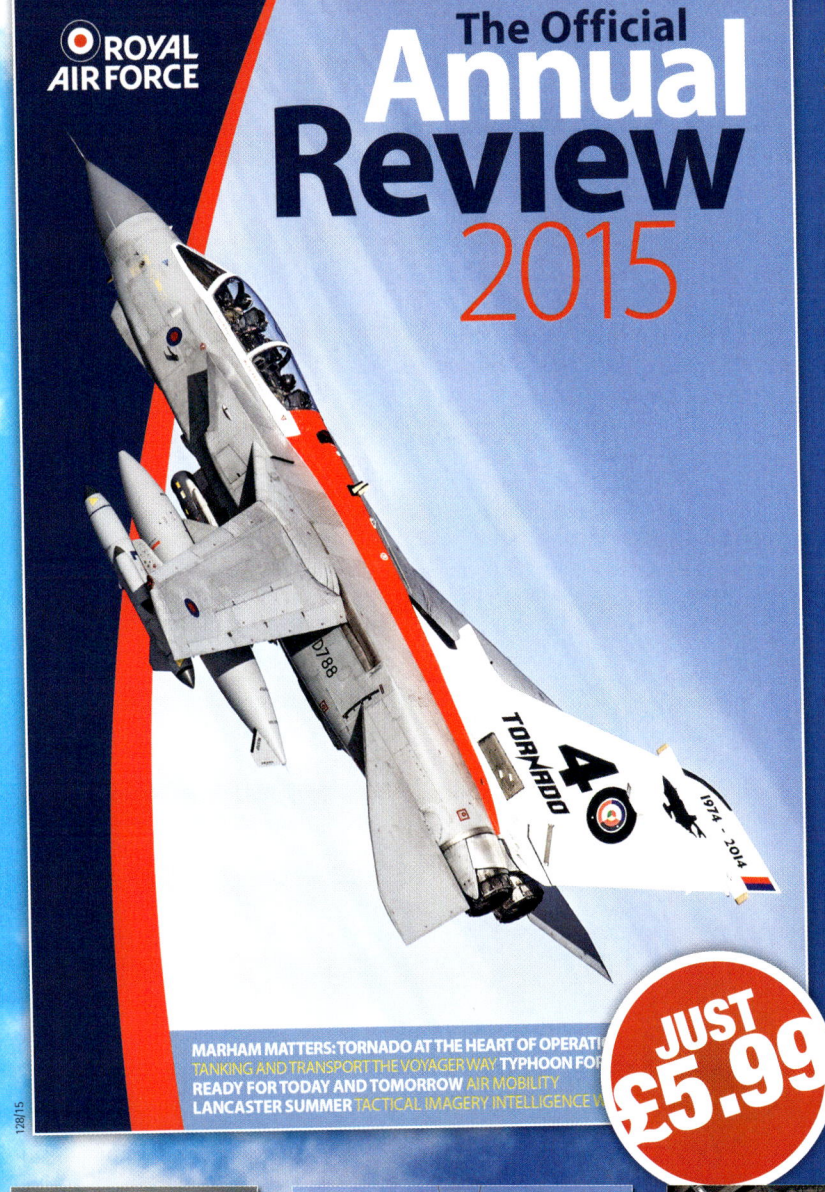

Produced by Key Publishing with exclusive access to the Royal Air Force, and featuring articles written with and by RAF personnel, *The Official RAF Annual Review 2015* is a 132-page special magazine that provides behind the scenes insight into the aircraft, equipment and people of one of the world's premier air forces.

HIGHLIGHTS INCLUDE:

TYPHOON FORCE: READY FOR TODAY AND TOMORROW

Typhoon Force Commander Air Commodore Philip Beach provides an update on RAF Typhoon capability and details his vision for the aircraft's future

MARHAM MATTERS: TORNADO AT THE HEART OF OPERATIONS

Group Captain Harvey Smyth, RAF Marham Station Commander looks back on a busy year of operations over Afghanistan, Africa and Iraq, with exclusive 40th anniversary Tornado air-to-air photography

TIW: THE EYES THAT GUIDE THE TALONS

A rare glimpse inside the Tactical Imagery Intelligence Wing, the RAF's premier reconnaissance imagery analysis and dissemination unit

AND MUCH MORE!

JUST £5.99

ORDER DIRECT
JUST £5.99 FREE P&P*

*Free 2nd class P&P on all UK & BFPO orders. Overseas charges apply.

Free P&P* when you order online at
www.keypublishing.com/shop

OR

Call UK: 01780 480404
Overseas: +44 1780 480404
Monday to Friday 9am-5:30pm

SUBSCRIBERS CALL FOR YOUR £1.00 DISCOUNT! SUBSCRIBERS CALL FOR YOUR £1.00 DISCOUNT!

OPERATIONS

Prelude to Battle: Denmark to Dunkirk

British forces fought a desperate campaign in Continental Europe a few months before the Battle of Britain began. It had been a campaign for which they were ill prepared, as historian and ex-fighter pilot Colonel Douglas C Dildy, USAF (Retd) explains

"The purpose of the [Fall Gelb] offensive will be… to win as much territory as possible in Holland, Belgium, and Northern France, to serve as a base for the successful prosecution of the air and sea war against England."
Hitler's *Directive No. 6 For the Conduct of the War*, October 9, 1939

The genus of the Battle of Britain lies in Adolf Hitler's aim to eliminate France and Great Britain from the conflict so that he could turn his Wehrmacht ('armed forces') against his hated enemy, the Soviet Union. Following a series of successful blumenkriege ('flower wars') – five bloodless victories that progressively stunned the Allies – and the August 23, 1939 signing of the Molotov-Ribbentrop Pact, which divided the 20-year old nation of Poland between Nazi Germany and Communist Russia, Hitler started World War Two with a full-blown invasion of that hapless nation.

Having allowed the previous episodes to pass with no more than political rhetoric and worthless accords – due almost entirely to the Allies' woeful unpreparedness for war, especially in terms of air forces – on August 25, France and Britain had pledged that if Germany invaded Poland, they would declare war. Undeterred, Hitler launched Fall Weiß ('Case White') on September 1, and three days later – ready for war or not – Britain and France found themselves once again in an armed conflict with Germany.

"Should the Army succeed in defeating the Anglo-French armies in the field and in seizing and holding a sector of the coast of the Continent opposite England, the task of the Navy and Air Force to carry the war to English industry becomes paramount."
Hitler's *Directive No. 9, Instructions for Warfare Against the Economy of the Enemy*, November 29, 1940

The Wehrmacht's 'Western Front' fielded only 25 army divisions (of 106 in total), 15 fighter groups, and eight bomber groups when Hitler unleashed it upon Poland. Once victory in the East was assured, a massive movement of men, equipment and aircraft across Germany began. To meet the new threat, the French mobilised 93 divisions and deployed 13 'groupe de chasses' (fighter groups), but had almost nothing in the way of offensive air power – 21 of 33 squadron-sized 'groupe de bombardments' were in the south of France or North Africa, re-equipping with more modern types.

While the British Expeditionary Force's (BEF's) contribution of nine fighting divisions mattered more symbolically than materially, the RAF made up for it by fielding two 'air forces'. One was tactical – the BEF's Air Component (BEF(AC)) of four squadrons of modern Hurricanes, plus army-cooperation (observation) and tactical reconnaissance units. The other was rather optimistically regarded as a 'strategic air force', the Advanced Air Striking Force (AASF), initially made up of ten single-engined Battle and two twin-engined Blenheim light bomber squadrons.

These 615 Squadron Gladiator pilots were at Vitry-en-Artois in early January 1940. Few encounters with the Bf 109 were required to instil a more sombre mood. All RAF (AHB)/© UK MoD Crown Copyright 2015

OPERATIONS

Smoke billows from a merchant ship and warehouse in Bergen, Norway, after RAF bombs struck them during a raid in April 1940.

In the sporadic aerial encounters that punctuated the Sitzkrieg or 'Phoney War', the Battle proved completely unsuited for modern combat, especially against the high-performance, cannon-armed Bf 109, so two Hurricane squadrons were reassigned to the AASF as escorts and airfield defenders, these being 'backfilled' by two squadrons of obsolete Gladiator biplanes.

"The development of the situation in Scandinavia makes it necessary to prepare for the occupation of Denmark and Norway… This would anticipate English actions against Scandinavia and the Baltic, secure our supplies of iron ore from Sweden, and provide our Navy and Air Force with expanded bases for operations against England."
Hitler's *Directive for 'Operation Weser-exercise'*, **March 1, 1940**

> In the so-called blumenkriege, Nazi Germany occupied the Rhineland in March 1936, then annexed Austria in April 1938 and occupied the Sudetenland that October. It occupied the rest of Bohemia-Moravia and annexed Lithuania's Memel district in March 1939.

As the opposing forces massed on either side of Belgium and the Maginot Line, Hitler became anxious that the repeated hostile encounters in Norwegian waters – such as HMS *Cossack's* February 16, 1940 attack on a German tanker in Jøssingfjord to rescue 299 prisoners – presaged a British occupation of Norway. Pre-empting Churchill's projected 'Plan R.4', Hitler launched Unternehmen Weserübung ('Operation Weser-exercise'), in which practically the whole Kriegsmarine delivered three divisions to seven locations along Norway's craggy, fjord-notched coastline. A Bf 109 gruppe (in Denmark), two Bf 110 long-range 'heavy fighter' gruppen (in Norway), one Ju 87 Stukagruppe and eight bomber gruppen flying He 111 and Ju 88 twin-engined medium bombers provided cover.

The Allied response was tardy and inadequate, landing four brigades at Åndalsnes, Namsos, and Narvik, initially without air support other than Royal Navy carrier-based aviation. Defeated in detail by an enemy with unprecedented air superiority, the RAF sent 18 Gladiators (No. 263 Sqn), but these lasted only three days. The Åndalsnes-Namsos expeditions were withdrawn on May 1-2, triggering a political crisis that resulted in the fall of Britain's Chamberlain Government.

The Narvik expedition was more successful, No. 263 Sqn returning – along with No. 64 Sqn with 18 Hurricanes – to help the French Alpine demi-brigade, Polish Podhale Brigade, and four Norwegian battalions drive the German Gebirgsjäger (mountain troops) out of the port city. Compelled by the German invasion of France and the Low Countries, this expedition too was withdrawn, HMS *Glorious* evacuating the two squadrons only for them to be lost when the carrier was sunk by two Kriegsmarine battlecruisers.

"The task of the Air Force is to concentrate strong offensive and defensive forces for action, with the focal point at Army Group A, in order to prevent the transfer of enemy reinforcements to the front and to give direct support to our own forces."
Hitler's *Directive No. 11*, **May 14, 1940**

By the time the Wehrmacht unleashed its mechanised whirlwind upon the Western Democracies, the Luftwaffe's Luftflotten (Air Fleets) 2 and 3 had gathered 26 Bf 109 and nine Bf 110 gruppen to support 40 bomber gruppen in the onslaught. The initial German air attacks destroyed half the Dutch air force and two-thirds of the Belgian, establishing aerial supremacy over the Low Countries that, in turn, resulted in veritable massacres of RAF and Armée de l'Air light bombers when they attempted to stem the steel tsunami.

In five days of operations the AASF was effectively destroyed, losing 93 of its 135 operational Battles. By the time the panzers were across the Meuse at Sedan and »

RAF officers inspect He 111 V4-DT, of 9./KG 1, which crash landed near Albert in the afternoon of May 10. It was one of seven III./KG 1 aircraft shot down by 85 and 607 Sqn Hurricanes. The bomber's crew surrendered to the unarmed keeper of a nearby British World War One military cemetery.

ROYAL AIR FORCE SALUTE 2015 | 15

OPERATIONS

German vehicles advance along the road at Donsbruggen, Germany, close to the Dutch border and Nijmegen.

A Battle gunner's view as the aircraft carries out a low-level attack on a German armoured column in northern France during June 1940.

Squadrons Then and Now

Number	Established	Initial aircraft	Aircraft in 1940	2015 role	Aircraft
3	May 13, 1912	Bleriot XI	Hurricane	Air Defence	Typhoon

charging headlong towards the Channel coast, the AASF was forced to revert to night bombing to salve its surviving squadrons.

Once the offensive was launched, BEF(AC) and AASF were reinforced with four more Hurricane squadrons. The Hurricane pilots experienced some sporadic, spectacular success, but overall were at the losing end of a battle of attrition. In the first six days BEF(AC) squadrons lost 30 Hurricanes shot down in exchange for nine Messerschmitts, but also accounted for 15 Stukas and 48 bombers destroyed, proving that both required fighter protection.

Despite assurances given by the War Cabinet following the impassioned (and now famous) appeal by Air Chief Marshal Hugh Dowding, head of Fighter Command, Churchill still required the RAF to despatch an additional 'ten fighter squadrons' to France. This was done by sending eight flights (half squadrons) to France and operating three squadrons and three 'composite squadrons' (composed of disparate flights) from Kent. The results – as Dowding predicted – were disastrous: by May 21, when the BEF(AC) evacuated France, 195 Hurricanes had been lost, 74 of them in combat. From this point on, Fighter Command's badly depleted No. 11 Group would have to challenge the Luftwaffe's aerial superiority over Flanders from its bases in England.

"The next object of our operations is to annihilate the French, English, and Belgian forces which are surrounded in Flanders… The task of the Air Force will be to break all enemy resistance of the surrounded forces, prevent escape of the English forces across the Channel, and to protect the southern flank of Army Group A."
Hitler's *Directive No. 13, Instructions on the Destruction of Forces in the Dunkirk Pocket*, May 24, 1940

The day the Admiralty initiated Operation Dynamo, the evacuation of troops from Dunkirk, No. 11 Group had 21 squadrons available, with a serviceable strength of 114 Spitfires, 137 Hurricanes, and 18 Defiants. Five

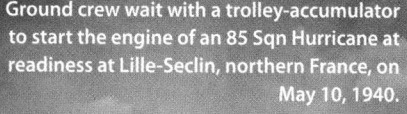

Ground crew wait with a trolley-accumulator to start the engine of an 85 Sqn Hurricane at readiness at Lille-Seclin, northern France, on May 10, 1940.

Below: As the situation worsened, RAF fighters provided cover over France from their UK bases. Here 56 Sqn Hurricanes depart for a sortie over France from North Weald, Essex, in May.

ROYAL AIR FORCE SALUTE 2015

OPERATIONS

Members of 226 Squadron pictured at Faux-Villecerf, France in May 1940, after withdrawing from Reims-Champagne airfield near Paris. The unit remained on active service on the Continent until mid-June.

Above: Bombs burst on troops massed on the east bank of the Meuse at Maastricht as 2 Group aircraft attack bridges and buildings in an attempt to block the German advance. Of 42 Blenheims despatched on the raids, 11 were shot down.

Spitfire squadrons were retained for home defence, leaving 16 units – about 200 fighters – to provide air cover over the beaches on an intermittent, rotational basis.

Almost completely inexperienced, saddled with outmoded and disadvantageous three-ship tactics, and flying beyond the effective range of the new Chain Home radar system, the British pilots operated under severe handicap against their battle-hardened adversaries.

In eight days of combat the Luftwaffe lost 36 Messerschmitts and 42 bombers to RAF fighters, but at a cost of 36 Spitfires, 45 Hurricanes, and eight Defiants, with 55 pilots killed and eight captured. In fact, 56 of these were shot down by the superb Bf 109E, generating a kill ratio of 2:1 in favour of the Jagdwaffe ('fighter force').

These losses, plus the 'wastage' of 386 Hurricanes and 74 pilots (56 killed in action and 18 prisoner of war) in France by the AASF's final withdrawal on June 18, left Dowding's command with 367 Spitfires and Hurricanes, with 36 unserviceable. Fortunately, aircraft production was able to keep pace with the losses – but replacing lost pilots was a far more critical problem. ⊙

Fighter reinforcement for the BEF(AC) and AASF came from Nos 3, 79 and 504 Sqns, which joined the BEF(AC)'s 85 and 87 Sqns (with 607 and 615 Sqns in the midst of conversion to the Hurricane), and No. 501 Sqn, which joined the AASF's Nos 1 and 73 Sqns

Below: A 220 Sqn, Coastal Command Hudson flies along the coast during the evacuation of the British Expeditionary Force from Dunkirk. The smoke in the distance is from burning oil tanks.

ROYAL AIR FORCE SALUTE 2015 | 17

PEOPLE

The Commanders
Dowding, Park and Leigh-Mallory

Three extraordinary men led Fighter Command through its greatest trial. As Air Cdre (Retd) Graham Pitchfork explains, they emerged victorious, but their relationship was difficult, with disagreement and serious clashes of character

Air Chief Marshal Sir Hugh Dowding, Air Officer Commanding-in-Chief Fighter Command during the Battle of Britain. Author's collection

Air Chief Marshal Sir Hugh Dowding was Air Officer Commanding-in-Chief (AOC-in-C) of Fighter Command in July 1940. The Command had four Groups, Numbers 10, 11, 12 and 13 led, respectively, by Air Vice-Marshal's Sir Quintin Brand, Keith Park, Trafford Leigh-Mallory and Richard Saul. The Battle was fought predominantly in the skies over southeast England, with the greatest burden falling on Park and his 11 Group squadrons, supported by those north of the River Thames and commanded by Leigh-Mallory.

Air Chief Marshal Sir Hugh Dowding – AOC-in-C Fighter Command

Hugh Dowding was born in 1882 at Moffatt, Dumfries and Galloway, and commissioned into the Royal Garrison Artillery in 1900. He served overseas for much of the next ten years, including six years in India. At the Army Staff College he took the opportunity to learn to fly at Brooklands and gained his 'wings' in 1913.

The outbreak of war saw Dowding at Farnborough, before service in France. His interest in wireless telegraphy led to his returning home to form the Wireless Experimental Establishment in April 1915, but he was soon back in France in command of 16 Squadron, tasked primarily with artillery spotting. In 1916 Dowding commanded the Ninth (Headquarters) Wing of the Royal Flying Corps during the Battle of the Somme, but after disagreement with Trenchard (then commanding the RFC in France) on tactics, he was sent to run the Southern Training Brigade at Salisbury. Here he spent the rest of the war, reaching the rank of brigadier.

Awarded a permanent commission in the Royal Air Force after the war, Dowding's first appointment was to HQ 1 Group at Kenley before serving as Chief Staff Officer, first at HQ Inland Area, Uxbridge and then at HQ Iraq. In 1926 he was moved to the Air Ministry as Director of Training where, for the first time, he was able to influence policy, and his strained relations with Trenchard (now the Chief of the Air Staff) improved. After an appointment as AOC Transjordan and Palestine, he was appointed in 1930 to the Air Council as Air Member for Supply and Research.

18 | ROYAL AIR FORCE SALUTE 2015

PEOPLE

Left: Sir Hugh Dowding, in civilian clothes, outside the Ministry of Information with a group of Battle of Britain personalities on September 14, 1942. Many of the pilots who served under Dowding were unhappy with his treatment after the battle. RAF (AHB)/© UK MoD Crown Copyright 2015

Left: Fighter Command badge. © UK MoD Crown Copyright 2015

From this time, and later, in 1935 as Air Member for Research and Development, Dowding was confronted with the increasingly complex technical matters associated with building a modern air force. One of his many activities was to encourage the development of advanced fighter aircraft based on the experiences gained in the Schneider Trophy events and it was largely on his initiative that the prototypes of the Hurricane and Spitfire were ordered in 1934.

Building Fighter Command

Dowding also showed the closest interest in the research being conducted into methods of detecting hostile aircraft and he gave strong support to the early experiments on radio detection finding (RDF, later called radar) in 1935. When Fighter Command was established at Bentley Priory in 1936, he was the natural choice to be its first AOC-in-C.

Most of the next four years were devoted to creating an intricate and effective system that combined his fighter squadrons, the RDF units and the various command and control organisations into an air defence structure that was well in advance of any other system in the world.

During this time he did not always enjoy a smooth relationship with the staffs in the Air Ministry, who he thought were obstructive as he sought improvements for his fighters, better airfields, the building of appropriate operations rooms, development of the Observer Corps and the introduction of an air raid warning system. These were just some of the things he fought for and his tenacity and foresight would later pay handsome dividends in the Battle of Britain. Dowding gained operational control of Anti-Aircraft Command and Balloon Command on the outbreak of war, completing the air defence system.

Dowding continued to press the argument that his fighter strength was far from adequate for the proper defence of the home base. Nicknamed 'Stuffy', he was an austere man with little time for diplomacy. In combination with his single-mindedness, this led to an awkward relationship with other senior RAF officers.

Irremediable Defeat

The erosion of his Hurricane force during the early stages of the Battle of France in May 1940 was intolerable to Dowding. He came under intense pressure from the Prime Minister and the French Government to send more fighters to the Continent, but he was convinced that the twin pillars of Fighter Command and the Royal Navy were the crucial factor in adequate home defence. So, on May 15, after five days of intense fighting and increasing aircraft losses, he warned the War Cabinet of the dire consequences if the current rate of wastage continued.

He wrote a letter, which many historians rate as one of the great documents in history, which concluded, "If the Home Defence Force is drained away in desperate attempts to remedy the situation in France, defeat in France will involve the final, complete and irremediable defeat of this country".

This unequivocal statement set out the stark reality of sending more of his precious fighters to France yet, for almost a month, Dowding would see his »

Below: Dowding escorted His Majesty King George VI and Queen Elizabeth during a visit to Fighter Command headquarters at Bentley Priory, near Stanmore, Middlesex, in September 1940. RAF (AHB)/© UK MoD Crown Copyright 2015

ROYAL AIR FORCE SALUTE 2015 | 19

PEOPLE

Dowding (saluting) and Leigh-Mallory stand uneasily together as they mark the third anniversary of the Battle of Britain. RAF (AHB)/© UK MoD Crown Copyright 2015 via author

11 Group, Fighter Command badge. © UK MoD Crown Copyright 2015

"If the Home Defence Force is drained away in desperate attempts to remedy the situation in France, defeat in France will involve the final, complete and irremediable defeat of this country".

ACM Sir Hugh Dowding, AOC-in-C Fighter Command

resources continue to slip away, particularly through the air cover he had to provide for the evacuation from Dunkirk, an action Churchill saw as the RAF's first victory over the Luftwaffe.

The heavy losses of his fighter force were serious, but Dowding had retained just enough of his aircraft and pilots to enable him to fight the Luftwaffe in the one place where they could be effective, over the United Kingdom, within the comprehensive air defence system he had built up.

Dowding recognised that the situation he faced was 'critical in the extreme', but the organisation he had created won the day. He saw his aim as simple; to prevent invasion by denying the Luftwaffe control of the air, but his personal role during the aerial battles was limited and the fighting, deployment and tactics were the responsibility of his Group commanders.

During the height of the Battle, there was a significant difference of opinion on tactics between Park and Leigh-Mallory, which threatened success. Dowding's critics feel that he should have been more aware of this issue and taken steps to resolve it.

At the end of the Battle he was aged 58 and more senior to the rest of the RAF's high commanders. He became increasingly remote and was considered uncooperative. There were those that favoured a more aggressive, albeit untried policy put forward by Leigh-Mallory for the use of his 'big wings'. There was also a feeling that, despite the success of daylight operations, there was inadequate response to the Luftwaffe's increasingly effective night operations. As a result, many believed there was a need for a change and Dowding was replaced as AOC-in-C of Fighter Command on November 13, 1940.

He retired from the RAF in 1942 and the following year was awarded a peerage, but was never promoted to the rank of Marshal of the Royal Air Force, an issue that rankled among his pilots. At the time of his death in 1970, the then Secretary of State for Defence, Dennis Healey, summed him up as: "one of those great men whom this country miraculously produces in times of peril."

Air Vice-Marshal Keith Park – AOC No. 11 Group

Keith Park was born in New Zealand in 1892 and educated in Dunedin, before spending three years as a cadet purser with the Union Steam Ship Company. He was granted war leave in December 1914, serving with a howitzer battery at Anzac Cove, Gallipoli and taking part in the Suvla Bay landings. He was commissioned and served with the British Army, being wounded on the Somme, before joining the Royal Flying Corps in December 1916 for pilot training.

Park flew the Bristol Fighter, took command of 48 Squadron and by the end of the war had accounted for 20 enemy machines. He was twice shot down and wounded, and awarded the Military Cross (MC) and Bar, the Distinguished Flying Cross (DFC) and the Croix de Guerre.

The King examined an anti-aircraft battery during his September 1940 visit to Northolt. Air Vice-Marshal Keith Park, at right, was on hand. RAF (AHB)/© UK MoD Crown Copyright 2015

PEOPLE

Nicknamed 'Stuffy', Dowding could seem distant and remote to those around him. RAF (AHB)/© UK MoD Crown Copyright 2015

His Majesty King George VI, visiting RAF Northolt on September 26, 1940, signs the 303 Squadron *Operations Record Book* while AOC 11 Group, AVM Keith Park, looks on. RAF (AHB)/© UK MoD Crown Copyright 2015

Squadrons Then and Now

Number	Established	Initial aircraft	Aircraft in 1940	2015 role	Aircraft
II	May 13, 1912	B.E. types	Lysander, Defiant (from August)	Air Defence	Typhoon
8	January 1, 1915	B.E.2c	Vincent, Blenheim, Swordfish	ISTAR	Sentry

Between the wars Park served in Egypt and commanded 111 (Fighter) Squadron at Duxford. He also served at HQ Fighting Area, before becoming the station commander at Northolt. After commanding the Oxford University Air Squadron, Park served as the air attaché in South America before promotion to air commodore in July 1938, to be the Senior Air Staff Officer at HQ Fighter Command, where Dowding was the AOC-in-C.

Under Dowding's direction, Park's chief concern was to employ the newly introduced, high-speed, heavily armed monoplanes (Hurricane and Spitfire) in combination with equally new radar and radio equipment to create an effective air defence against the growing danger of German air attacks. This daunting task was complicated by peacetime restrictions on realistic training.

11 Group

Park was promoted air vice-marshal (AVM) to be AOC 11 Group in April 1940, charged with the defence of London and southeast England. There was no senior RAF leader with a better understanding of Fighter Command and its units, and Dowding had great faith in his ability.

Park's first operational task was to provide fighter cover for the evacuation of Dunkirk. He regularly flew his own Hurricane to oversee operations and took part in the final patrol. Reflecting on this time he believed the operations had been vital and gave Fighter Command invaluable experience.

During the first phase of the Battle of Britain, from July to early September, 11 Group protected the most vital area from Southampton to Norwich, defending London from all approaches. During this intense period Park visited all the stations under his command, every evening, by Hurricane.

His strategy, approved by Dowding, was to place his squadrons near radar stations and break up enemy formations well in advance, before they could reach and bomb their targets. These tactics proved successful, but towards the end of the Battle, Park's handling of his fighters and Dowding's overall strategy were the subject of an informal enquiry, instigated, primarily, by AOC 12 Group (AVM Leigh-Mallory) who employed his squadrons in larger 'wing' formations having had time, thanks to the position of his units further north, to amass five to seven squadrons. The differences between the two commanders became so pronounced that the Air Council had to intervene.

In December 1940 Leigh-Mallory replaced Park. After a period as the AOC of a flying »

12 Group, Fighter Command badge. © UK MoD Crown Copyright 2015

Park kept in close touch with his squadrons during the Battle of Britain, visiting their stations in his personal Hurricane. RAF (AHB)/© UK MoD Crown Copyright 2015

ROYAL AIR FORCE SALUTE 2015 | 21

PEOPLE

training group, Park went on to serve with distinction as AOC Malta during the most difficult period of the assault on the island and later became AOC-in-C Middle East, before taking up the appointment of Allied Air Commander, South-East Asia Command. He was knighted three times and retired from the RAF in December 1946.

Air Chief Marshal Sir Keith Park died in February 1975. On September 15, 2010, the 70th Anniversary of the Battle of Britain, a permanent memorial statue of him was unveiled in Waterloo Place, London. The statue, in view of New Zealand House, faces the direction that the young pilots who fought in the summer of 1940 would have looked as they went to meet their enemy.

Air Vice-Marshal Trafford Leigh-Mallory – AOC No. 12 Group

Trafford Leigh-Mallory was born in July 1892 and after reading history and law at Magdalene College, Cambridge, joined the Army and was commissioned into the Lancashire Fusiliers in October 1914. He was wounded in France in January 1916 and during his recovery joined the RFC to train as a pilot. He remained on the Home Establishment until taking command of 8 Squadron, operating in the army co-operation role from Bertangles, France. He was awarded the Distinguished Service Order (DSO).

After the war Leigh-Mallory commanded II (Army Co-operation) Squadron, before spending a number of years in the Air Ministry. He later commanded 22 (Army Co-operation) Group and was Commandant of the School of Army Co-operation before joining the staff of the Army Staff College. In July 1931 Leigh-Mallory returned to the Air Ministry and later commanded 2 Flying Training School. In 1935 he moved to Iraq, first as the Senior Air Staff Officer and then as AOC, where his squadrons were involved primarily in supporting the Army.

Air Vice-Marshal Trafford Leigh-Mallory, AOC 12 Group during the Battle of Britain. Author's collection

12 Group

Leigh-Mallory took command of 12 Group in December 1937, having never flown or worked in an air defence role. He was responsible for the defence of the industrial Midlands and commanded, in effect, a rear echelon force. With more warning of the approach of enemy formations, he had the time to form up his squadron into larger wings, with a consequent increase in firepower. However, these 'big wings' lacked the speed and flexibility required to intercept the enemy bomber force before it reached its targets, resulting in friction with Park and his squadron commanders. On September 7, the Luftwaffe switched its attacks to London and, with enemy bomber formations concentrating on one predictable target, Leigh-Mallory's tactics were more successful.

Following an Air Council meeting on October 17 and the removal of Dowding and Park, Leigh-Mallory became AOC of 11 Group. In early 1941 he turned his squadrons onto the offensive, escorting small forces of bombers in an attempt to tempt the Luftwaffe into combat. It was largely unsuccessful and the operations were ended in November. However, his knowledge of the needs of the other services was invaluable during the ill-fated Dieppe raid, when one of the messages he received was 'air co-operation faultless'.

Leading Fighter Command

In November 1942 Leigh-Mallory was appointed AOC-in-C, Fighter Command. In the following July he was nominated by the British Chiefs of Staff to plan the activities of all air forces based in the United Kingdom and earmarked for the support of the invasion of Europe. His appointment as Allied Air Commander-in-Chief was confirmed in December with the rank of air chief marshal.

Leigh-Mallory's appointment was not a popular decision. The arrangement for the command and control of the air forces was complex and seen by many as an extra headquarters in the air force chain of command. Despite being the C-in-C, he did not have control of the strategic bomber forces and his role caused constant problems, placing Leigh-Mallory in a difficult position. Nevertheless, he persevered and played a key role in the planning and execution of the air offensive. Many admired him for his dignity and Eisenhower paid tribute to his devotion to duty.

By the end of the campaign it was decided that an overall air commander was no longer needed and Leigh-Mallory's appointment finished in October. He was appointed to be Allied Air Commander in South-East Asia Command. Heading off for his new role, he took off with his wife from Northolt in an Avro York on November 14. The aircraft disappeared and only in June 1945 was its wreckage found in the French Alps. In an ironic twist of fate, Keith Park was chosen to take the appointment that Leigh-Mallory had been unable to fulfil.

Air Chief Marshal Sir Trafford Leigh-Mallory was the most senior RAF officer to lose his life during World War Two. He died near the summit of a mountain, just as his oldest brother George, who had perished near the summit of Mount Everest in June 1924.

Middle right: 10 Group, Fighter Command badge. Led by AVM Sir Quintin Brand, 10 Group played a minor role in the Battle of Britain. © UK MoD Crown Copyright 2015. **Right: 13 Group, Fighter Command badge. Air Vice-Marshal Richard Saul's 13 Group took a small but important supporting role in the Battle.** © UK MoD Crown Copyright 2015

Park signed this photograph of himself in April 1941. RAF (AHB)/© UK MoD Crown Copyright 2015

22 | ROYAL AIR FORCE SALUTE 2015

The Club at the heart of the RAF

Enjoy the beautiful surroundings of a heritage listed Club in London overlooking Green Park and the Bomber Command Memorial. Membership of the RAF Club offers a host of benefits, including access to 92 bedrooms, first-class dining, private meeting and banqueting rooms and a thriving social and events programme.

Membership is open to those who hold or have held commissions in the RAF, PMRAFNS, RAF Reserve Forces and Commonwealth and Allied Air Forces. Other types of membership are available.

The Royal Air Force Club,
128 Piccadilly, London, W1J 7PY

Email: admin@rafclub.org.uk
Facebook: The Royal Air Force Club
Twitter: @TheRAFClub

For more information: visit www.rafclub.org.uk, call 020 7399 1001 or call in at reception. REF: SALUTE

OPERATIONS

Battle Joined

The RAF's victory in the Battle of Britain saved the country from defeat. Air power historian and former fighter pilot Colonel Douglas C Dildy, USAF (Retd) describes the life and death struggles of the long summer of 1940

Although, from the British perspective the Battle of Britain began on July 10 as the RAF first encountered the Luftwaffe over the Channel, these engagements were part of a harassment campaign (Störangriffe) derived from Hitler's *Directive No. 9*. Nothing more ambitious was attempted because, after moving to bases within range of Britain, the Kampfgeschwadern (bomber wings) needed time to recuperate and regroup. During the intense six-week Western Campaign, the two Luftflotten had lost 438 of their 1,120 twin-engined bombers. By late July the frontline bomber force was back up to 1,131 aircraft, with another 129 in Norway.

The initial phase of operations began on July 19, with attacks on Dover harbour. Almost daily, six Fliegerkorps ('Flying Corps', three in each Luftflotte) attacked ships in the Channel, sinking 18 small steamers and four destroyers, prompting the Admiralty to suspend merchant shipping through the Straits of Dover during daylight. Fliegerkorps I raided Dover repeatedly, culminating in an attack that caused the Royal Navy to withdraw its destroyer flotilla.

Defending against these raids, during July, No. 11 Group lost 64 day fighters (of 145 losses total). Far more serious was the loss of another 42 pilots (19 of them missing in the Channel – there was no air-sea rescue service worthy of the title), causing Dowding to direct that all combat must occur within gliding distance of land. It was little consolation that Luftwaffe units lost 54 bombers, 12 Stukas and 45 Messerschmitts in combat during July. »

OPERATIONS

"What General Weygand called the Battle of France is over. I expect that the Battle of Britain is about to begin."
Prime Minister Winston Churchill's address to Parliament, June 18, 1940, four days before the surrender of France

These 610 Sqn Spitfires were airborne on July 24, 1940, during the Battle's opening phase.
All RAF (AHB)/© UK MoD Crown Copyright 2015

OPERATIONS

Two squadrons flew the ill-fated Defiant into the Battle of Britain, 264 and 141. These aircraft, belonging to the former, were flying from their Kirton-in-Lindsey base during July.

"The aim of [Operation Sea Lion] will be to eliminate the English homeland as a base for the prosecution of the war against Germany and, if necessary, to occupy it completely."

Hitler's *Directive No. 16, On Preparations for a Landing Operation Against England*, July 16, 1940

> On the day *Directive No. 17* was issued, Fighter Command mustered 367 serviceable Spitfires and Hurricanes (of 570 total) and 1,434 pilots. The two Luftflotten's fighter commands (Jafü – short for Jagdfliegerführer – 2 and 3) had assembled 702 serviceable Bf 109s (of 813 total) for the offensive.

Churchill's expectation was correct. Euphoric over the surprisingly fast and relatively easy conquest of France, on July 2 Hitler – despite the fact that Wehrmacht pre-war planning never considered a cross-Channel invasion of Britain – began toying with just such a notion and ordered the three services to provide assessments for this contingency.

They submitted independent studies on July 16. The Luftwaffe's proposal was a revision of the year-old 'Studie Blau', which envisaged defeating Britain through a quixotic strategic bombing campaign. Two weeks later, in a meeting at Hitler's Berchtesgaden HQ, the three divergent approaches were hammered into a provisional concept of operations, issued on August 1 as *Directive No. 17*.

Commonly and erroneously called an 'invasion plan', this instruction was never more than a compilation of the requirements that each service would fulfil to make an operations plan viable. It established tasks, set logistics and signals arrangements, and required the preparations to be completed by September 15.

No joint command or staff was established to undertake the mission of invading Britain, as there had been for Weserübung, resulting in no actual assault planning being accomplished. While the services were making their preparations and the Luftwaffe began its task of attempting to destroy the RAF, Hitler and the Nazi leadership assumed an odd, hopeful-yet-doubtful 'wait and see' approach.

"In order to establish the necessary conditions for the final conquest of England… I therefore order the Luftwaffe to overpower the English air force with all the forces at its command, in the shortest possible time. The attacks are to be directed primarily against flying units, their ground installations, and their supply organisations, but also against the aircraft industry."

Hitler's *Directive No. 17, For the Conduct of Air and Sea Warfare against England*, August 1, 1940

Smarting from Churchill's rejection of his July 19 'appeal to reason' peace overture and dissatisfied with the Luftwaffe's limited raids against coastal shipping, Hitler ordered Reichsmarschall Hermann Göring to step up its attacks into a full-blown offensive air campaign against the RAF. In this order, the Luftwaffe was directed that: "the English air force must be so reduced morally and physically that it is unable to deliver any significant attack against the German crossing." The following day Göring's headquarters (the Oberkommando der Luftwaffe, or ObdL) issued its *Preparations and Directives for Unternehmen Adler* (Operation Eagle).

Göring, the corpulent, vainglorious leader of the Luftwaffe, was a politician, not an

The strain of combat is etched into the face of Sqn Ldr Brian 'Sandy' Lane, commanding 19 Sqn, after a sortie in September 1940. Flt Lt WJ 'Farmer' Lawson is at left, with Flt Sgt George 'Grumpy' Unwin right.

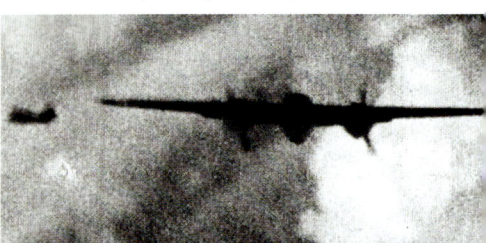

This Do 17Z's starboard engine is smoking badly after taking hits, while at least one crewman has taken the decision to abandon the machine.

OPERATIONS

Fighter Command is unlikely to have prevailed without the Chain Home radar installation and associated fighter control system. Security around the radar sites was tight and they came in for frequent air attack.

Adolf Gysbert 'Sailor' Malan was among many pilots that excelled during the Battle. He is shown here as a group captain in 1944.

air power authority – he had not flown an aircraft since 1922, had no knowledge of – or experience in – air campaigning, and had only overseen the development and expansion of the Luftwaffe as a basis for power and influence, leaving doctrine, technological development and combat operations to the professionals.

Now that his personal prestige was 'on the line', he took a sudden, intrusive interest in directing the Luftwaffe's 'showcase' campaign. ObdL's 14-day attack plan was designed to 'roll back' the RAF, bombing airfields and aviation industries in three phases, each advancing progressively closer to London. For daylight attacks London was considered the geographical extent of daylight bomber operations, dictated by the range limitations of escorting Bf 109s.

For the Germans, the battle for Britain began on August 12, with preliminary bombardment of six radar stations and three coastal fighter airfields, intended to 'open the door' for the major assaults the next day.

Adlertag (Eagle Day) saw Luftflotten 2 and 3 mounting 1,485 bomber and fighter sorties (several large raids in the morning were cancelled due to weather), Fighter Command countering with 727 aircraft. Anticipating that the opening attacks had prompted Dowding to reinforce 11 Group from his northern establishment, the next operation (August 15) included Luftflotte 5, launching 63 He 111s and 27 Ju 88As from Norway and Denmark, escorted by 34 twin-engined Bf 110 and Ju 88C Zerstörern ('Destroyers'). Nos 12 and 13 »

RAF Aircraft 1940: Boulton Paul Defiant

Boulton Paul's Defiant resulted from erroneous pre-war thinking that a turret-equipped fighter might overcome a perceived weakness in combat aircraft featuring only fixed-forward firing armament, by allowing a gunner to lay fire through a much wider field of engagement. It was a concept not entirely without merit, since air tacticians widely believed that enemy bombers would attack unescorted and en masse, allowing squadrons of turret fighters to engage from abeam, outside the range of defensive fire and without the need to manoeuvre to reattack after each firing pass.

In reality, the requirement produced a fighter encumbered by the turret and gunner, the installation adding drag and weight. The 1,030hp Rolls-Royce Merlin III powered the Mk I Defiant and Hurricane alike, but the latter offered twice the firepower in an airframe 32% lighter.

The prototype Defiant flew for the first time on August 11, 1937 and first deliveries were made to 264 Sqn in December 1939. The Dunkirk evacuation provided a backdrop for the type's first operational sorties on May 12, 1940, when Luftwaffe pilots assumed that it was conventionally armed and perhaps mistook it for the Hurricane. The result was 38 enemy aircraft destroyed on that first day and 65 by the end of the month.

But German pilots learned quickly that the Defiant could be attacked with impunity from below or head-on, the aircraft's lack of speed and agility generally preventing the pilot from manoeuvring to place the hapless gunner in a firing position before the Defiant had been mortally wounded. There could be no result other than defeat and as the Battle of Britain began in earnest, Defiant losses mounted rapidly. On July 19, six Bf 109Es attacked nine 141 Sqn Defiants off Folkestone, downing six, and by the end of August the type had been withdrawn from day fighting.

The Defiant's two-man crew made it a suitable candidate for night fighting, however. An improved, more powerful Defiant Mk II was subsequently developed and although performance remained inadequate for day fighting, equipped with AI.Mk IV radar as the Defiant NF.Mk IA, it successfully countered German bombers through the desperate winter of 1940/41, racking up more kills than any other night fighter of the period.

A total of 1,065 Defiants was built, the type increasingly serving in second-line roles from 1941, including air-sea rescue, electronic countermeasure and target towing. The last operational Defiant was withdrawn from target-towing duties in April 1945.

This 264 Sqn Defiant Mk I is shown as it appeared just before the Battle of France, when the type remained untried in combat. © Pete West

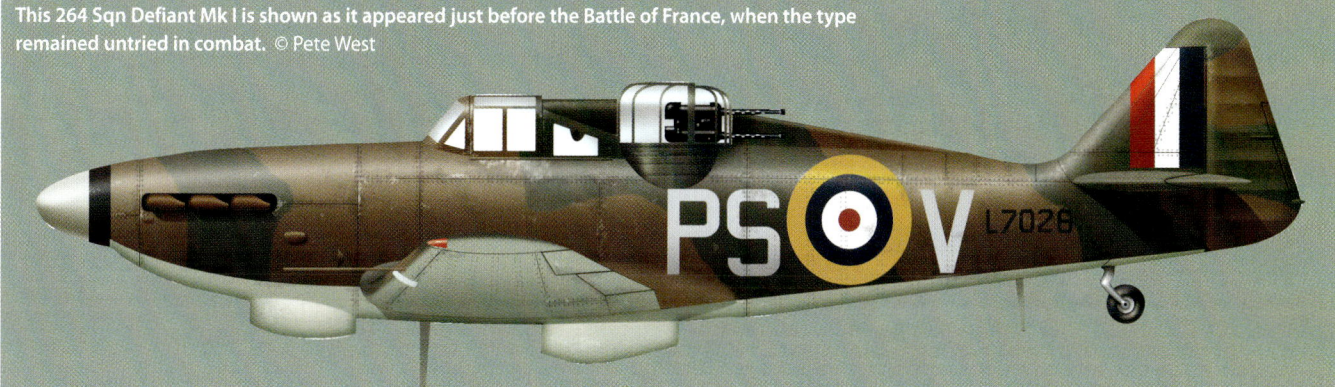

ROYAL AIR FORCE SALUTE 2015 | 27

OPERATIONS

These Hurricanes are flying in the RAF's originally preferred fighter formation, as groups of three aircraft in vee, or 'vic', layout. Designed primarily for use against bombers, these tactics proved restrictive against the Bf 109, whose pilots used a superior Schwarm formation of four aircraft. The RAF later adopted the German format as the so-called 'finger four' formation.

RAF Aircraft 1940: Supermarine Spitfire

Synonymous with the Battle of Britain, the Supermarine Spitfire is nonetheless widely recognised as being numerically less important at the time than the Hawker Hurricane and, accordingly, to have scored fewer kills. The Hawker and Supermarine fighters were similarly armed with eight 0.303in (7.7mm) machine guns and powered, by the 1,030hp Merlin II or III engine, but the Spitfire was of more modern construction, lighter, smaller and considerably faster than the relatively conventional Hurricane.

The latter's conservative design helped ensure the RAF had large numbers of easily maintained, rugged fighters when it needed them most, but the Spitfire's technological superiority and inherent potential for development meant it was a machine of the future, quickly eclipsing the Hurricane to become one of the most successful fighter aircraft ever built.

Remarkably, Supermarine was primarily established as a builder of flying boats and floatplanes, the latter pure racing machines for the Schneider Trophy competition, in which Britain ultimately triumphed with the Supermarine S.6B. The Spitfire was only its second attempt at a fighter, designer Reginald J. Mitchell having first penned the Type 224, a disappointing monoplane that lost out in competition with the Gloster SS.37 biplane that became the Gladiator.

Convinced he could do better, Mitchell set to work again, drawing on his work with the racing seaplanes to create the radical new Type 300, based on the new Rolls-Royce PV.12 engine, which matured as the Merlin.

The design showed promise and the Air Ministry drew up specification F.37/34 around it. The prototype flew for the first time on March 5, 1936 and flew well, but there were teething problems to overcome and considerable work required to mould it as a frontline warplane. Mitchell died on June 11, 1937 while this work was under way and it was Supermarine's former chief draughtsman Joe Smith, promoted as chief designer, who saw the fighter into service.

Gun Trouble

Problems with gun freezing at altitude and in productionising the airframe took the best part of two years to solve, so that the first Spitfire Mk I was not delivered to 19 Squadron at RAF Duxford until August 1938. But still the aircraft continued to evolve, with changes to the cockpit canopy and replacement of the original fixed-pitch, two-bladed propeller with a three-bladed, two-pitch or variable-pitch unit better able to harness the Merlin's power.

By September 1939 ten Spitfire squadrons were operational, and 19 were ready to engage the Luftwaffe during the Battle of Britain. The Hurricane was by far the more numerous aircraft in the Battle, with 30 squadrons available, but the Spitfire emerged the more effective fighter, accounting for 529 enemy aircraft, including 282 Bf 109s, while the Hurricane downed 656 machines, 222 of them Bf 109s.

The standard eight-gun armament was never really adequate in combat, especially against bombers with self-sealing fuel tanks and armour protection, and several undoubtedly made it back to base damaged, when a cannon-armed fighter might have finished them off. A handful of cannon-armed Spitfire Mk IB aircraft was therefore issued to 19 Sqn during the Battle, but the weapons jammed frequently and the installation, although paving the way for the later Mk VB, was generally unsatisfactory.

With the more powerful Merlin XII installed, the Spitfire Mk II also emerged during the Battle of Britain, entering service with 611 Sqn in August 1940. The majority was of the Mk IIA with eight machine guns, but the Mk IIB was also built, with 20mm cannon. Subsequent Mk II variants were produced for long-range escort missions as the RAF turned to the offensive, and for air-sea rescue. Early in 1941, trials with Mk I airframes modified to take the yet more powerful Merlin 45 began. These aircraft were effectively to Mk V standard and it was with this mark that the Spitfire began to show its true versatility.

The Spitfire excelled as a fighter and reconnaissance aircraft, and gave a good account against ground targets. The navalised Seafire was always a handful on deck, but nevertheless proved effective. The RAF flew its last operational Spitfire sortie over Malaya, on April 1, 1954, a Griffon-engined PR.Mk XIX reconnoitring rebel positions.

This Spitfire Mk I was with 19 Sqn in October 1938. The squadron was involved in a great deal of propaganda work and its number featured on the fin of many of its Spitfires. Although this machine retained the two-bladed propeller, it had already been fitted with the 'blown' cockpit canopy, in place of the flat-topped unit originally installed. © Pete West

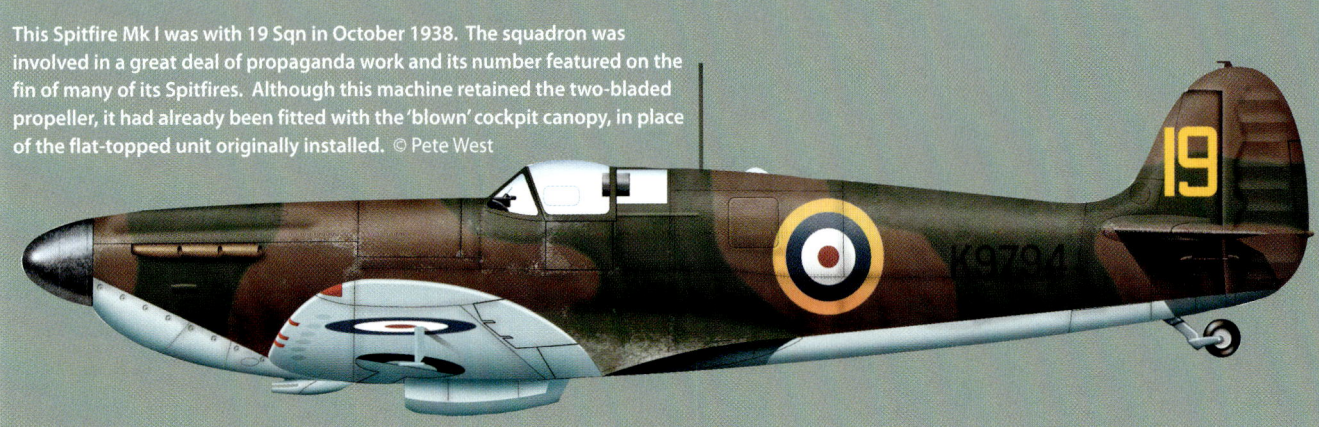

28 | ROYAL AIR FORCE SALUTE 2015

OPERATIONS

Pilot Officer Jack Ross took time to pose with his 17 Sqn Hurricane at Debden in September 1940. The aircraft crashed into the sea after combat with a Bf 109 on September 24, Plt Off Bird-Wilson bailing out safely. Ross was posted missing after ditching his 134 Sqn Spitfire in the Irish Sea on January 6, 1942.

This 87 Sqn Hurricane pilot was adjusting his Mae West life jacket before a sortie from Exeter on November 20.

James 'Ginger' Lacey was among the Battle's top-scoring pilots, achieving 23 kills between May and October 1940, over France and the Channel. Here he sits in the cockpit of a 501 Sqn Spitfire in May 1941.

A 92 Sqn Spitfire shot down this 9./KG 27 He 111 during an attack on Cardiff docks on August 14.

Groups responded with five squadrons (42 fighters), downing 16 bombers and seven Messerschmitts, for the loss of one Hurricane.

In fact, during Adlertag the Zerstörergruppen lost 21 Bf 110s in exchange for five Hurricanes. Specifically designed as a long-range escort fighter, the Zerstörer had proven incapable of performing its mission – it could barely defend itself, much less the bombers it was escorting – and was effectively eliminated from the contest.

Adlerangriff's ('Eagle Attack's') first phase operated across a broad 280-mile (450km) wide front. It attempted to eliminate Coastal and Bomber Command bases – these containing units that could interfere with an attempted invasion – as well as fighter airfields, culminating in heavy attacks on August 18. While the primitive coastal Chain Home radars provided timely early warning and adequate initial vectors of the attackers, the system's lack of accurate height information and dependence on visual-only tracking (by the Observer Corps) overland, limited the sector controllers' ability to complete intercepts. This frequently resulted in the side that saw the other first having the initial advantage when formations clashed. By now Fighter Command had lost 171 aircraft and 154 pilots, while shooting down 350 Luftwaffe aircraft, 37 of them Stukas.

Phase II
In the meeting that determined and disseminated Reichsmarschall Göring's guidance for Phase II of the Battle, faulty intelligence assessments convinced Luftwaffe leaders that Phase I was successfully completed, but adjustments were needed for the second wave of attacks. The apparently ineffective strikes against coastal radar stations would »

The Italian air force struck at the UK on November 11, suffering grievous losses to Fighter Command. Number 257 Sqn was in the thick of it, claiming 8½ destroyed and four damaged. Here three of the unit's Hurricanes return to their Martlesham Heath base during the month.

"We have reached the decisive period in the air war against England. The vital task is to turn all means at our disposal to the defeat of the enemy air force. Our first aim is the destruction of enemy fighters.
Reichsmarschall Hermann Göring, meeting with Luftwaffe commanders and staff officers, Karinhall, August 19, 1940

OPERATIONS

These 41 Sqn Spitfires were up during October 1940, although the further aircraft, X4178/EB-K was shot down on October 15 with the loss of Sgt Philip Lloyd.

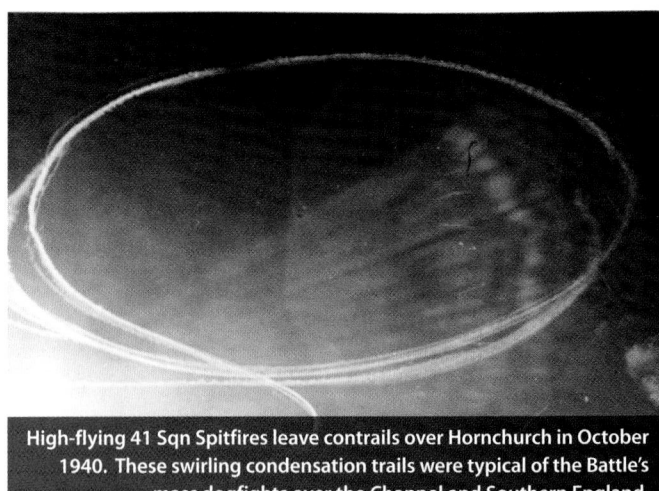

High-flying 41 Sqn Spitfires leave contrails over Hornchurch in October 1940. These swirling condensation trails were typical of the Battle's mass dogfights over the Channel and Southern England.

be discontinued. To preserve the obsolescent, fixed-gear Stuka dive-bomber to support the proposed invasion, it was withdrawn. More critically, heavy losses of twin-engined bombers meant that close escort (Jagdschutz) by Bf 109s – a restrictive mission that, due to large differences in fighter and bomber speeds, put the escorts at a serious tactical disadvantage – were now required, as well as freie Jagd ('free hunt') fighter sweeps to engage intercepting RAF fighters and destroy them.

Consequently most of Jafü 3's fighter units were transferred to Luftflotte 2. From this point on, Generalfeldmarschall Hugo Sperrle's Luftflotte 3 would primarily conduct night attacks against industrial targets, while Generalfeldmarschall Albert Kesselring's Luftflotte 2 'took the war to the enemy' with daylight raids against 11 Group airfields closer to London. The movement of six Jagdgruppen required several days, postponing renewed operations until August 24.

Luftflotte 2 began Phase II with 1,030 sorties, making major attacks against Manston (subsequently abandoned), Hornchurch and North Weald airfields. The tempo and intensity steadily increased, with 1,450 sorties flown a week later and including heavy attacks on Biggin Hill, Debden, Hornchurch, Croydon and Eastchurch. Kesselring's raids saturated Air Vice-Marshal Keith Park's No. 11 Group – on a 165-mile (266km) front – overwhelming the responding fighters and forcing an unfavourable exchange ratio, compelling Park to prioritise defending his sector stations, allowing other targets to be bombed without interference.

Within another week, six of the seven (all save Northolt) sector stations were heavily damaged, repeatedly disrupting communications links with the Fighter Command Operations Room at Bentley Priory – the sole source of target location information – frequently putting Park's Spitfire and Hurricane pilots at untimely disadvantage. Even with AVM Trafford Leigh-Mallory's 12 Group 'feeding the fight' from the north by September 6, Dowding lost 273 aircraft and 231 pilots, while the effort cost Kesselring 308 fighters and bombers.

By the end of the first week of September, Fighter Command was in desperate straits. Dowding wrote, "The rate of loss was so heavy that fresh squadrons became worn out [no longer operationally viable] before convalescing squadrons were ready to take their place." By September 7, his reserves of fighters in maintenance and storage – despite deliveries of new aircraft – had dwindled from 518 (on July 6) to 292. More critical was the loss of virtually irreplaceable fighter pilots, reducing squadron manning from 26 to 16 (on average), with only 500 (of 1,023) being combat experienced – the remainder having less than 20 hours on fighters.

By the same token, Nazi leadership was dissatisfied with Göring's results. At the end of August Kriegsmarine commander, Großadmiral (Grand Admiral) Erich Raeder complained to Hitler that the prerequisite of aerial supremacy had not been achieved – and his assessment was that "in the current German air attacks these conditions could not be created soon" – prompting a postponement of the proposed invasion to September 21.

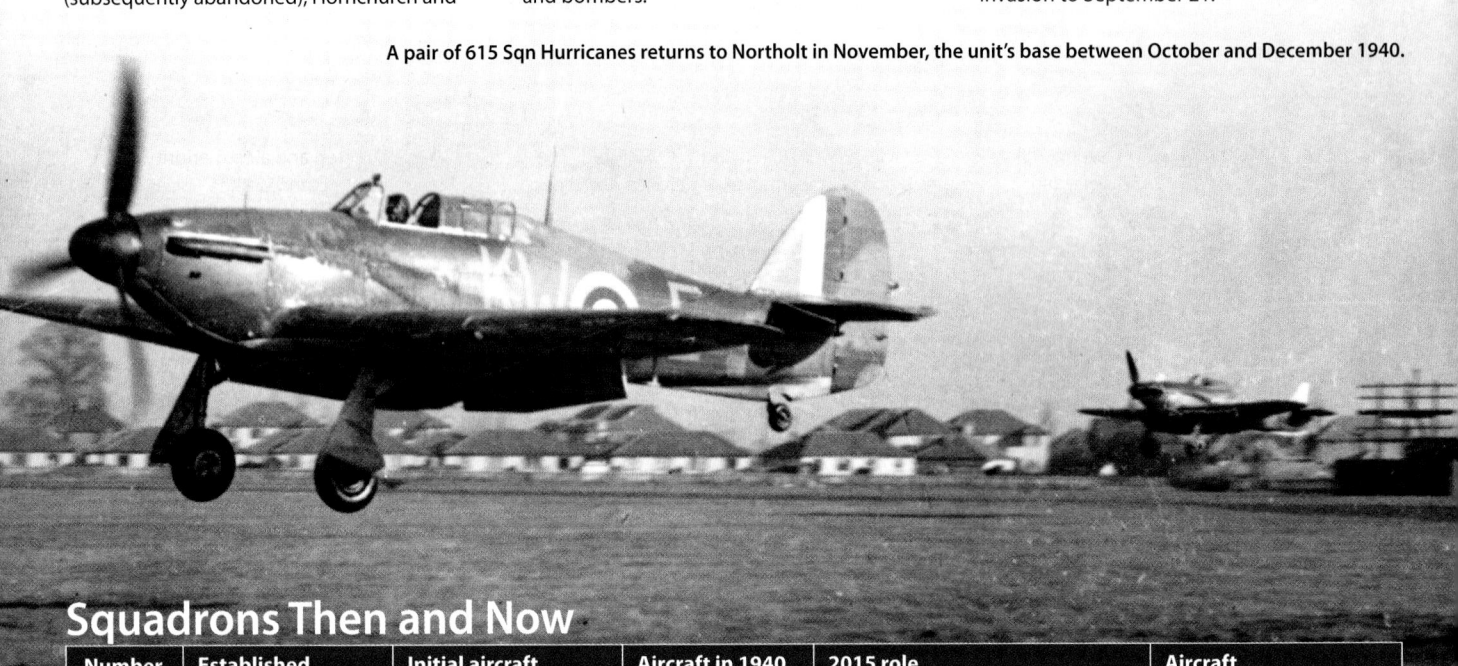

A pair of 615 Sqn Hurricanes returns to Northolt in November, the unit's base between October and December 1940.

Squadrons Then and Now

Number	Established	Initial aircraft	Aircraft in 1940	2015 role	Aircraft
17	February 1, 1915	B.E.2, DH.2, Scout	Hurricane	Operational Evaluation	Lighting II
41	July 14, 1929	F.B.5	Spitfire	Operational Test and Evaluation	Tornado and Typhoon

OPERATIONS

Barrage balloons were used over London and other cities as a last-ditch defence against low-flying bombers.

"We have no chance of destroying the English fighters on the ground. We must force their last reserves… into combat in the air."
Reichsmarschall Hermann Göring, meeting with Luftflotte commanders, Karinhall, September 3, 1940

Just when Luftflotte 2 had No. 11 Group 'on the ropes' – Dowding was on the verge of deciding to withdraw Park's units north of the Thames, a decision that would have ceded air superiority over southeast England to the Luftwaffe and given Göring the victory – the Reichsmarschall's frustration and impatience prompted him to switch the focus of the offensive from the destruction of RAF fighters at their bases to 'luring the RAF into a fight' by attacking London.

To Kesselring this had the perceived advantage of striking the British Empire's vital economic centre – especially the London docks – and to Hitler of retaliating for the RAF's attempted night bombing of Berlin on August 25/26. Additionally, sensing his reputation and future were now at stake, at this point Göring assumed direct control of air operations.

> Göring had 623 operational Bf 109s as the Luftwaffe turned its attention to London. Dowding could muster just 350 serviceable Spitfires and Hurricanes in defence.

On September 7, the first attack – 348 bombers covered by 617 fighters approaching in a massive 20-mile (32km) wide formation – surprised Park's controllers by initially feinting towards various sector airfields before turning against London, causing numerous 'missed intercepts'. The heavy attacks substantially damaged the East End docks, Woolwich Arsenal, and factories and oil installations along the Thames – 448 civilians were killed and 1,337 injured. The limitations of the interior air defence network, as well as dwindling combat experience and disadvantageous tactics, ensured the continued drain on fighters and pilots. The attack cost Park 21 fighters in exchange for 13 Bf 109s.

Fateful Decision
However, German bomber losses continued to mount; consequently, as operational commander, two days later Göring made his final, fateful decision: increase the awkward and unworkable close escorts of the bombers at the expense of the free-ranging and effective freie Jagd fighter sweeps. The lower altitudes and slower speeds necessary for the escorts to maintain station with the bombers gave the RAF fighters the advantages of speed, initiative, altitude, speed and, above all, 'fighting spirit'.

The anticipated climax to the campaign came on September 15, 277 bombers, escorted by 650 fighters, arrowing straight for London – no feints this time – in a 10-mile (16km) wide stream of warplanes approaching in two large waves. The Germans expected much of this attack – ObdL predicted it to be 'the decisive blow'.

Numbers 11 and 12 Groups responded with 336 defensive sorties. While they only shot down 16 German bombers and five escorts, after a month of attacks Fighter Command was still not beaten and air superiority over southeast England was no closer to attainment. Frustrated by Göring's inability to meet this requirement, two days later Hitler postponed Unternehmen Seelöwe indefinitely and the following day he authorised the dispersal of the 1,704 river barges and 149 sea-going transports the Kriegsmarine had gathered for the proposed invasion.

> During the nine-day Phase III period of the Battle, after London became the primary target, the RAF lost 131 fighters while the Luftwaffe lost 174 aircraft in combat.

The air campaign continued with sporadic raids for the rest of the month, culminating in the final major daylight attack of the war (173 bomber and 1,000 fighter sorties) on September 30. For the first time in the whole Battle, RAF fighters »

OPERATIONS

This He 111 was one of many bombers that attacked London on September 7. It is passing over the Thames at Wapping.

London's East End took a pounding on September 7, these Do 17s adding to its suffering as they flew close to Woolwich Arsenal.

London fireman at work during the Blitz.

significantly outperformed their adversaries, shooting down 16 bombers and 27 Bf 109s for the loss of 16 Spitfires and Hurricanes. Following this heavy loss, bombing raids steadily decreased and massed formations virtually disappeared.

The Night Blitz

Attempting to comply with *Directive No. 9*, the Luftwaffe's night bombing of Britain began on June 2/3, with small formations targeting industrial areas, shifting later that month to aircraft factory and airfield locations.

Few Kampfgruppen were trained for night bombing, but almost all experienced bomber pilots were qualified in night instrument approaches and landings. Radio beacons installed at the Luftflotten airfields aided recovery (especially for fuel-starved fighters) and these were augmented by the 42-48MHz Knickebein ('crooked leg') long-range, radio beam navigation system, which was received by the bombers' Lorenz instrument-approach equipment. Using this rudimentary system, Luftwaffe night bombing proved far more accurate than concurrent RAF nocturnal operations. Over the next ten weeks, 16 industrial plants, 14 ports and 13 airfields were targeted.

When Göring decided to focus daylight attacks against Fighter Command airfields in southeast England (Adlerangriff Phase II) and concentrated his Bf 109s in Kesselring's Luftflotte 2, Sperrle's Luftflotte 3 transitioned almost exclusively to nocturnal operations. To increase accuracy, as well as the weight of night attacks, Sperrle was assigned the 'pathfinder' Kampfgruppe 100 (KGr 100 – from Luftflotte 2) on August 17. This group, flying 41 He 111H-3s – used the narrow-beam 66.5-75MHz X-Gerät ('X-gadget') night bombing system that was more precise, had multi-targeting capability, and a 180-mile (290km) range.

Attacks continued to be small, widespread, and inaccurate – the RAF began the 'electronic war' in late July, countering with 'meacons' (masking beacons) to disrupt Knickebein operations – until the last week in August, when Sperrle doubled his effort with heavy attacks on south and western ports, especially Merseyside, delivering 496 tons of bombs in 629 sorties during a sustained four-night bombardment.

RAF night intercept capability was in its infancy and its radar system was generally ineffective over land, so German losses – reduced to about one third (2% of sorties

OPERATIONS

RAF Aircraft 1940: Bristol Beaufighter

Through an odd combination of wings, aft fuselage, empennage and undercarriage from its Beaufort torpedo-bomber, and a new forward fuselage and centre section, Bristol produced an exceptional two-seat fighter. It began work privately, but the RAF warmed to the concept and was fully behind it by July 17, 1939 when the first prototype Beaufighter (Beaufort-fighter) made its initial flight.

Powered by a pair of 1,400hp Bristol Hercules III radial piston engines, the Beaufighter proved somewhat slower than anticipated and was considered unsuitable as a day fighter. Nevertheless, it was heavily armed, with six 0.303in machine guns in the wings and four 20mm cannon in the nose, and when the Luftwaffe began upping the pace of its nocturnal bombing offensive, the Beaufighter came into its own.

Equipped with AI.Mk IV radar, it was a far more effective night fighter than the stopgap Blenheim, and joined Fighter Command's Fighter Interception Unit in August 1940 as the Beaufighter Mk IF.

Five frontline squadrons received the type during September and the first victory came on November 19/20, when Sqn Ldr John Cunningham used his 604 Sqn aircraft to down an enemy machine. Subsequent developments saw the Beaufighter remain in service throughout the war and beyond, although primarily in the maritime strike role at which it proved to excel.

This Beaufighter Mk IF was in service with 604 Sqn. Note the AI.Mk IV antennas on the wing leading edge. © Pete West

flown) of daylight operations – were almost exclusively due to crashes during attempted night landings and from anti-aircraft artillery.

Following the August 25/26 RAF bombing of Berlin's municipal farms (not the intended target), Sperrle was ordered to bomb London, and Göring's September 3 orders (Adlerangriff Phase III) made the British capital his primary target. On the initial attack four days later, Sperrle's night bombers followed Kesselring's daylight assaults with 247 sorties, adding to the conflagration and destruction of the East End industrial areas. Starting on September 7, London was bombed on 57 consecutive nights, destroying and damaging more than one million homes and killing more than 40,000 civilians.

Even after the disheartening battle of September 15, Sperrle's night raids continued – more as 'punishment' (Strafe Angriff) than for any strategic or operational reason. In October he was ordered to despatch 250 bombing sorties nightly – 150 against London and 100 striking Merseyside, the Midlands, and western ports – augmented by another 50 from Luftflotte 2.

During the next 34 weeks London was bombed 48 times, with multiple major attacks also hitting Birmingham, Liverpool, Plymouth, Bristol, Glasgow, Southampton, Portsmouth and Hull, while eight other cities were bombed once. The Night Blitz lasted until May 21, 1941 when the Luftwaffe had to reorganise and deploy eastwards for Unternehmen Barbarossa (Operation Barbarossa), the invasion of Soviet Russia, slated to commence one month later.

Battle Won

Officially, for the RAF the Battle of Britain ended on October 31, 1940. Sadly – and ironically – the last real casualty of the successful defensive struggle over southeast England was actually its victor. In part because of Fighter Command's inability to defend against the Luftwaffe's night bombing attacks, ACM Hugh Dowding was relieved of his post, being replaced by Air Marshal Sholto Douglas on November 25.

Politicians good and bad are prone to hyperbole – 'over the top' pronouncements made to engender public support and motivate mass enthusiasm or determination. Churchill and Hitler were both masters at this. Despite their overblown, emotional and evocative rhetoric in the summer of 1940, each was absolutely correct about one thing.

Churchill was right in saying: "Upon this battle depends the survival of Christian civilisation." Hitler was also right: "…the English homeland [proved to be the] base for the prosecution of the war against Germany."

To that end, Britain and the Western Allies owe thanks to Hugh Dowding and the 'Few'.

Number 41 Squadron took this Spitfire, purchased with funds raised by the Observer Corps, on strength in November 1940. Photographed with OC Sqn Ldr Donald Finlay in January 1941, the aircraft was lost in April after transfer to 54 Sqn.

Sqn Ldr Stanford-Tuck, OC 257 Sqn, stands with a unit Hurricane and pilots after the engagement with Italian aircraft on November 11.

ROYAL AIR FORCE SALUTE 2015 | 33

CAPABILITY

An Aerospace Battle Manager's station at RAF Boulmer, one of the UK's Air Defence Control and Reporting Centres.
© UK MoD Crown Copyright 2015

Air Defence: 2015

The fundamentals of air defence laid down prior to the Battle of Britain and exercised so thoroughly in determining victory remain as relevant today as ever. Flight Lieutenant Lucy Williams, an Aerospace Battle Manager at RAF Boulmer, explains

Based on the new technology of radar, Air Chief Marshal Hugh Dowding developed what became known as the Dowding System. Operational just in time for the outbreak of war, it was the first air defence system capable of integrating information from radar and ground observers, and using this product to command ground-based defences and fighter aircraft.

So successful was the system that it remains the basis of how the Royal Air Force secures our skies today, although there have been many changes. Modern aircraft fly much faster, our radars see much further and Fighter Controllers have become Aerospace Battle Managers (ABMs). But the task itself, to defend the nation, remains exactly the same and carries just as much importance.

Dowding would undoubtedly recognise many of the benefits and challenges of modern radar technology. A primary obstacle during the Battle of Britain was the task of processing raw radar information. Teams of Filterer Officers analysed data to determine where aircraft were, identify them and track them to produce a recognised picture of the air that could be used by commanders.

Now computers process much of the raw radar data, but that processed information would be useless without the hard work of the ABMs, including the teams of Identification Officers, who work tirelessly 24 hours a day, 365 days a year, analysing, identifying and tracking all the aircraft in our skies and producing the Recognised Air Picture for UK and NATO air defence commanders. And although radar technology is vastly improved, there are new challenges – jamming and stealth aircraft have made the job as difficult today as it ever was.

The constantly updated Recognised Air Picture is exported not only around the country as it once was, but also around coalition partners. Using a combination of familiar technology in radios and telephone landlines, and newer technology, including tactical data links, the Identification Officers' output is shared instantly.

The National Air Defence Operations Centre at High Wycombe coordinates domestic air security, but the UK also has responsibilities to NATO security, coordinated by the Combined Air Operations Centre in Uedem, Germany. This centralised command ensures commanders have information from a variety of sources, allowing them to make informed decisions. They then task the most appropriate air defence unit to carry out any required mission.

34 | ROYAL AIR FORCE SALUTE 2015

CAPABILITY

The Sentry provides a versatile, rapidly deployable radar surveillance capability. Operating at altitude, its powerful radar system 'sees' well over the horizon. © UK MoD Crown Copyright 2015

Below: Type 45 destroyer HMS *Dragon* was in the Middle East during 2013. This class of vessel is an important component in UK air defence capabilities.
L(Phot) Dave Jenkins/© UK MoD Crown Copyright 2015

Weapons Controllers

The Weapons Controllers are a subset of ABM and an essential component in our air defence. Their function is closely related to that of the Cold War ground controlled interception (GCI) units, and GCI remains a core role, but as air power capabilities have increased, so has the contribution of the Weapons Controller.

With access to a real time picture of the air battle via the Identification Officers, the Weapons Controllers not only vector friendly fighters onto enemy or unknown contacts, but also use the advantage of having the big picture to manage the battle as it develops. This delegation of responsibility from the centralised commanders enables rapid decision making and is a key element of the RAF's effectiveness, just as it was with Sector Commanders and Sector Controllers during the Battle of Britain.

The basics of the Dowding System remain successful today because they provide a foundation from which operators can adapt and respond to changing threats. During the Battle of Britain the enemy was clearly defined and identified, but that is no longer the case. UK and NATO air defence systems must react to a whole spectrum of potential threats from unpredictable terrorist activity to the conventional threat of other nations with their own air power capabilities.

As aviation technology has developed, the skies over and around the UK have also become increasingly congested. Aircraft that do not always submit flight plans through the civilian air traffic system, including Russian military aircraft, do not come under the control of civilian air traffic agencies and can pose a risk to flight safety as they transit busy air routes. Although they fly in international airspace, it is airspace in which the UK is responsible for the safe passage of flight. Typhoons are therefore scrambled to escort these unannounced aircraft, accurately identifying their position to the civilian control agencies so that they can safely route other traffic around them.

ASACS

With such an array of possible threats the RAF has developed and expanded upon the original Dowding System, not least with the Air Surveillance And Control System (ASACS). The surveillance aspect of the system draws upon permanent military and civilian radars, airborne radar aboard the Sentry AEW1 and shipborne radar on the Royal Navy's Type 45 destroyers.

The control element is extremely flexible and provided from one of the UK's two Control and Reporting Centres, at RAF Boulmer, Northumberland and RAF Scampton, Lincolnshire, a Sentry or a Type 45. Bringing together these capabilities to act in concert makes UK air defence highly effective, agile and adaptable.

In an unpredictable world it is important to keep these capabilities well practised. The ASACS is therefore exercised regularly, on a small scale with scrambles of individual quick reaction alert (QRA) aircraft and on a large scale with joint, multinational exercises that integrate with the Royal Navy and Army, as well as NATO and coalition partner nations.

As it was during the Battle of Britain, it is clearly still a case of 'the many supporting the few'. From the Identification Officers and the Weapons Controllers of the ABM branch to the air traffic managers, engineers and air-to-air refuelling tanker squadrons, there are many personnel supporting every QRA Typhoon. The success of ACM Dowding's original system lay in its ability to network a variety of capabilities using military and civilian systems. This remains the core of the RAF's operating procedures – it is the combined effect of many teams working together that ensures the continued safety of our skies.

CAPABILITY

Air Defence: 1940

Success in the air often came down to the courage of the RAF's pilots and the quality of their equipment, but defeating the Luftwaffe en masse would have been impossible without Britain's complex air defence network. The Air Historical Branch's Seb Cox explains

CAPABILITY

In a scene that sums up much of the UK's air defence control system in 1940, WAAF plotters work in the underground operations room at HQ Fighter Command, Bentley Priory. A senior officer studies the unfolding events from the viewing deck above. RAF (AHB)/© UK MoD Crown Copyright 2015

The Battle of Britain surely ranks alongside the Battles of Trafalgar and Waterloo as one of the most significant in British history. As with the Battle of Trafalgar, it lifted the threat of invasion; like Waterloo it limited the ambitions of an expansive European power in thrall to a megalomaniac. It was the first significant strategic defeat suffered by Adolph Hitler's Third Reich during World War Two. In the longer term, the Battle ensured that Britain could serve as an 'unsinkable aircraft carrier', enabling the Western Allies, including the USA and Canada, to launch their invading armies into continental Europe on D-Day.

The iconic vision of Spitfires and Hurricanes battling to preserve our democratic freedoms as they swept into action against large formations of German aircraft is an accurate one. However, it gives us only a partial understanding of what was a far more complex picture with a myriad cast of characters and a host of participating organisations, extending well beyond the RAF fighter pilots, sweating in their cramped cockpits high above the hop fields of Kent.

The air battles of 1940 were a struggle for supremacy rooted in a fiercely technological domain, where science and its application were as important as the courage and skill of the pilots. Britain was no stranger to air attack. Indeed, the story begins more than two decades earlier, when German Zeppelin airships and giant heavier-than-air bombers attacked London during World War One. The sight of formations of bombers flying apparently unmolested over the capital in broad daylight in the summer of 1917 caused a political storm, and the subsequent enquiry led directly to the formation of the RAF.

The Prime Minister, David Lloyd George, appointed the razor-sharp South African General Jan Christian Smuts, to investigate. He recommended that the effective aerial defence of the nation required a single professionally qualified and expert air service. His recommendation was approved and the necessary legislation put in place. As a result, on April 1, 1918, the Royal Air Force was formed, although steps had already been taken to create an effective air defence organisation for the British Isles.

Air Defence Defined
It was quickly recognised a century ago that the basic requirement for effective air defence was a system comprising several constituent parts. The first, the observation element, identified and located the enemy aircraft, while the second, an efficient communications system, sent the information as rapidly as possible to an air defence operations centre.

At the operations centre the information could be displayed in an understandable form quickly enough to enable the air defence commander to react by alerting anti-aircraft (AA) gun batteries and despatching fighter aircraft to intercept and shoot the enemy down. All parts of the system, identification and location, dissemination and display, command and control, fighter interception or AA fire control, had to function efficiently and in concert to achieve the desired end result – the destruction of the enemy.

The system developed in World War One involved observation by military personnel (some using concrete 'acoustic mirrors' for sound detection of aircraft), police and railway officials. Curious as this latter arrangement might appear, it was in fact a sensible and imaginative innovation. The railway network at the time was an important strategic asset to the country, boasting stationmasters and a dense patchwork of stations extending across large parts of the country. Just as importantly, these were linked together by telephone and telegraph, which provided that most vital component – rapid communication.

Operations rooms with map tables and other communications equipment were established in London, one being located at Liverpool Street Station. Eventually, a central control room was set up in Horse Guards and 25 sub-controls around the country passed details of 'plots' on raiders. There were ten 'plotters' seated at the map table, each with a headset connecting him to several sub-controls.

Colour-coded counters with arrows were placed on the map tables to depict the tracks of hostile aircraft and airships, and there were indicators to show where bombs had been dropped. The colours on the counter corresponded to five-minute coloured segments on the operations room clock, which thus indicated how old the plot was. 'Stale' plots more than ten minutes old were removed from the table. The air defence commander, General EB Ashmore, sat in a raised gallery, giving him an unobstructed view of the map table, and could talk directly to any sub-control.

By the time of the Armistice, Ashmore and his team had thus more or less solved the organisational problems associated with air defence. The foundations of the later air defence system, which came to be known as the Dowding System, had their origins in Ashmore's organisation, known as the London Air Defence Area (LADA).

The technological issues that LADA faced were less easily addressed. The acoustic mirrors were not particularly successful, and the limited results of enemy air attacks owed as much to the technical shortcomings of German aircraft as to the rapid improvement of UK air defences. However, the acoustic mirrors were the focus for some of the earliest attempts at co-operation between scientists and the military in the air defence field. This relationship, although not without its difficulties, would bear far more significant fruit in a later conflict.

Air Defence Under Pressure
In the 1920s, as now, defence spending came under intense pressure. However, this did not mean that UK air defences were entirely neglected. Under the Treaty of Versailles, Germany was forbidden military aircraft, leaving France as the only major power theoretically capable of threatening the UK from the air. The 1920s air defence system was therefore designed to address that »

ROYAL AIR FORCE SALUTE 2015 | 37

CAPABILITY

potential, if unlikely, eventuality. A number of committees investigated various aspects of the air defence problem and produced recommendations for a new approach, drawing on the experience of the LADA and creating separate zones for AA guns and fighters (to avoid friendly fire incidents).

The Aircraft Fighting Zone originally extended from Duxford, near Cambridge, to Devizes in Wiltshire. The outer edge of this Zone was about 35 miles (56km) inland from the coast, a distance dictated by the amount of warning expected of an incoming raid combined with the time it took the contemporary biplane fighters to climb up to 14,000ft – the height at which it was anticipated the bombers would fly.

There was an Outer Artillery Zone in front of the Aircraft Fighting Zone, and an Inner Artillery Zone behind it, mainly covering London. The Aircraft Fighting Zone was sub-divided into ten Sectors, each with a front of about 15 miles (24km). The four Sectors to the south and east of London were to be defended by two fighter squadrons, and the others would have one squadron. A further three squadrons would be stationed near the coast to intercept and harass the incoming raids as early as possible. Observer posts were to be established across Southern England, linked to observer centres; those on the coast were to be equipped with acoustic mirrors. In October 1925 an Observer Corps (later Royal Observer Corps) was established, using volunteer civilians to man the observer posts.

Defensive Reorientation

In the 1930s, following Hitler's rise to power and the establishment of the Luftwaffe, the air defence system was progressively reorientated from south to east and extended to cover the whole country. Of course, it was anticipated that France would be allied with Britain in the event of war and that the threat from Germany would come from across the North Sea. However, the rapid development of aviation during the 1920s and 1930s served to complicate the issue.

The German Gotha biplane bombers of 1917 had flown at a stately 70mph (110km/h), but by the 1930s, their sleek monoplane Dornier and Heinkel descendants could reach almost 200mph (320km/h). With enemy bombers flying at such speeds, there would be less time to mobilise the air defence system against them.

The advent of an aggressive potential enemy capable of threatening the UK so worried the government that it set up a Committee for the Scientific Survey of Air Defence, with a membership that included several distinguished scientists. The very first meeting of this committee in January 1935 heard a proposal from Mr (later Sir) Robert Watson-Watt of the National Physical Laboratory on the possibility of detecting aircraft using reflected radio waves – the principal of what is now known as radar. This required Treasury approval for the expenditure of some £10,000, and Air Marshal Sir Hugh

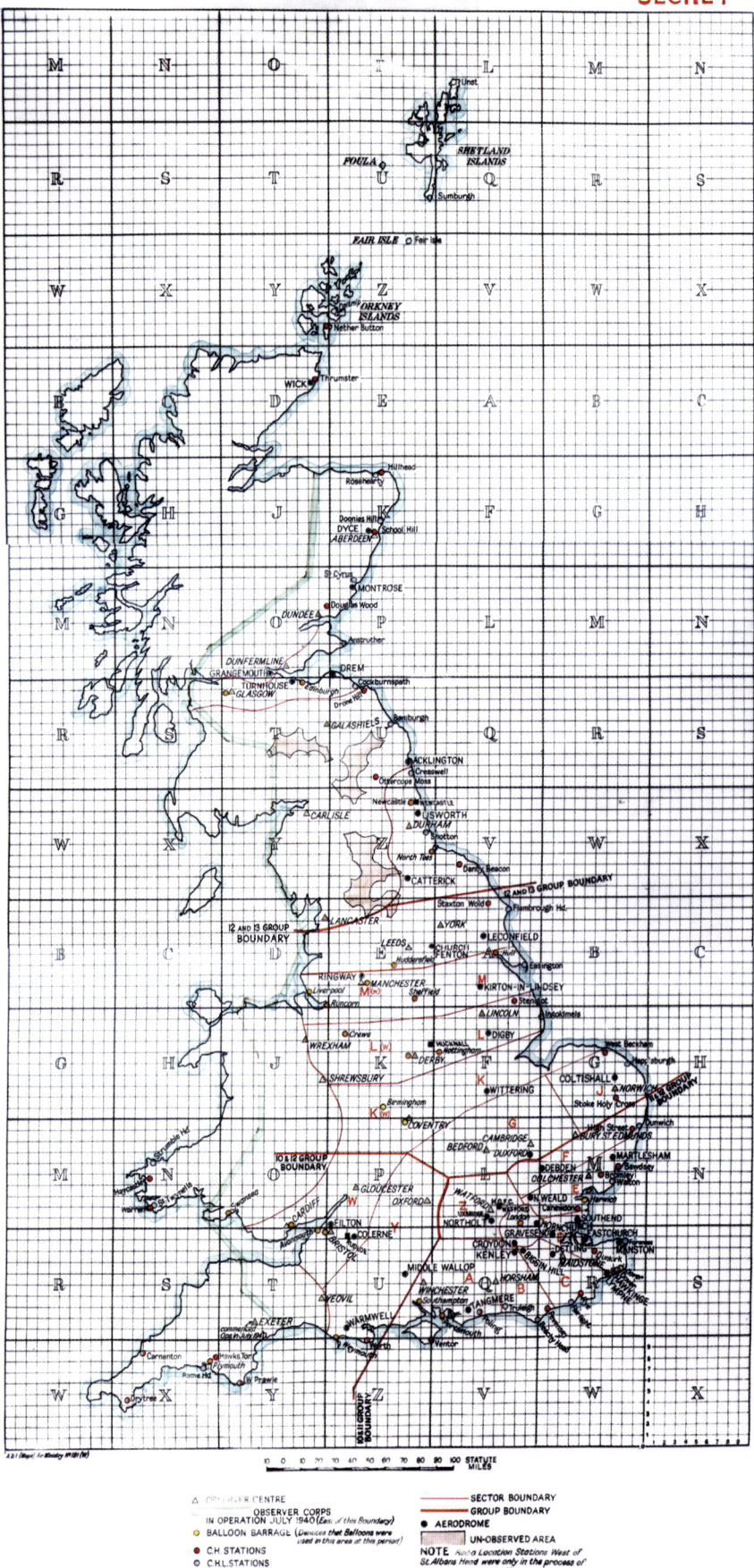

Dated July 1940, this map depicts the division of UK airspace into Groups and Sectors for the purposes of fighter control. Chain Home (CH) and Chain Home Low (CHL) radar stations are shown, as are airfields, balloon barrages and Observer Corps coverage. *RAF Museum*

CAPABILITY

Fighter Command's squadrons relied on the RAF's comprehensive early warning and control network to scramble them in time to reach and engage incoming enemy formations. These 85 Sqn Hurricanes were airborne on October 5, 1940, with Sqn Ldr Peter Townsend leading. RAF (AHB)/© UK MoD Crown Copyright 2015

"From the map references relayed to the Ops Room the squadrons could be scrambled to deal with the approaching enemy aircraft."
Patricia Clark (nee Robins), WAAF plotter

Dowding, the senior officer responsible for research and development for the RAF, wisely considered that this would more probably be forthcoming if some basic evidence was available.

Dowding therefore arranged for an RAF aircraft to be made available to Watson-Watt. The latter, with help from AF Wilkins, set up a crude experiment in the middle of a field near Weedon, Northamptonshire. At this location, on February 26, 1935, Watson-Watt and Wilkins parked a van with a radio receiver connected to an antenna slung from wooden poles and linked to a cathode ray oscilloscope. Meanwhile, Flt Lt RS Blucke approached the nearby town of Daventry in a Handley-Page Heyford biplane bomber. Blucke proceeded to fly a predetermined route backwards and forwards between Weedon and Daventry, where there was a BBC Radio short-wave transmitter. In the field below, the receiver was tuned to the signal from the BBC, which showed as a straight line on the oscilloscope; however, as Blucke's aircraft passed, it reflected the radio waves, producing a distinct spike on the oscilloscope trace.

Radar Reality
Watson-Watt immediately wrote a memo entitled *Detection and Location of Aircraft by Radio Methods* and presented it to the Air Ministry next day. Radar was born. Much work and further experimentation was necessary to turn this first, very crude, almost comical experiment into a functional early warning system integrated into the UK's air defences. Nevertheless, this humble beginning was to have the most profound effect on the outcome of the Battle of Britain. Dowding duly got his money from the Treasury, and that notoriously parsimonious organisation actually sanctioned expenditure of £12,300 in the first year; much more was to follow.

A research station was established for Watson-Watt and a team of scientists at Bawdsey Manor in Suffolk, and the Treasury approved the construction of an experimental chain of five radar stations to cover the Thames Estuary, while the Air Ministry suspended all expenditure on the acoustic mirrors it had been building.

Despite many hiccups and setbacks, RAF senior officers were convinced by 1937 that a full chain of radar stations should be built to protect the east coast. By the outbreak of war in September 1939, 20 radar stations were in operation, and further expansion followed »

Observer Corps' posts were strategically sited around the country, personnel detecting and plotting all aircraft over their area. Information, including the height and track of friendly and hostile machines, was passed to the local control centre. Dated April 1941, this photograph shows a typical post. RAF (AHB)/© UK MoD Crown Copyright 2015

Hopton-on-Sea's Chain Home Low Air Ministry Experimental Station (AMES) Type 2 installation in 1945. It has an array on the 185ft (56m) tower and a second on the 20ft (6m) gantry. RAF (AHB)/© UK MoD Crown Copyright 2015

Early radar equipment was large and relatively crude, requiring considerable skill to operate well. This is the transmitter room of an AMES Type 2 CHL station. RAF (AHB)/© UK MoD Crown Copyright 2015

under the impetus of live hostilities; 27 more radars were operational before the Battle of Britain.

Experiments had also been conducted at the other end of the 'system', whereby the plots originating at the radar stations were displayed on the operations room map tables at the newly established Fighter Command, and at Group and Sector headquarters lower down the chain, interception orders then being passed by radio telephone to squadron commanders in the air.

In addition to building the radar stations, all the necessary communications facilities had to be installed, linking radars, observer posts and Observer Corps centres with Fighter Command Headquarters at Bentley Priory, near Stanmore, and connecting the Fighter Command operations room with Group and Sector operations rooms.

Vital Communications

This communications network, linking the component parts of the system, would prove to be of vital importance to UK air defence in 1940. By the time the Battle of Britain began, the Luftwaffe's bases were far closer to the UK than they had been at the start of the war. A German fighter squadron based in the Pas de Calais could cross the Straits of Dover in just six minutes. However, the German bombers were based further inland and, heavily laden with bombs and fuel, they had to climb slowly to their operational altitude. The Luftwaffe's Bf 109 fighters were handicapped by their relatively short endurance, which is why they were based further forward on aerodromes near the coast. There they would wait for the bombers to approach, before taking off and joining up into much larger formations.

This process took a little time and, as the formations assembled, they began to appear on British radar screens. This generally provided about 20 minutes' warning of their approach. The radar station would report the raid through constantly open telephone lines to Bentley Priory, where the plots were received in a filter room and placed in the appropriate map square on the filter room map table. The function of this room was literally to filter the plots, combining

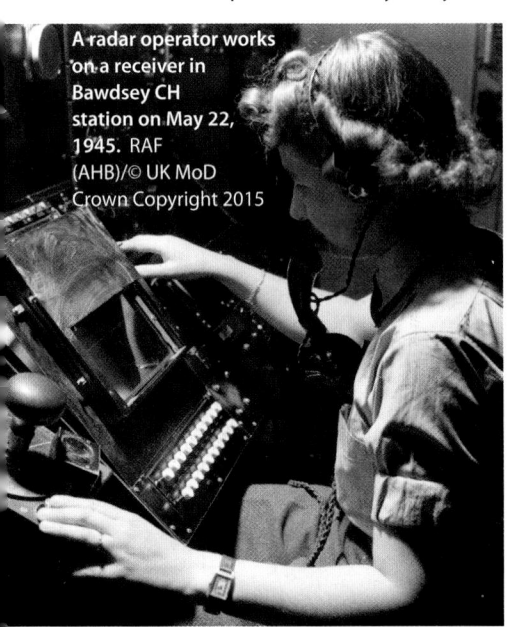

A radar operator works on a receiver in Bawdsey CH station on May 22, 1945. RAF (AHB)/© UK MoD Crown Copyright 2015

Defiant crews in August 1940, awaiting the Sector controller's call to scramble. RAF (AHB)/© UK MoD Crown Copyright 2015

40 | ROYAL AIR FORCE SALUTE 2015

Above left: **Taken at HQ 11 Group, RAF Uxbridge in October 1942, this image illustrates how plotters received information on aircraft positions through earphones, then carefully plotted their courses on table maps for the controllers.** Above right: **This May 1945 photograph shows an East Coast receiver room with one of the two RF7 receivers (left) and the Mk 3 console (right) in use.** both RAF (AHB)/© UK MoD Crown Copyright 2015

those from different radars and weeding out extraneous returns, which might be flocks of geese or meteorological phenomena.

When the filterer officer was sure that a plot was genuine, it was allocated a hostile raid number and a 'teller' would speak into her microphone (most tellers were Women's Auxiliary Air Force (WAAF) personnel) and pass the details of the hostile raid plot. Her words would simultaneously echo in the headphones of WAAF 'plotters' in every operations room in the affected region, from Fighter Command at Bentley Priory right down to the Group and Sector levels. Instantly and simultaneously, the plotters would place the appropriate plot counter in the correct map square on all the operations room map tables throughout the system. From the first radar contact to the operations room plot appearing, the process took about four minutes.

There were now around 16 minutes left, but it took a Spitfire squadron in a battle climb 14 minutes to reach 20,000ft and a Hurricane squadron a few minutes longer. So the controllers at the Group HQ, who determined which fighter squadrons were to be scrambled to intercept incoming raids, had very little time to make the right decision if they were to intercept.

As the radars tracked the raid, the plotters moved the counters across the map table using croupier-like rakes; as in Ashmore's LADA, the arrows showing the track were colour-coded according to the colour on the face of the segmented clock in the operations room. Plots older than 15 minutes were removed from the table.

Patricia Robins was a WAAF plotter and explains the job first hand: "The information received by the plotters in the filter rooms from the coastal radar stations was processed by the filterers and relayed by an operator on the telephone to the ops room. From the map references relayed to the ops room the squadrons could be scrambled to deal with the approaching enemy aircraft. Speed was, therefore, essential, and the urgency of our work became even more apparent when the blitz started.

"I think there were about 30 around the table on a shift. We were an assorted bunch of young women from very varied backgrounds, but there was never any discord between us. We were all dedicated to our work and totally concentrated on what we were doing.

"On occasions we would receive SOS signals from one of our planes damaged so badly it was about to come down in the Channel. We were then able to plot its anticipated ditching position and the ops room could alert the necessary rescue craft."

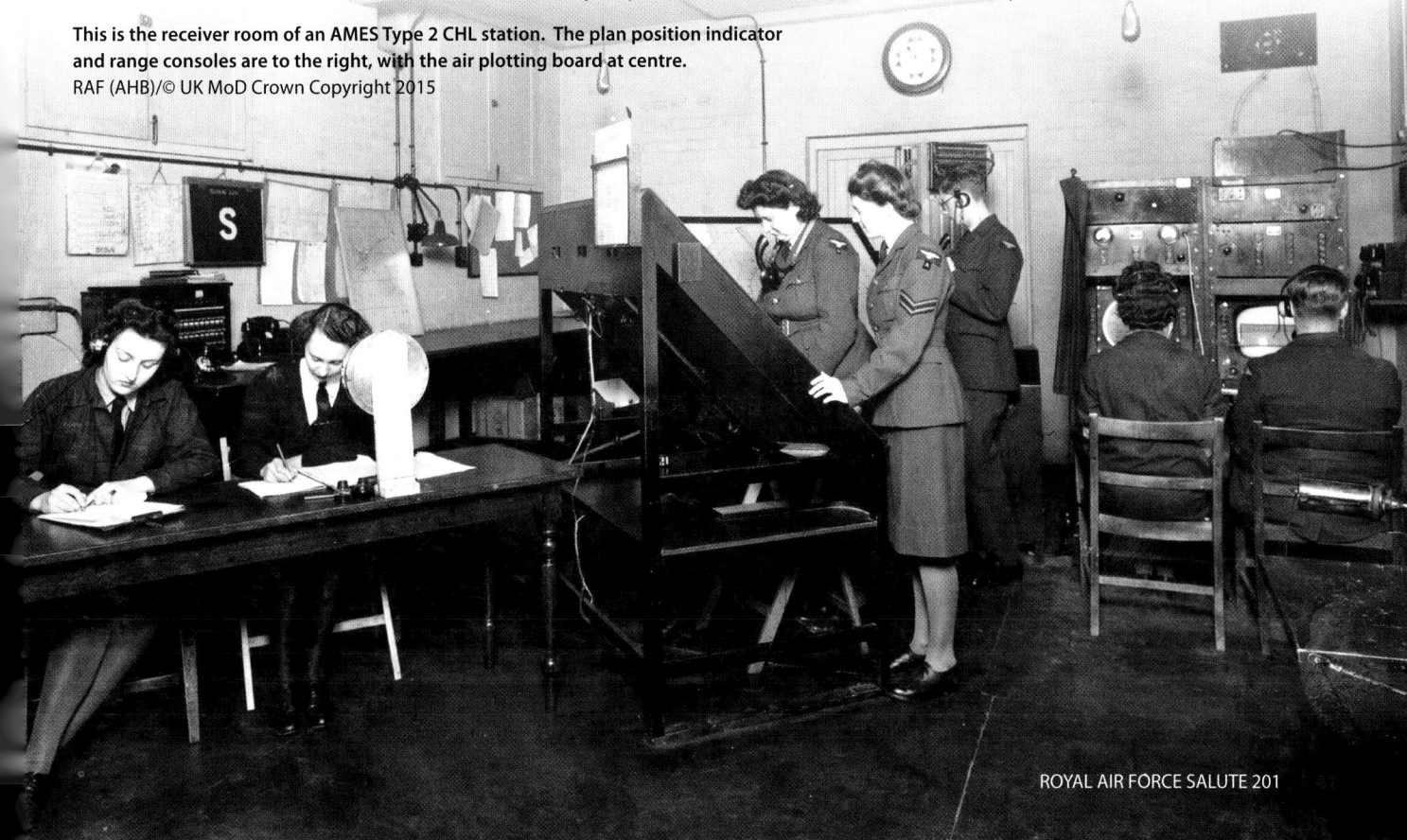

This is the receiver room of an AMES Type 2 CHL station. The plan position indicator and range consoles are to the right, with the air plotting board at centre.
RAF (AHB)/© UK MoD Crown Copyright 2015

CAPABILITY

Telephone operators, in the Sector 'G' Operations Room at Duxford, take reports from Observer Corps' posts. RAF (AHB)/© UK MoD Crown Copyright 2015

The Filter Room at Fighter Command HQ. RAF (AHB)/© UK MoD Crown Copyright 2015

Scramble!

Once his mind was made up, the controller at the responsible Group HQ would lift his phone and tell the switchboard operator to connect him to the relevant Sector station. The Sector controller's phone would ring and he would hear the Group controller's voice issuing instructions to scramble the relevant squadrons and confirming the altitude at which they should patrol, and the patrol area.

The orders were crisp and to the point, wasting few words. Thus, "Scramble 92 and 72, Patrol Canterbury, Angels 25," meant 92 and 72 Squadrons were to be sent into the air immediately, climb to 25,000ft and form a patrol line over the city of Canterbury.

The Sector controller repeated the words to ensure they were correctly understood and then put the phone down. He then turned to the phone connected directly to the squadron dispersal huts on the airfield. When the phones in the dispersal huts rang, every pilot lazing in the bunks in the hut, or outside in deck chairs, or on the grass, sat bolt upright and stared at the individual who lifted the receiver. As soon as he shouted "Scramble!" they ran towards their aircraft.

Parachutes would have been placed on the wing or the seat, and the ground crew, who never strayed far from their charges, helped the pilots buckle them on, slip into their cockpits and do up their straps. Then the engines all around the dispersal spluttered and roared into life, brakes were released and the fighters began to move, bouncing and rolling across the grass in a pell-mell race to get airborne.

Once the aircraft left the ground, the fighter leader called up the Sector controller for instructions. It was then the Sector controller's task to direct them towards the enemy via radio-telephone, his initial order being the course to steer, together with "Make Angels 25". As more information was received on the strength and direction of the raid, he would pass this to the squadrons and change the vectors as necessary to bring them over Canterbury or adjust their course to meet the enemy.

All tracking of raids that had crossed the English coast was the responsibility of the Observer Corps, since the radars looked out to sea, not inland. The margins for error were small, but the vital communications links between the component parts of the system allowed just enough time for the defences to react.

Talking about her work as a radar operator, former WAAF Yvonne Axon emphasised the importance of minimising errors for accurate interceptions: "We were connected directly to Fighter Command, telling them what to put on the table. In other words we said: 'I think we have an aeroplane…' Actually, it could be three, or a squadron, or might well be a group of 60 fighters. They all looked very much the same. You had to sound terribly confident. If what you said was right, then the fighter boys were sent up to that spot, or where that spot would be in five minutes' time. We were always there in the right place at the right time – that is, most of the time."

Thus the radars, Observer Corps and filter and operations rooms gathered, filtered, disseminated and displayed the information in usable form. But they made up only those elements of the air defence system designed to tell commanders what was going on. Moreover, while the commanders benefited immeasurably from this heightened situational awareness, they had still to decide what resources to use, despatch those forces to intercept, and manoeuvre them into contact with the enemy, which was no mean feat in a fast-moving, three-dimensional battle. ⊙

The result of successful detection, plotting, reporting and control was an engagement with the enemy, as far away from British targets as possible. Here Heinkel He 111 bombers are under attack. RAF (AHB)/© UK MoD Crown Copyright 2015

key SHOP

For a great selection of aviation and transport books, DVDs, magazines and models visit:

www.keypublishing.com/shop

ROYAL AIR FORCE museum

Come for a flying visit – stay the day

- Group Tours available on request
- The Battle of Britain Hall – London
- The National Cold War Exhibition – Cosford
- Full calendar of family events

FREE ADMISSION

Explore the story of the RAF, aviation and the men & women who transformed our world.

Cosford: T: 01902 376 200   London: T: 020 8205 2266
Email: cosford@rafmuseum.org   Email: london@rafmuseum.org

www.rafmuseum.org

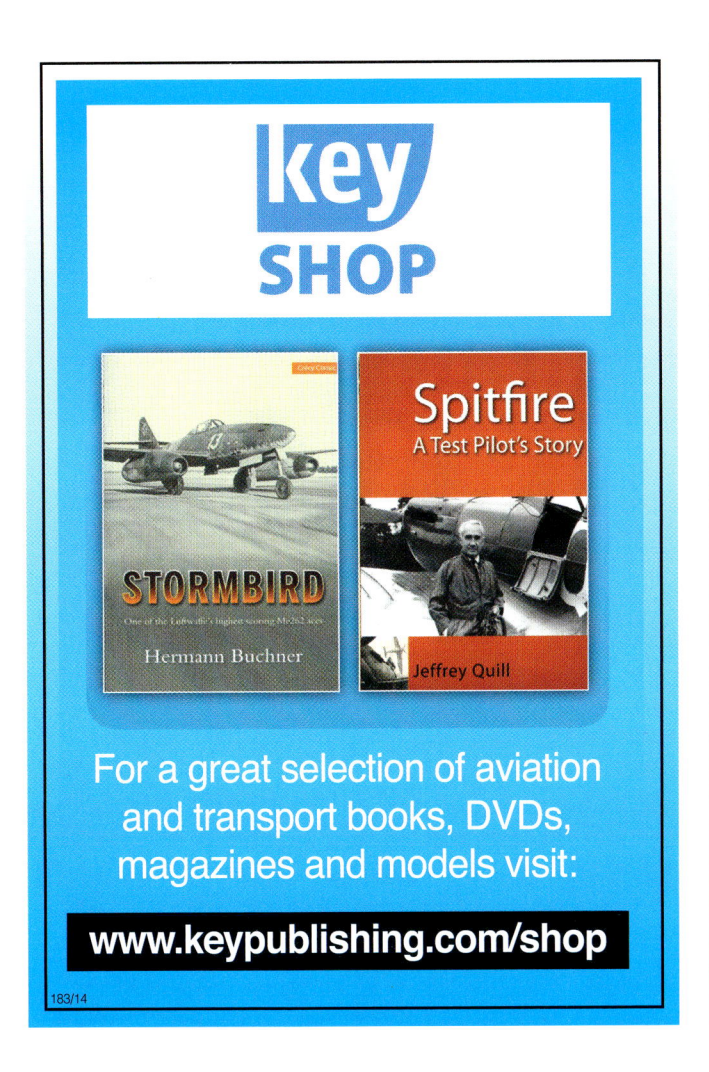

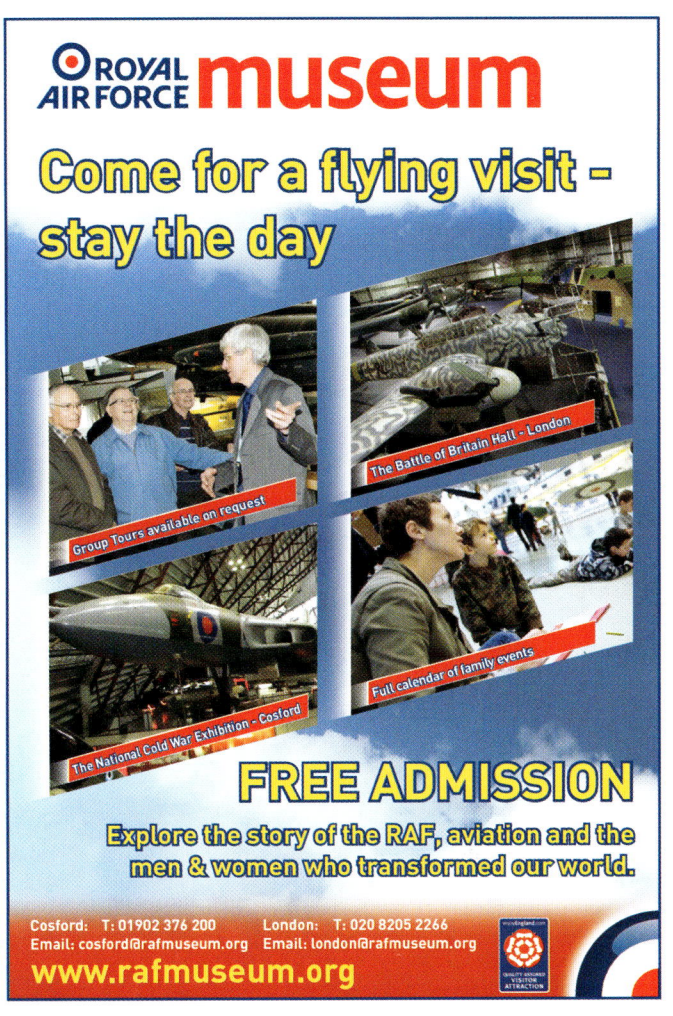

THE DEVELOPMENT, COMBAT HISTORY AND THE ACES WHO FLEW THEM

Produced by a team of some of the most highly-respected aviation journalists in the business, 'Famous Fighters of World War 2' is a **100-PAGE SPECIAL** publication timed to celebrate the 70th anniversary of VE Day.

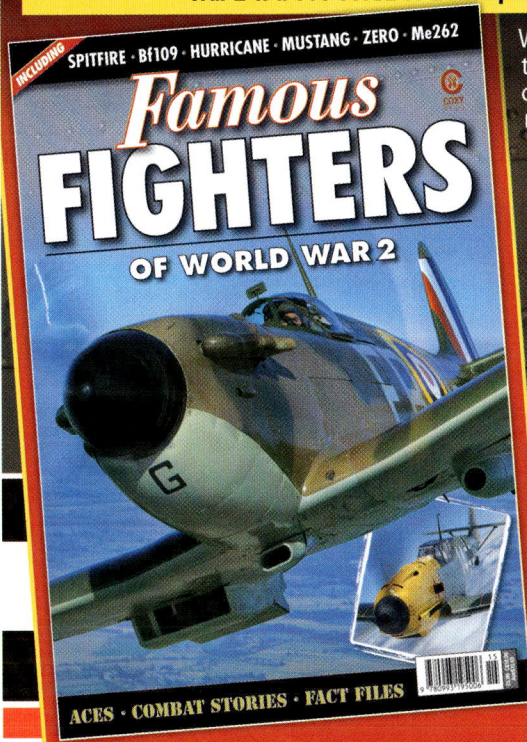

INCLUDING SPITFIRE · Bf109 · HURRICANE · MUSTANG · ZERO · Me262

Famous FIGHTERS OF WORLD WAR 2

ACES · COMBAT STORIES · FACT FILES

We hold the iconic fighter aircraft of World War Two in such reverence, that it is sometimes difficult to comprehend that they were designed for one purpose, and one purpose only. They were the lean, mean, killing machines of their time, a time when rapidly advancing technology honed the aircraft into a war-winning weapon that influenced every theatre of the conflict.

Arranged in chronological sequence, we look at the top ten fighters of the conflict, their development, combat history and the aces that flew them. From the eternal grace of the Spitfire to the futuristic Me262, this special publication pays tribute to them all.

AIRCRAFT INCLUDE:
SUPERMARINE SPITFIRE, HAWKER HURRICANE, MESSERSCHMITT BF109, **FOCKE-WULF FW190,** MESSERSCHMITT ME262, **P-51 MUSTANG,** P-47 THUNDERBOLT, **AND MANY MORE!**

Order Direct:
JUST £5.99 FREE P&P*

*Free 2nd class P&P on all UK & BFPO orders. Overseas charges apply.

Free P&P* when you order online at
www.keypublishing.com/shop

OR

Call UK: 01780 480404
Overseas: +44 1780 480404
Monday to Friday 9am-5:30pm

KEY MAGAZINE SUBSCRIBERS CALL FOR YOUR £1.00 DISCOUNT!

HERITAGE

Synchro 75
Battle of Britain Tribute

For 2015 the Battle of Britain Memorial Flight has joined forces with RAF Coningsby's 29 (Reserve) Squadron to create a very special Synchro team of Typhoon and Spitfire. Paul E Eden visited the Lincolnshire station to find out more

HERITAGE

The Battle of Britain Memorial Flight's Hurricanes and Spitfires will be the focus of attention in this 75th anniversary year of the Battle of Britain. In particular, Spitfire Mk II P7350 is a survivor of the campaign, albeit having suffered the ignominy of being shot down in its closing stages. Hurricane Mk II LF363 also pays tribute to the Battle, with its 1 Sqn colour scheme replicating that of the Mk I flown by Plt Off Arthur 'Taffy' Clowes, who scored ten Battle of Britain kills with the squadron.

Four Eurofighter Typhoon operators share BBMF's RAF Coningsby base, among them 29 (Reserve) Squadron, latterly provider of the Typhoon Display Team, presenting a spectacular solo aircraft routine. This year the unit is providing a second display jet, as half of the Spitfire/Typhoon Synchro Display, known to the pilots simply as Synchro and the world as @RAFSynchro75 on Twitter and Instagram.

A Typhoon FGR4 single-seater has been painted in stunning Battle of Britain camouflage with the aspiration of presenting this aircraft alongside a Spitfire, serviceability allowing. The scheme replicates the colours and markings of the Hurricane I flown by Flight Lieutenant James Nicolson VC DFC, allowing Synchro to present a dynamic opposition routine representing both primary Battle of Britain fighters.

In an ideal world, P7350 would fly as the second Synchro, but the aircraft was less than enthusiastic about the coming display season and at the time of writing in late May had yet to emerge from winter serving; at 75 years old it can perhaps be forgiven a little grumpiness. The team worked-up and gained its public display authorisation using BBMF's Spitfire Mk IX, but the VB, XVI or XIX could also serve. Whichever appears for a given display, audiences will witness the classic silhouettes of Spitfire and Typhoon, two world class fighters 60 years apart in concept, in the same piece of sky.

Synchro Pilots

Flight Lieutenants Antony 'Parky' Parkinson and Ben Westoby-Brooks are the Spitfire and Typhoon Synchro pilots. Ben is a Qualified Pilot Instructor on Typhoon, training new pilots and instructors on the type; he flew combat over Libya during Operation Ellamy in 2011. Parky also flew Typhoon, but has been with the BBMF for eight years. For him the Synchro display is a recreation of a similar show flown in 2010, but for Ben it's his first taste of display flying. Early in May they spoke to *Salute* about Synchro and the forthcoming season.

"The Spitfire and Typhoon routine was really well received when we did it in 2010," says Parky. "Because it's just a little different and went so well last time, the Air Officer Commanding 1 Group was very keen that it should be done again to honour the guys from 75 years ago – the Few get fewer, but they are still around.

"For that reason, the Royal Air Force wanted to massively celebrate the 75th and a really effective way of doing that is to put a Spitfire »

The Synchro Typhoon, ZK349, is used daily on 29(R) Sqn, as is the unit's solo display aircraft. Here they depart Coningsby in a pairs take-off for a training sortie. © Christiaan Lowe

Flight Lieutenant Ben Westoby-Brooks flies with Wg Cdr Justin 'Hells' Helliwell in BBMF's Battle of Britain-painted Hurricane, for a Battle of Britain 75th anniversary formation. The Synchro team uses a Spitfire rather than a Hurricane, but with the Flight's Mk II reluctant to begin the new season, the Hurricane flew for the photo shoot. © Richard Paver

HERITAGE

"It's in 249 Sqn colours with James Nicolson's name on it. It's a living memorial, his aircraft in effect, 75 years on…"

Flight Lieutenant Ben Westoby-Brooks, Synchro Typhoon pilot

The display work-up used Spitfire Mk IX MK356. © Christiaan Lowe

Although any of the BBMF Spitfires could fly the Synchro display, the hope is to use Mk II P7350. Photo © John M. Dibbs

46 | ROYAL AIR FORCE SALUTE 2015

HERITAGE

ZK349's stunning colours represent those of the Hurricane I flown by Flt Lt James Nicolson to shoot down a Messerschmitt Bf 110 during the Battle of Britain. Nicolson remained with his blazing aircraft to attack the enemy, receiving the Victoria Cross for his actions. © Richard Paver

and Typhoon together. What's really brilliant is that we have a Spitfire that actually flew in the Battle of Britain and we've painted the Typhoon in exactly the same green and brown camouflage."

Ben Westoby-Brooks explains how the Typhoon's camouflage was chosen: "With Typhoon colour schemes there's generally some tail art, and that was the initial plan for the 75th. But we thought about how few veterans were left and wanted to paint the full colours in their honour. What's really great is that lots of people at Coningsby, including the engineers, SERCO and the paint shop, and the hierarchy all the way up to Air Command, found ways to say 'yes'.

"All the BBMF's aircraft tell a story of what happened at the time and we've been able to do that with the Typhoon. It's in 249 Sqn colours with James Nicolson's name on it. It's a living memorial, his aircraft in effect, 75 years on, and the story behind it is incredible."

The routine itself is little changed from 2010's, as Parky explains: "We already had approval for a synchro display that involves either two Spitfires or a Hurricane leading a Spitfire; it's always an option although we don't always do it.

"We do a little close formation, then a dynamic split and the two aircraft end up manoeuvring, pointing towards each other and crossing. This time we arrive with Ben en echelon, whereas the aircraft were in line astern throughout before."

Ben: "It was amazing the first time we flew together in early April. I came up alongside the Spitfire and looking across at it I was thinking: 'It's right there!' I'm just a few feet away, looking at it in its element. Brilliant!"

Asked if the radically different performance characteristics of the two aircraft make for challenging flying, Parky says: "Essentially, if we fly at the same speeds we should always cross 'in the middle', but because it's fairly standard flying for me, I'd say Ben has the more difficult job. I just position my Spitfire and it's Ben's responsibility to make sure the formations work – he's formating on me."

Ben admits there's been a lot to take onboard, although working with Parky, an ex-Red Arrow, must have eased that process. "There are lots of subtle nuances to learn, as well as making sure all the crosses are in the middle. I hadn't realised the wind would have such an impact for example and we have to take it in turns to correct our speed to make the cross accurate. We both have to be doing it right to make it work. We talk to each other constantly."

Interestingly, the Typhoon remains a regular line jet, used in the daily flying cycle just like any other 29(R) Sqn aircraft. Ben says: "It looks fabulous on the line, everyone loves to see it. And in the mornings when we're planning, there's a bit of discussion at the authoriser's desk as to who's going to get what aircraft. There's a variety of reasons why people think they should take it!"

Parky concludes: "Essentially we're showing that technology's moved on, but the task remains much the same. More importantly, it's a way of showing the veterans the effort the Royal Air Force has gone to to make sure the 75th is remembered. A striking, unusual display is a very good way of getting the public interested and appreciating the importance of the anniversary."

Thoughts From the Boss

Behind every BBMF appearance, whether country fete flypast or Royal International Air Tattoo display, lays a masterpiece of planning, coordination and engineering skill, pitted against the inevitable challenges of flying old aeroplanes. Every season is a busy one and the Flight is more in demand than ever when significant anniversaries come around. Squadron Leader Dunc Mason, OC BBMF, explains the motivation behind the Flight's work and its importance to the RAF and the nation.

"This year marks the 75th anniversary of the Battle of Britain; the Royal Air Force's highest battle honour. The Battle of Britain Memorial Flight will commemorate the event as a reminder of the sacrifices made by the 'Few' who did not return, as well as celebrating the lives of those who survived and those that remain with us now.

"The Battle of Britain Memorial Flight will mark the event with numerous flypasts alongside the civilian warbird community, over London and various other memorial sites across the country, from July to October. These will evoke memories of the Battle and instil a renewed pride in our military, reminding the public that the Royal Air Force is still defending the nation and protecting the UK's interests around the world to this day. It is vital that we uphold the memory of the events that took place in the dark days of 1940 and show that the spirit and ethos of the Royal Air Force is just as strong today as it was 75 years ago.

"Lest we forget…"

GREAT SUBSCRIPTION OFFERS FROM KEY

SUBSCRIBE
TO *YOUR* FAVOURITE MAGAZINE
AND SAVE

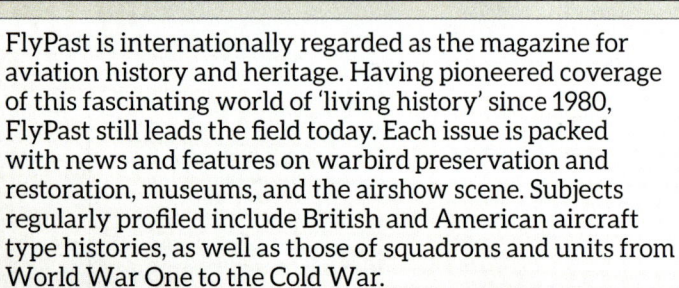

RAF SALUTE SPECIAL 2015

FlyPast is internationally regarded as the magazine for aviation history and heritage. Having pioneered coverage of this fascinating world of 'living history' since 1980, FlyPast still leads the field today. Each issue is packed with news and features on warbird preservation and restoration, museums, and the airshow scene. Subjects regularly profiled include British and American aircraft type histories, as well as those of squadrons and units from World War One to the Cold War.

www.flypast.com

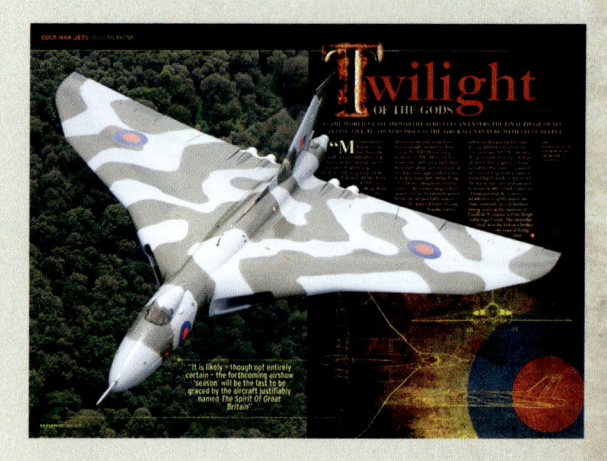

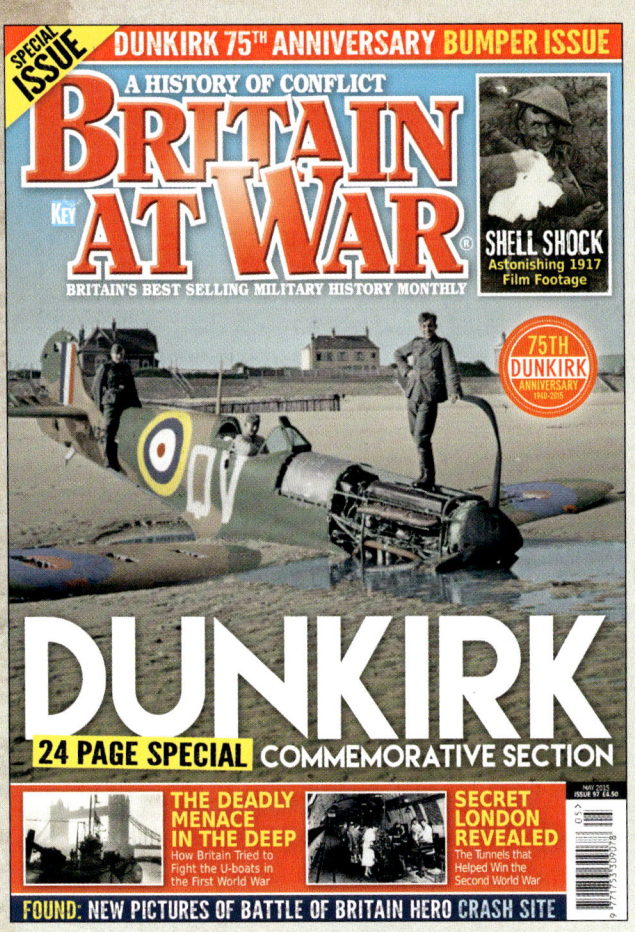

Britain at War is dedicated to exploring every aspect of Britain's involvement in conflicts from the turn of the 20th century through to modern day. From World War I to the Falklands, World War II to Iraq, readers are able to re-live decisive moments in Britain's history through fascinating insight combined with rare and previously unseen photography.

www.britainatwar.com

Aeroplane traces its lineage back to the weekly The Aeroplane launched in June 1911, and is still continuing to provide the best aviation coverage around. With a distinct emphasis on military aircraft from the 1930s to the 1960s, the magazine features such icons as the Spitfire, Hurricane, Lancaster and many more.

www.aeroplanemonthly.com

ALSO AVAILABLE DIGITALLY:

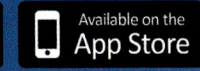

Available on iTunes Available on the App Store Available on Google play Available on BlackBerry Available on kindle fire Available on PC, Mac & Windows 8

Available on PC, Mac, Blackberry and Windows 8 from pocketmags.com

559/15

FOR THE LATEST SUBSCRIPTION DEALS

VISIT: www.keypublishing.com/shop

PHONE: (UK) 01780 480404   (Overseas) +44 1780 480404

PEOPLE

For Valour 1940

Through the desperate days of 1940, first in defence of continental Europe and later in the Battle of Britain, five RAF personnel were awarded the Victoria Cross for actions of supreme courage. Air Cdre (Retd) Graham Pitchfork tells their stories

Flying Officer Donald Garland. all author's collection unless otherwise stated

Flying Officer Donald Garland and Sergeant Tom Gray

Ten squadrons of Fairey Battles deployed to France in September 1939 as the spearhead of the RAF's Advanced Air Striking Force (AASF), although at this early stage of World War Two, the so-called 'Phoney War', there was little air activity other than reconnaissance sorties.

Among the Battle units, Number 12 Squadron had moved to Amifontaine, south of St Quentin, northern France, by the spring of 1940. One of its more senior pilots, Flying Officer Donald Garland was the fourth son of Doctor Garland and his wife Renee. Born in County Wicklow, Ireland, on June 28, 1918, he was accepted for a short service commission in July 1937. After completing his pilot training, he joined 12 Squadron.

Aged 21, Garland's first significant war sortie was on the night of April 21/22 when the squadron launched four Battles on 'Nickel' (propaganda leafleting) raids. Garland was tasked to drop his over Koblenz, Germany, and to carry out a recce of the Rhine Valley, completing both tasks successfully.

The observer in the fourth aircraft on that sortie was Sergeant Tom Gray, the fourth of seven brothers, five of whom joined the RAF. He enlisted as an aircraft apprentice in August 1929 and spent the next three years as one of 'Trenchard's Brats' at RAF Halton, Buckinghamshire, learning the trade of Aeroengine Fitter II(E). He was serving on 40 Sqn, operating Fairey Gordon biplanes, when he volunteered for flying duties as an 'airman gunner'. After several postings, he reached No. 12 in February 1938 and trained as an observer.

Bridge Attacks

On May 10, the Germans launched their blitzkrieg through the Low Countries and into France. The AASF and Bomber Command were soon in action, suffering heavy casualties from Luftwaffe fighters and ground defences. By the 12th it was already evident that the Germans were making great advances.

Number 12 Squadron came to readiness at 0400hrs and, three hours later, received orders to attack and destroy two bridges over the strategically important Albert Canal in Belgium. These stated that the bridges must be "destroyed at all costs". Six aircraft were required and when the commanding officer called for volunteers, all the crews stepped forward. He decided to send those who had been placed on standby.

Garland had just been appointed to command 'B' Flight following the loss of its

50 | ROYAL AIR FORCE SALUTE 2015

PEOPLE

Sergeant Tom Gray.

Flight Lieutenant Roderick Learoyd.

Sergeant John Hannah.

commander the day before. He was tasked to lead the second section of three Battles. Tom Gray would fly as his observer and Leading Aircraftsman (LAC) Lawrence Reynolds as gunner.

One of the Battles was unserviceable on start-up, but the remaining five launched just before 0900hrs. Eight No. 1 Sqn Hurricanes flew ahead to protect from German fighters, but they were heavily engaged over the target and powerless to help the Battles.

Murderous Fire

The leader of the first section, Fg Off Norman Thomas, elected to carry out a dive-bombing attack from 9,000ft, but Garland chose to strike from low level. Light anti-aircraft batteries ringed the two bridges at Veldwezelt and Vroenhoven and the Battles soon began falling to their murderous fire.

Garland led his formation to the metal bridge at Veldwezelt at very low level, before pulling up to 1,000ft for a shallow dive attack. His Number 2 was shot down by flak and the third of the trio dropped its bombs before crashing. Garland pressed home his own attack and released his four 250lb bombs despite his aircraft being hit repeatedly; bombs gone, the Battle dived into the ground, killing its three-man crew.

The bridge was damaged and some reports suggested that Garland's aircraft may have hit it and exploded. Some of the Hurricane pilots claimed to have seen bombs bursting near the target and later accounts stated that the western truss of the bridge had been destroyed. But all five Battles were lost, while two crews perished and two were captured. The pilot of the fifth aircraft was taken prisoner following a forced landing. Local people buried Garland and his crew and, after the war, they were reinterred in the Commonwealth War Graves Commission cemetery at Heverlee, Belgium.

Family Sacrifice

On June 11, it was announced that Garland and Gray had been posthumously awarded the Victoria Cross (VC), the first two airmen to receive the supreme award during World War Two. The third member of the crew, LAC Reynolds, received no award because he was not in a 'decision making' position. Many people at the time, and since, have questioned the failure to recognise Reynolds.

Tom Gray was only the second airman to receive the Victoria Cross (Flt Sgt Thomas Mottershead was awarded the VC posthumously on February 12, 1917) and the only Halton apprentice to receive the medal. The families of Garland and Gray paid a heavy price for the victory against Germany. All three of Garland's brothers died serving in the RAF and two of Gray's brothers also made the ultimate sacrifice.

Flight Lieutenant Roderick Learoyd
Roderick Learoyd joined the RAF on a short service commission in 1936, and after completing his training as a pilot he joined 49 Squadron to fly the Hawker Hind light bomber. After moving to Scampton, Lincolnshire in March 1938, the unit became first to convert to the Handley Page Hampden.

Learoyd flew on the initial Hampden raid of the war, seeking German naval units, but there were few operations during the Phoney War. Following Hitler's blitzkrieg into the Low Countries and France, however, 49 Squadron saw plenty of action on bombing raids and mine-laying sorties. By mid-August 1940, Learoyd had flown 24 operations.

On the night of August 12/13, 11 Hampdens were tasked against the »

Hannah remained in hospital for many weeks after his heroic actions, but his health was never fully restored. RAF Scampton Archive/© UK MoD Crown Copyright 2015

ROYAL AIR FORCE SALUTE 2015 | 51

PEOPLE

aqueduct that carried the Dortmund-Ems canal over the River Ems north of Münster, Germany. Learoyd took off at 2000hrs and arrived over the canal on time in half moonlight, which reflected off the water. He stood off as the first aircraft made its attack at 100ft, approaching through an intense barrage of light flak. The second Hampden in was shot down and the third so badly damaged that the crew were forced to bale out.

Learoyd was fifth to attack, by which time the anti-aircraft fire was at its fiercest and the gunners and searchlight operators fully aware of the bombers' line of approach. He let down to 150ft and, just short of the release point, searchlights blinded him as the aircraft took two shells that tore through the starboard wing. Despite the intense flak, Learoyd held the badly damaged bomber steady, allowing the bomb aimer to release the weapons.

Safe Return

After clearing the target, the crew assessed the state of their aircraft. In addition to the severe damage to the wing, the hydraulic system was badly shot-up, causing the flaps to droop and increase drag. Learoyd coaxed the Hampden across the North Sea and arrived over Scampton before first light. Concerned that the undercarriage and flaps might not work properly, he elected to wait until dawn before attempting to land. By the time the Hampden was safely on the ground, it had been airborne for almost nine hours.

Several awards resulted from this valiant attack and Learoyd was awarded the Victoria Cross for "high courage, skill and determination… and an example which is unsurpassed."

He went on to serve on 83 Squadron before commanding 44 Squadron, the first Avro Lancaster unit. Later he instructed at a bomber Operational Training Unit (OTU) and left the RAF as a wing commander in 1946.

Sergeant John Hannah

Sergeant John Hannah was a wireless operator/air gunner with No. 83 Sqn, based at RAF Scampton on the Hampden. On the night of September 15/16, 1940 the squadron was tasked against invasion barges at Antwerp, Belgium, marking Hannah's 12th operational sortie.

Born at Paisley, west of Glasgow, in 1921, Hannah gave up a career as a shoe salesman to enlist in the RAF on August 15, 1939. He passed through 2 Electrical and Wireless Training School at Yatesbury, Wiltshire in 1939, then 4 Bombing and Gunnery School, West Freugh, Dumfries and Galloway, in 1940 and went on to 16 OTU at Upper Heyford, Oxfordshire, where he became a wireless operator/air gunner.

Hannah first experienced the Hampden with 16 OTU and continued on the type with his first operational unit, 106 Squadron at Thornaby, Yorkshire. He arrived on July 1, 1940, but had moved on to 83 Squadron by mid-August.

Under Fire, On Fire

As the bombs fell from P1355, Hannah's aircraft on September 15/16, flak ignited a fierce fire that quickly enveloped his position. With both fuel tanks pierced, there was every chance of the blaze spreading. Now the gunner baled out, but Hannah chose to remain with the aircraft.

The fierce fire buckled the door in his compartment and he had to use all his strength to open it to reach the fire

Squadrons Then and Now

Number	Established	Initial aircraft	Aircraft in 1940	2015 role	Aircraft
1	April 13, 1912	Nieuport 17 (from March 1916)	Hurricane	Air Defence	Typhoon
27	November 5, 1915	Martinsyde Elephant (from June 1916)	None (disbanded 1939, reformed February 1941)	Support Helicopter	Chinook
72	July 2, 1917	Martinsyde Elephant (from December)	Gladiator, Spitfire	Flying Training	Tucano

RAF Aircraft 1940: Fairey Battle

Fairey flew its Day Bomber prototype for the first time on March 10, 1936. The aircraft matured into the production Battle, having been designed against a requirement for a two-seat, single-engined monoplane able to carry a 1,000lb bombload over a range of 1,000 miles at 200mph.

The machine was to replace the Hawker Hart, a high-performance biplane easily eclipsed by the new breed of monoplane fighters and satisfied all aspects of the requirement, albeit with a crew of three – pilot, observer/navigator and wireless operator/gunner. This was a time of expansion across the RAF and 155 aircraft had been ordered off the drawing board in 1935. They were the first of 2,185 Battles, 1,156 built by Fairey and the remainder by Austin Motors.

The Battle marked the first operational use of Rolls-Royce's exceptional Merlin engine and was largely without vice, although the design of its rear canopy left much to be desired. A single 0.303in (7.7mm) machine gun was available to the gunner, who fired the weapon from his position aft in the cockpit, where the canopy unfortunately directed the slipstream directly into his face. A second weapon of similar calibre was mounted in the starboard wing, but since the Battle was no dogfighter, the rear gun amounted to its only defence.

Deliveries of production aircraft began in May 1937 and in excess of 1,000 Battles had been delivered by the outbreak of war.

The type represented the major striking power of the AASF, but from May 10, 1940 the first desperate daylight raids against the advancing enemy revealed the Battle's extreme vulnerability. Poorly armed, the aircraft fell in droves to fighters and anti-aircraft defences, and after 35 of a force of 63 Battles failed to return from strikes on May 14, it was largely withdrawn from combat.

Nevertheless, the Battle served on as a useful trainer and target tug, especially in support of the Commonwealth Air Training Plan, under which Battles flew in Australia and Canada.

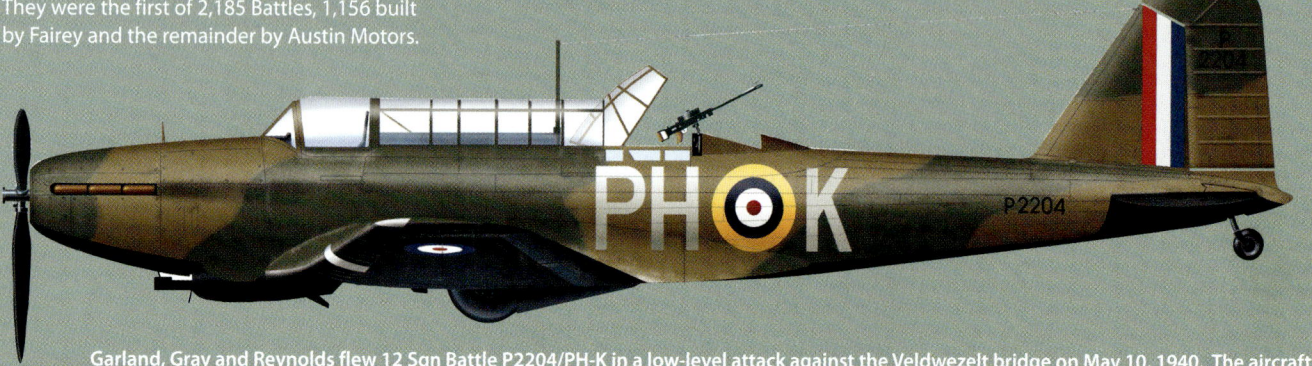

Garland, Gray and Reynolds flew 12 Sqn Battle P2204/PH-K in a low-level attack against the Veldwezelt bridge on May 10, 1940. The aircraft was shot down and all three men killed; Garland and Gray were posthumously awarded the VC for the mission. © Pete West

52 | ROYAL AIR FORCE SALUTE 2015

PEOPLE

RAF Aircraft 1940: Handley Page Hampden

Hampden Mk I P1355/OL-W was the 83 Sqn, Bomber Command aircraft that Sgt Hannah fought so hard to save on September 15/16, 1940. © Pete West

Built to Air Ministry specification B.9/32 of September 1932, the unusually configured Handley Page H.P.52 twin-engined bomber featured an extremely narrow, very deep fuselage just wide enough to accommodate the pilot's seat. The pod-like forward section diminished aft into a slim 'boom' that mounted the tailplane and twin vertical tail surfaces.

First flown on June 21, 1936, and subsequently named Hampden, the aircraft achieved a maximum speed of 254mph (409km/h) and could land at just 73mph (117km/h) thanks to its Handley Page leading edge slats. Powered by a pair of 1,000hp Bristol Pegasus XVII radial piston engines, the Hampden hauled a maximum bombload of 4,000lb (1,814kg) over 1,200 miles (1,931km).

On August 15 the Air Ministry ordered 180 Hampdens and subsequently ordered 100 of a derived aircraft powered by Napier Dagger engines and named Hereford. This unreliable powerplant doomed the Hereford to failure and the majority was relegated to training. Meanwhile, the first Hampden deliveries were to No. 49 Sqn at Scampton in September 1938, where the aircraft replaced Hawker Hind biplanes.

Ten Hampden squadrons were operational at the outbreak of World War Two, the type's early reconnaissance missions passing without enemy contact. However, as soon as the bomber met Luftwaffe fighters the inadequacy of its defensive armament was painfully exposed. Five out of 11 aircraft despatched in daylight to observe activity in the Heligoland Bight were shot down.

Switching to nocturnal operations improved the Hampden's chances of survival, but armament remained as two fixed-forward firing 0.303in machine guns, with pairs of similar weapons on flexible mounts in the upper and lower aft 'corners' of the fuselage.

Over the winter of 1939/40 the Hampden squadrons became extremely efficient in night mining sorties, albeit at continuing cost to Luftwaffe fighters. The aircraft remained as a primary Bomber Command asset, joining the Armstrong Whitworth Whitley in the Command's first raid against Berlin in August 1940 and continuing in the bombing offensive until September 15/16, 1942, when No. 408 (Royal Canadian Air Force) Sqn flew the type's last operational Bomber Command mission.

The Hampden had embarked upon a new torpedo-bombing career in April 1942, however, when Coastal Command began taking aircraft modified to launch torpedoes and redesignated Hampden TB.Mk I. The variant was active in RAF and Soviet hands in defence of the northern convoys and achieved its final success, against a U-boat, with 455 (Royal Australian Air Force) Sqn on April 4, 1943.

extinguishers. He also noted that his parachute was smouldering, but ignored it to tackle the fire. He fought the inferno in the confined area for ten minutes, the bomber remaining under heavy anti-aircraft fire as Hannah almost succumbed to the heat and fumes. With the extinguishers exhausted, he beat out the flames with his logbook, ammunition exploding around him as he finally put out the fire.

The he crawled forward to the pilot, who was shocked by the severity of Hannah's burns. Despite these serious injuries, the young man crawled forward again, to ascertain if the navigator was alive, only to find that he had baled out. Hannah helped his pilot navigate back to Scampton, where the severe damage caused by the fire became evident, including the total loss of his own parachute.

He spent several weeks in hospital recovering from second-degree burns, and learned there that he had been awarded the Victoria Cross for "displaying courage, coolness and devotion to duty of the highest order." He was the youngest airman ever to be awarded the supreme award for gallantry. Invalided from the RAF in December 1942, he died aged 25 in June 1947.

Flight Lieutenant James Nicolson
Only one Victoria Cross was awarded to a fighter pilot during World War Two, Flt Lt James Nicolson receiving the supreme award for gallantry in action during the Battle of Britain. Born in April 1917, Nicolson joined the RAF in December 1936 and, after pilot training, was posted to 72 Squadron to fly the Gladiator. Assessed 'above average', he excelled in air-to-air firing. The squadron re-equipped with the Spitfire and, following the outbreak of war, Nicolson flew patrols off the east coast without seeing action.

In May 1940 he was posted to a newly formed Hurricane squadron, No. 249, as a flight commander. Once the squadron had worked up to operational efficiency it moved south »

Flight Lieutenant James Nicolson.

ROYAL AIR FORCE SALUTE 2015 | 53

PEOPLE

to Boscombe Down, Wiltshire, just as the Battle of Britain intensified.

On August 16 Nicolson took off on his first patrol with the unit, leading two other Hurricanes towards Southampton at 15,000ft, where he spotted three Junkers Ju 88 bombers but could not catch them. Shortly afterwards, cannon shells thudded into his Hurricane as the formation was 'bounced' by Bf 109s. Both his colleagues were shot down.

Badly wounded, and with his aircraft on fire, Nicolson prepared to bale out, but then a Bf 110 appeared in his sights. Abandoning any idea of taking to his parachute, he closed on the enemy aircraft, determined to destroy it. His bullets raked the Bf 110 and he continued firing as it tried to escape. With flames enveloping his cockpit, and the skin peeling from his hands, he abandoned the Hurricane and, after a struggle, managed to pull the ripcord of his parachute.

Back in the Air

His uniform in tatters and suffering from severe burns and wounds, Nicolson's situation was no less dangerous as he drifted down – 'friendly' soldiers fired on him, wounding him further. His doctors expected him to die, but he gradually recovered and in November it was announced that he had been awarded the Victoria Cross.

By February 1941 Nicolson was back in the air as a fighter instructor, before heading for India. Here he commanded Beaufighter-equipped 27 Squadron for a year, flying ground-attack missions in support of the 14th Army; for his leadership and gallantry he was awarded the Distinguished Flying Cross (DFC).

Nicolson later served as a wing commander on the air staff of the 3rd Tactical Air Force and in April 1945 joined Headquarters RAF Burma. Anxious to experience the bombing operations he was responsible for tasking, he joined a 355 Squadron Consolidated Liberator crew for an operational sortie on May 2, 1945. The bomber caught fire en route to the target and crashed into the Bay of Bengal. A search found two survivors, but the gallant Battle of Britain fighter pilot was lost. ◉

RAF Aircraft 1940: Hawker Hurricane

Among the most iconic RAF aircraft, the Hawker Hurricane was the result of Hawker chief designer Sydney Camm's genius and determination in the face of Air Ministry conservatism. Officials doubted the structural integrity of the new monoplane layout, preferring the trusted biplane configuration for its predictable behaviour and manoeuvrability.

The contemporary Gloster Gladiator, Fiat CR.42 and Polikarpov I-15 series were among the latest and highest performing biplane fighters from Britain, Italy and the USSR, but although their airframes were more advanced, in design and fighting philosophy they were merely an extension of World War One concepts. Camm was convinced that the performance of a heavily armed monoplane, powered by one of the new generation of high-power aeroengines would more than compensate for its lack of manoeuvrability compared to a biplane. The earliest encounters between Bf 109s and Gladiators and I-15s more than proved the point.

Hawker began work on the Hurricane in 1933, with lacklustre support from the Air Ministry. Camm used the proven structural techniques used in Hawker's biplanes, including the Fury fighter, to create the new monoplane. Power came from the Rolls-Royce PV.12, which would mature as the Merlin. The first prototype flew on November 6, 1935, by which time official interest was sufficient for specification F.36/34 to have been drawn up around it.

With trials under way, the Air Ministry's order for 600 of the aircraft soon to be named Hurricane came after the fact, since Hawker had examined the darkening situation in Europe and gambled on tooling up for a 1,000-aircraft production run on the basis that the RAF would need to expand very rapidly.

Ultimately, more than 14,000 Hurricanes were built on production lines in Britain and Canada. There was a naval Sea Hurricane variant, while the initial RAF version, the Mk I, was soon outperformed in the fighter role, but formed the basis for an excellent ground-attack aircraft. Later Hurricanes mounted 12 0.303in machine guns, four 20mm cannon, pairs of 40mm anti-tank guns and bombs; the type also pioneered operations with rockets, paving the way for the Hawker Typhoon attacks that proved devastating when the Allies returned to Europe in 1944.

Battle of Britain Hurricane

But the RAF fought through the 'Phoney War' and the Battle of Britain with the Hurricane Mk I. The aircraft entered service in December 1937 and 19 squadrons were equipped by the outbreak of war, generally with improved Hurricanes featuring three-bladed variable-pitch or constant-speed propellers, replacing the original two-bladed unit and metal, rather than fabric-covered wings.

Among the new breed of fighters, including the Spitfire and the Fleet Air Arm's Fairey Fulmar, armed with eight machine guns, by summer 1940 the Hurricane's performance was insufficient to match the Bf 109 on equal terms, so that the Hurricane squadrons tackled Luftwaffe bombers, leaving the Messerschmitts to the Spitfires. In combat the inadequacy of 0.303in machine gun rounds against armoured bombers equipped with self-sealing fuel tanks was immediately apparent and many damaged bombers might well not have returned to base had the Hurricane mounted cannon or heavy machine guns as the Bf 109 did.

Nonetheless, the Hurricane accounted for more enemy aircraft destroyed during the battle than all other defences combined, its rugged, simple structure withstanding damage and making for relatively easy repair. With Spitfire production still ramping up, Hawker's bold decision to build Hurricanes regardless of official doubts ensured that the RAF had as many fighters as possible to resist the German onslaught of summer 1940.

Flt Lt James Nicolson remained in the cockpit of Hurricane Mk I P3576/GN-A after the aircraft had been hit on August 16, 1940. With the aircraft burning around him he manoeuvred to engage and shoot down a Bf 110.
© Pete West

AVIATION LEATHERCRAFT®

BRITISH CRAFTSMANSHIP AT ITS BEST

Irvin Original and Lightweight Flying Jackets, Sheepskin Gilets, Flying Helmets and Goggles. Leather Flying Jackets of Famous Squadrons: Red Arrows® BBMF® 79 Squadron® Registered Trade Marks belonging to the MoD

THE ORIGINAL WW11 IRVIN® FLYING JACKET

Moto-Lita Ltd. Thruxton Industrial Estate Thruxton Airport Andover, SP11 8PW.
Tel: +44(0)1264 772811

WWW.MOTO-LITA.CO.UK   WWW.FLYING-JACKET.COM

Please call for a catalogue or visit us
9am-4pm Mon-Thurs. 9am-12 noon Friday.

CAPABILITY

Fighter Stations
Old and New

Pilots Douglas Bader (left) and Alexander Hess at Duxford. © IWM

Royal Air Force Lossiemouth became a fighter station for the first time in 2014 and is now a cornerstone of UK air defence. RAF Duxford, now IWM Duxford, was a sector station and key airfield in 12 Group during the Battle of Britain. Paul E Eden draws surprising comparisons between them

Among the younger Royal Air Force flying stations Lossiemouth, on the Moray coast of Scotland, began operations as a training establishment with Airspeed Oxfords and North American Harvards in spring 1939. In April 1940, 46 Maintenance Unit (MU) formed, tasked with the preparation of newly delivered aircraft for service and taking 17 Hurricanes as its initial 'customers'.

As the MU work expanded, Lossiemouth also played host to the first of many bomber detachments, its position in northeast Scotland ideal for launching attacks across the North Sea at targets in Norway. The first such operations sent Blenheims to attack Stavanger in mid-April and similar raids continued into August, by which time the Battle of Britain was in full swing.

This pattern of training and hosting bomber detachments continued throughout the war, most famously resulting in the November 1944 destruction of *Tirpitz*, when Lossiemouth, Kinloss and Milltown launched 9 and 617 Sqn Avro Lancasters against the battleship as it lay moored in Alten fjord.

In the immediate post-war period Lossie transferred to Royal Navy ownership, but passed back to the RAF in 1972, hosting search-and-rescue helicopters and Avro Shackleton AEW.Mk 2 early-warning aircraft, for its first taste of air defence. The SEPECAT Jaguar

These 19 Sqn pilots are outside what is now IWM Duxford's education office. © IWM

56 | ROYAL AIR FORCE SALUTE 2015

CAPABILITY

Hangar 3 at Lossiemouth, with an impressive collection of 1(F) and 29(R) Sqn Typhoons inside. Both squadrons were involved in the Battle of Britain. SAC Connor Payne/© UK MoD Crown Copyright 2015

Looking at Duxford today, the three double hangars to the left were present during the Battle of Britain. The technical buildings behind are also little changed, as is the domestic site across the road. © IWM

arrived in 1974 and the Blackburn Buccaneer from 1980, continuing Lossie's training work (with operational conversion units (OCUs) for both types) and its traditional attack role. The 'Bucc' added an anti-shipping capability until it was retired in 1994. When the Jaguar also departed, in 2000, Lossie became a Panavia Tornado station and it maintains a 'Tonka' presence today, in the shape of XV (Reserve) Squadron, the Tornado GR4 OCU.

Lossiemouth had never held a quick reaction alert air defence commitment until Nos 1(F) and 6 Squadrons moved in from RAF Leuchars with their Typhoons. Both units arrived in 2014, the straightforward transfer of QRA from one Scottish base to another testament to the hard work and detailed preparation that preceded the transfer.

RAF Duxford

Back in 1940, RAF Duxford, Cambridgeshire was, like RAF Lossiemouth today, a premier fighter station. The Spitfire was introduced into service at Duxford and the airfield was a vital Dowding System sector station within 12 Group. It also became a centre for Czech pilots when 310 Sqn formed there on Hurricanes, while that most famous of Battle of Britain pilots Douglas Bader briefly flew Spitfires there, before returning with his 242 Sqn Hurricanes late in August 1940.

The station then became pivotal in the 'big wing' controversy between Leigh-Mallory and Park, the former employing the tactic to the full and adding the weight of 302 (Polish) Sqn and 611 Sqn to the concept from September. Ironically, Park had commanded 111 Sqn at Duxford in 1927.

Similar to Lossiemouth, Duxford had opened as a training establishment, but during World War One. Today the airfield is owned by the Imperial War Museum and its infrastructure, as much as its exhibits, is considered historically significant on an international scale, especially since some original 1917 buildings remain.

The station's training commitment continued into 1919, but it also hosted several operational units, including No. 8 Sqn, which arrived with Bristol F.2B Fighters in May and disbanded the following January – it was No. 8 that flew Shackletons from Lossiemouth five decades later. Duxford returned to training duties after 8 Sqn departed, but soon began its long career as a fighter station alongside its sister airfield at nearby Fowlmere.

This switch to air defence required considerable infrastructure and a major building programme was underway in 1923, equipping the station for 19 and 29 Squadrons, and their Sopwith Snipe fighters. Expansion continued and although Duxford relinquished its training role, 111 Sqn arrived with Snipes and Gloster Grebes, the three based squadrons then progressing through increasingly modern equipment, including the Armstrong Whitworth Siskin IIIA and Gloster Gauntlet. At the same time, new buildings continued to be erected and older structures modified, a process paralleled at Lossiemouth many years later as it too took on an air defence role.

Air Defence at Lossie

A great deal of building work and other changes prepared Lossie for its new air defence role but, as Station Commander Group Captain Mark Chappell explains, there is more to do: »

Newly arrived at Lossiemouth in June 2014, 6 Sqn lines up on the pan alongside Lossie's control tower. SAC Scott Ferguson/© UK MoD Crown Copyright 2015

ROYAL AIR FORCE SALUTE 2015 | 57

CAPABILITY

Station Adjutant Sqn Ldr Copley in his office at RAF Duxford in 1940. © IWM

Plt Off Wallace Cunningham, Sub-Lieutenant Arthur Blake RN and New Zealander Flg Off Francis Noel Brinsden, with pet, rest between sorties at Fowlmere in September 1940. RAF (AHB)/© UK MoD Crown Copyright 2015

"Infrastructure changes are still under way. There are some new squadron facilities, but there have also been extensive modifications to existing buildings. Our ability to generate a Quick Reaction Alert (Interceptor) North (QRA(I)N) capability has been at the forefront of our infrastructure programme."

This QRA(I)N responsibility provides air defence against threats around the north of the country, a similar commitment at RAF Coningsby, Lincolnshire taking care of the south. It provides the equivalent of the Battle of Britain 'scramble', albeit on a smaller scale and without the desperate peril of 1940.

Although there is little operational comparison with 1940, the well publicised upswing in Russian military flying in recent years has tried Lossie's QRA capabilities many times. How has the station coped, with just two fully operational squadrons and extensive training commitments? "The extra edge afforded by any operational activity intensifies the focus of all those involved," says Gp Capt Chappell, "whether it is responding to Russian Long Range Aviation, a potential terrorist threat or participating in Baltic Air Policing. The opportunity to use skills and procedures beyond the training environment is generally welcomed by all military personnel."

The station is also working to field a third Typhoon squadron: "In addition to 1(F) and 6 Squadrons, II(AC) Squadron is building up to becoming our third declared Typhoon squadron by the end of the year. This will allow for a further distribution of our QRA(I)N commitment, but also require an increase in the training requirements that we need to achieve. Our exercise programme is intrinsic to the maintenance and development of our skills. Some of the best training opportunities are only available through high-end multinational exercises and we need to maintain a sufficient tempo in order to allow us to participate in them."

Scramble!

During the Battle of Britain, Duxford's Hurricane and Spitfire squadrons sat at readiness, pilots in flying kit waiting near their aircraft, ready to dash out to the machines, don parachutes and start engines. Fast, accurate ground crew work was essential to get the pilots into their cockpits and safely strapped in, engines running.

Take-off was into wind; Duxford being a grass aerodrome, its fighters were not restricted to the one or two runway orientations offered by an airfield with hard surfaces. Ground crew were also in attendance for rearming and refuelling, as well as regular maintenance, all done in the field, preparing aircraft for the next scramble. More challenging work, including battle damage repairs, could be done in one of the station's hangars, but when damage was more extensive, especially on the Spitfire, airframes were despatched to specialist repair centres.

The addition of a concrete runway aside, Duxford remains largely as it was in 1940, allowing visitors the opportunity to see, touch, feel, hear and even smell the airfield as it was

Above: Duxford had a large and important presence of Canadians, Czechs and Poles. Here a 312 (Czech) Squadron Hurricane receives attention. RAF (AHB)/© UK MoD Crown Copyright 2015

Below: Lossiemouth launches a 6 Sqn 'Q jet', the equivalent of a scramble at Duxford or any of the Battle of Britain fighter stations. QRA scrambles are a regular occurrence. Sgt Stu Fenwick/© UK MoD Crown Copyright 2015

CAPABILITY

Armourers replenish the guns on 310 Squadron Hurricane I P3143/NN-D at Duxford on September 7, 1940.
RAF (AHB)/© UK MoD Crown Copyright 2015

Visiting Duxford

IWM Duxford is open to visitors all year round, providing them the opportunity to walk through one of the best preserved World War Two fighter stations in existence. It features a vast, exceptional collection of aircraft and artefacts, including the restored Sector 'G' Operations Room, and runs an annual air show programme. For 2015 this includes The Battle of Britain Anniversary Air Show, scheduled for September 19/20 and likely to include participation from the RAF Battle of Britain Memorial Flight.

A comprehensive range of tours and activities designed especially for children is also offered, especially during school holidays. More information is available at www.iwm.org.uk/duxford

Fowlmere provided additional space as more squadrons arrived at Duxford. No. 19 flew Spitfires from the base, where this group, including Sqn Ldr 'Sandy' Lane, talks with the unit intelligence officer.
RAF (AHB)/© UK MoD Crown Copyright 2015

when fighter pilots were taking off in the desperate defence of the nation.

Jump forwards 75 years and QRA(I)N at Lossiemouth represents that Battle of Britain scramble, and there are remarkable similarities between the two. Group Captain Chappell explains the basics of the task: "QRA(I)N jets operate from a HAS [hardened aircraft shelter]. Maintenance continues to be performed outside on the line or in a hangar, depending on the complexity of the fault. First line maintenance is carried out by RAF manpower, second line and beyond is carried out under the control of BAE Systems at RAF Coningsby. This work is supplemented by elements of RAF personnel and demonstrates how the RAF and industry work together to ensure the RAF meets its operational commitments."

Key Differences

The similarities in mission between 1940 and 2015 are striking, but the Service has evolved considerably. Today's RAF draws on personnel from a multitude of backgrounds, for example, and there are no restrictions for female aircrew. "The RAF, and this station, can rightly be proud of how we have embraced change with respect to the composition and equal opportunities afforded to our personnel," says Gp Capt Chappell.

"That is not to say that any organisation is perfect, but we make huge effort to ensure that we constantly evaluate and assess our performance in this area. One of our key management strategies is to retain our people. A significant difference between the RAF of 1940 and today is the training burden required to get our personnel 'combat ready'. We won't retain trained and experienced personnel if we don't provide a culture and workplace that satisfies their aspirations. Therefore, it is in our interest to work as hard as we can to provide the environment that can achieve that."

Group Captain Chappell completes his tour at Lossie in November. Reflecting on the job so far, he says: "Commanding a premier RAF station is an honour and privilege, and being Station Commander at RAF Lossiemouth will no doubt be one of the highlights of my career, especially at such a significant time in its history. I recognise the significance of the squadrons under my command and the traditions that they bring with them, but at the same time I'm always impressed by the people who work on those squadrons now. We're under different pressures and expectations today, and I think that it's the endeavour and fortitude of our people that remains the common theme throughout any prestigious squadron's existence. When I hear of challenges that have been overcome by a positive attitude and a will to get the job done it makes me think that the equipment may change, the challenges we face may change, but our people's wonderful attitude is something that resonates.

"Because of the changes the station has gone through during my tenure, the main challenge I've faced as Station Commander has really been about time management, but I've had tremendous support and witnessed a magnificent work ethic from my colleagues, and felt an overwhelmingly positive attitude about the RAF from local organisations and the extremely supportive people of Moray. I may be the figurehead here at RAF Lossiemouth, but it is our people, our whole force, that are our greatest asset. We have to value them, invest in them and nurture them." ⊙

ROYAL AIR FORCE SALUTE 2015 | 59

THE RAF COLLECTION

Remembering the battle for the skies

Our RAF collection of figures pays tribute to the heroes of the Royal Airforce for their hard work and sacrifice during World War II.

Hand-crafted in our matte finish style and incorporating highly detailed sculpting plus shading and highlighting in the painting to produce extraordinary figures, perfect for display on a diorama or as a gift.

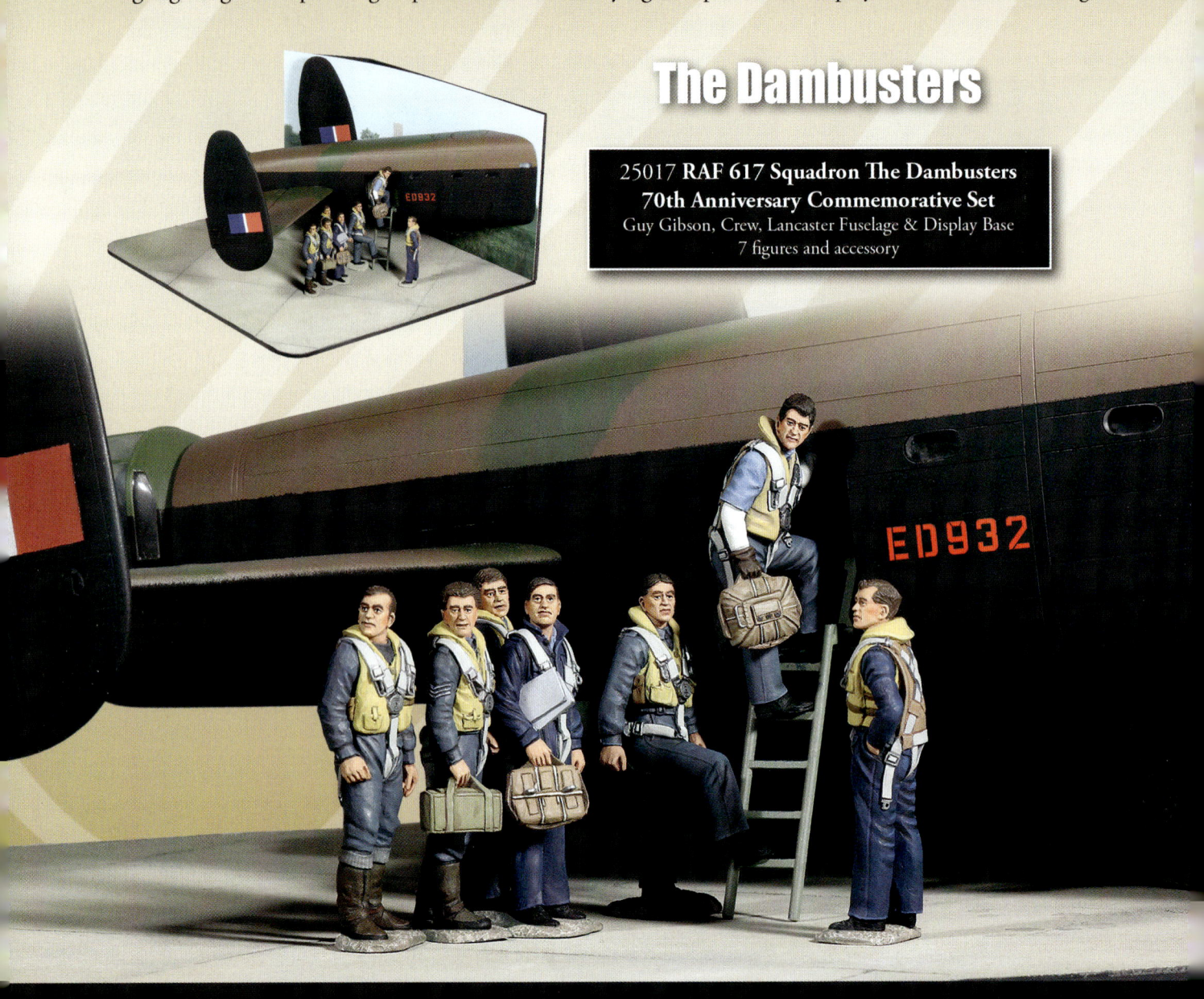

The Dambusters

25017 RAF 617 Squadron The Dambusters 70th Anniversary Commemorative Set
Guy Gibson, Crew, Lancaster Fuselage & Display Base
7 figures and accessory

Please visit http://britain.bachmann.co.uk to find your nearest retailer

25018 RAF Commemorative Set
WAAF with Bicycle, 1943
2 Piece Set

25027 RAF Pilot with Model
Spitfire and Child
2 Piece Set

25021 RAF Military Policeman
1 Piece Set

25019 RAF Fighter Pilot 1943
with Faithful Companion
2 Piece Set

25025 'I'll Be Seeing You' RAF
Pilot and Girl Kissing Goodbye
2 Piece Set

25026 RAF Lewis Gunner, Spotter
& Sand Bag Emplacement
5 Piece Set

25022 Air Marshall Sir Arthur
'Bomber' Harris
1 Piece Set

Bachmann Europe Plc. Moat Way, Barwell, Leicestershire. LE9 8EY

PEOPLE

WAAFs at War

PEOPLE

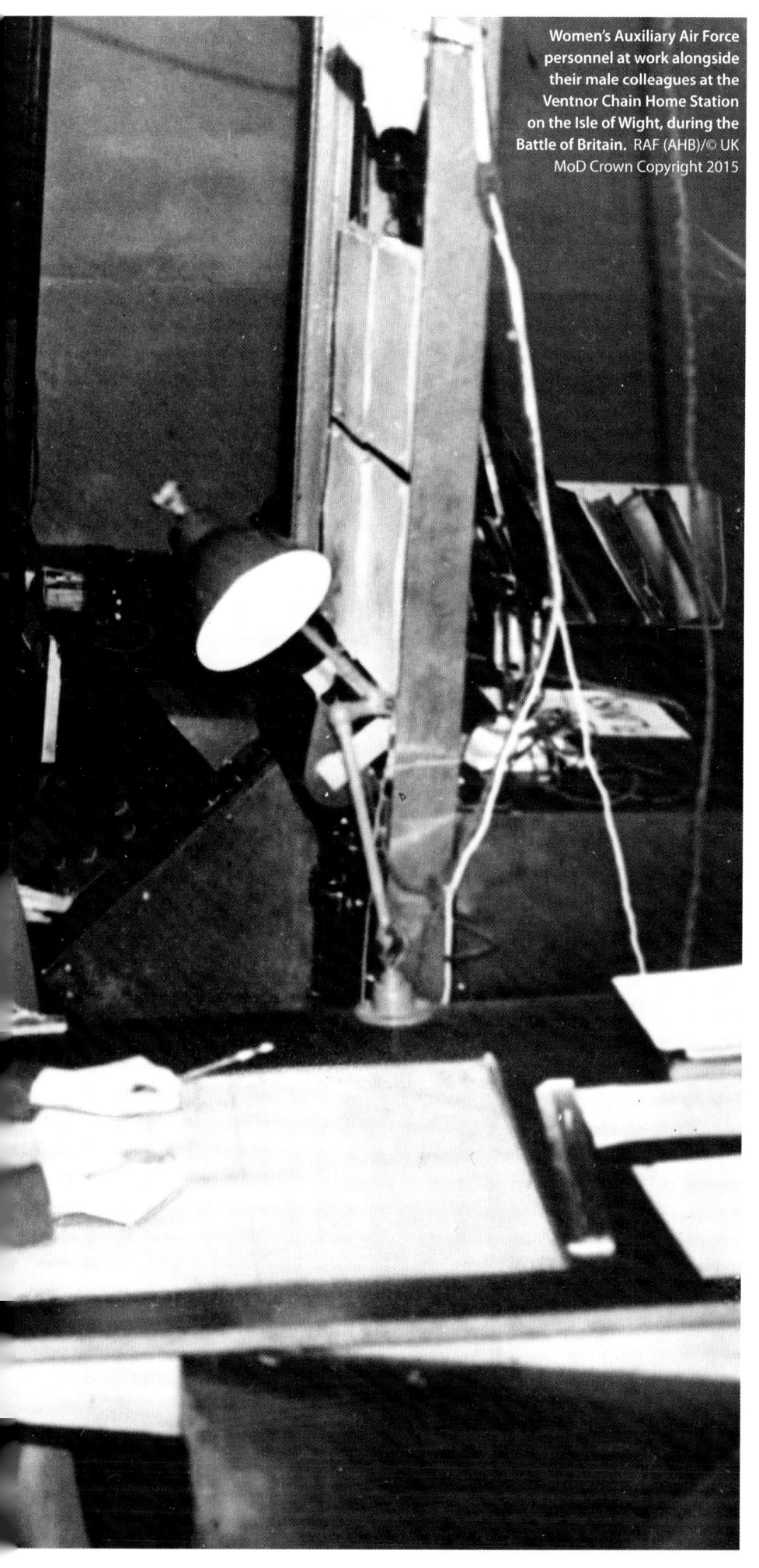

Women's Auxiliary Air Force personnel at work alongside their male colleagues at the Ventnor Chain Home Station on the Isle of Wight, during the Battle of Britain. RAF (AHB)/© UK MoD Crown Copyright 2015

Although women were shielded from direct combat during World War Two, they quickly found battle-winning roles in the UK's air defence network. As filterers, plotters and radar operators they worked arduous shifts, often coming under attack from enemy aircraft, as these veterans recall

On June 28, 1939 the Women's Auxiliary Air Force (WAAF) was created from the Auxiliary Territorial Service. The WAAFs were initially offered fairly mundane jobs, but one task was far from dull and so secret that few knew about it. After selection as Clerk Special Duties, WAAFs were trained as radar operators, plotters or tellers.

Initial training for radar operators was at RAF Bawdsey, Suffolk. Among other instruction, recruits learned the high-end skills they would need to extract information from radar displays. Their subsequent postings were generally to radar units on the frontline of Britain's air defence network, albeit designated as Air Ministry Experimental Stations to preserve secrecy.

August 1940 saw the first direct attacks against radar units, placing their personnel – including the newly trained WAAFs – directly in harm's way. After a series of raids on August 12, Air Chief Marshal Dowding signalled the radar units, expressing his satisfaction and pride in the behaviour of the WAAF personnel in the face of attack.

Those selected as plotters and tellers were trained at RAF Leighton Buzzard, Bedfordshire, the headquarters of 60 Group. Here they were further streamed to become either filter plotters and tellers, or operations room plotters and tellers. The term 'plotters and tellers' does little justice to the importance of these vital operational roles.

The system of 'telling' information from the radars to the filter centre and then to the numerous operations rooms across the Dowding System using landlines and a formatted telling sequence was time consuming. But with time of the essence, both the plotters and tellers had to be quick, dexterous and precise, so as not to cause additional delays that could cost lives.

Throughout 1940, WAAFs were increasing employed on frontline radar units and at Fighter Command, Group and Sector operations rooms and within the filter centre at RAF Bentley Priory. They were also employed in training roles at Leighton Buzzard and Bawdsey.

In this 75th anniversary year, Eileen Younghusband, a former Filterer Officer who »

PEOPLE

worked at Fighter Command Headquarters, said: "I hope that the vital contribution that WAAF Clerks Special Duties and Filterer Officers made to the success of the Battle of Britain and the overall outcome of the war will finally become fully recognised."

Filter Plotter

Early in 1941, aged just 19, Eileen volunteered for service with the Women's Auxiliary Air Force. After brief technical training she was sent as a filter plotter to 10 Group, RAF Rudloe Manor, where she learned the essential role that the filter centre would play throughout the war. Later, as a filterer officer, she was posted to Fighter Command HQ at Bentley Priory; her watch covered the D-Day landings and she subsequently played a role in tracking the first V-2 rocket to reach the UK – it landed on Chiswick on September 8, 1944.

Although she began her vital work after the Battle of Britain, recollections in her book *One Woman's War* paint a vivid picture of the lives of these brave, highly trained women. She writes: "'Must be under twenty-one, with quick reactions, good at figures – and female.' These were the prerequisites for members of the WAAF seeking to work as plotters, or officers in the filter room. The women chosen ranged from psychology and science students, young actresses, county debutants, grammar school high flyers, to daughters of famous people – novelists, painters, musicians and vicars. But they were without exception dedicated to their work.

"Several of the airwomen and officers I met were volunteers from the day war started. They had been chosen because they were young, quick-witted and bright. There was no time to train them in those early days, they learnt on the job.

"We all kept our work secret; it was impressed on us how vital it was that the enemy should not know how the system worked. As far as my family were concerned, I told them I was covered by the Official Secrets Act. We had very little communication with the other parts of the Group Headquarters since Special Duties personnel lived a somewhat isolated existence from the rest of the camp.

"The mental stress and physical strain were intense. The filter room plotter officers had brothers, boyfriends, cousins who were in the squadrons of fighters or bombers they could see on the table. They would track out 500 bombers and perhaps only 450 returned, but they never let us down. There was no hysteria, no crying, they just went on doing their job hour after hour. It was frenzy. It was organised chaos. Those girls, those filter plotters… I can never speak too highly of. They were wonderful."

Novel Service

Patricia Robins joined the WAAF in 1940. Assigned to Special Duties, she was sent to Leighton Buzzard with five other girls for training as plotters. Her first posting was to 10 Group HQ, RAF Rudloe Manor where she

> "Several of the airwomen and officers I met were volunteers from the day war started".
> Eileen Younghusband, Filterer Officer

Eileen Younghusband worked as a Filterer Officer at Fighter Command HQ.
© UK MoD Crown Copyright 2015

Eileen Younghusband in March 2015.
AC Cathy Sharples
© UK MoD Crown Copyright 2015

worked in the filter room, first as a plotter then as a filterer.

"When it became necessary for the male plotters to be released for active duties," she writes in her autobiography *You Never Know*, "we females were recruited to replace them. At first there were doubts as to whether females would be capable of coping with the work, but it soon became apparent that we were more than capable of doing so.

"Our work was highly secret, as were all aspects of the Dowding System concerning radar, and we were obliged to sign The Official Secrets Act. As most of us were very young, our parents wished to know what we would be doing once we left home, but we were not allowed to inform them of anything but our whereabouts. We worked shifts, including an eight-hour night shift, and had occasional 48-hour and 72-hour passes, as well as a week's leave.

"I spent the first three years of my war service at RAF 10 Group near Bath. At Rudloe Manor an appropriate filter room had not yet been built and when I started work there it was in a barn converted for the purpose. Lights often failed and we made do with candles. It was extremely cold at times on night duty, but we were allowed to wear our great coats. Not long after I arrived, an underground block was built with a spacious filter room, canteen, and other necessary facilities. Non-commissioned personnel, the plotters, lived in Nissen huts

PEOPLE

Patricia Robins initially worked in the filter room at 10 Group HQ, at RAF Rudloe Manor. © UK MoD Crown Copyright 2015

Patricia Robins in January 2015. SAC Lee Matthews © UK MoD Crown Copyright 2015

containing iron bedsteads. Three square, straw-filled pallets known to us as biscuits served as mattresses. A year later I was commissioned and had my own room and even a girl known as a 'batwoman', to clean my buttons, shoes, room and so on.

"When weather prohibited flying and there was no activity, plotters remaining attached to their earphones were permitted to occupy themselves with books, embroidery, letter writing, etc. I had been working briefly as a junior sub-editor on a magazine and thought I would try my hand at writing short stories in order to augment my service pay. To my surprise they were published, and I continued to do this whenever time permitted. When the war ended I progressed to writing novels as a career." (Married as Patricia Clark, she wrote under her maiden name of Patricia Robins and later as Claire Lorrimer.)

An Ordinary Airman

Joan Grogono joined the WAAF at the very beginning of the war and learnt filtering on-the-job at Bentley Priory. She served at 11 Group and 13 Group. "One of the first officers I met," writes Younghusband, "was Flying Officer Grogono, known to all as 'Grog'. She did almost every job there was in the filter room except controller, which was confined to male officers. She was one of the first commissioned Special Duties WAAFs and was soon working on the balcony as a filter officer. She can still recall the names of all the radar stations on the south coast that reported to 11 Group filter room from the outbreak of the war, and even the colour of their plots."

Thinking back to 1940, Grog said: "I wanted to do something for my country. I was an ordinary airman, but I learned how to filter by watching. I never went on a course.

"You don't expect to be special. We joined up to save the country. You just do a job and get on with it. The people who were filtering to start with were very young and had to learn a lot more when they got onto the plotting table. There wasn't anything special about it. You just did it. We all got on extraordinarily well; there was no sort of bitchiness. Everybody worked together. It's a different atmosphere altogether in wartime.

"When the filter room was underground, we also lived underground. Once, when somebody put something wrong down the loo, it overflowed and we had to walk around in the swill. You never thought about it. What happened happened, and we accepted it – one time we had a run of German measles and they would come around and take our temperatures.

"We couldn't have cleaners in the filter room so we had to clean the floor ourselves. We used to put wet tea leaves down and sweep them up. And nobody ever polished the table. We were too busy, although when the weather was bad and nothing happened, we used to sit upstairs. We even played cards once or twice.

"For 30 years we weren't allowed to talk about it. My family never knew what I did, so we never talked about it. We had Wrens [Women's Royal Naval Service, WRNS, known popularly as Wrens] living in our Mess – they were part of Bletchley Park and they didn't know what we did either.

"When it was all over and I left the Service, I don't think we realised how shocked we were. I worked for a very short time. I went back home, but once you've been in the Service, you can't go back home again. You're treated as a child and we weren't any more…"

Birthday Watch

Barbara Saks joined up as Barbara Brown on April 22, 1940. After two weeks' basic training at West Drayton she was posted to Kirton-in- »

Joan 'Grog' Grogono learned the exacting skills of a filterer on the job at RAF Bentley Priory. © UK MoD Crown Copyright 2015. **Barbara Brown, now Saks, during the war.** Barbara Brown

ROYAL AIR FORCE SALUTE 2015 | 65

PEOPLE

Lindsey, Lincolnshire as a WAAF plotter. She recalls the events of September 15, when the Luftwaffe flew some of the heaviest raids of the Battle of Britain. Concentrated in two main attacks directed at London, the first hit a little after midday and the second around 2pm.

"It was a Sunday and my 23rd birthday. 'A' watch (my watch) was on duty in the operations room at RAF Kirton-in-Lindsey, on the morning shift, 8am to 1pm. It was the usual slow Sunday morning, two or three pilots practicing take-offs and landings after breakfast. Nothing unusual.

"Then intelligence came through that the Luftwaffe was sending over a second wave of bombers and fighters, bigger than the first, and a message went out all over Britain for every available pilot and plane to report to the South. We had two squadrons of Spitfires and two squadrons of Hurricanes at that time, and they were all scrambled. We plotted them off the table. After the bustle of their leaving, there was no more activity, and it was very quiet, everyone left to his or her own thoughts.

"Then came news that most of our pilots had returned to base, some having to land on other aerodromes on the way back, and a few who didn't make it back. Among those was a friend of mine – a quiet man with a great sense of humour. We shared the same interests, music and the theatre. It was a horrible afternoon, tears being shed. Then later came the news that he had been shot down, ditched in the Channel and been taken prisoner, but no one knew where."

Radar Operator

Yvonne Axon was a radar operator based at Dover during the Battle of Britain. Speaking in 1991 she recalled: "We had five hours on, ten hours off. We sat in a very dark room in front of a cathode ray tube, with a horizontal line about an eighth of an inch thick with a ratio gauge of about nought to 50. A little wiggle along that line meant an aeroplane – on the other hand a flight of seagulls or a good cloud did exactly the same. You had to 'judge your wiggle'. It was jolly hard work."

The near constant threat of attack added desperately to the strain of the job. "On average during the summer, we were dive bombed or strafed about ten times a day. We didn't have any shelters or sandbags outside the door and of course our enormous masts were only too visible. Things got terribly busy at that time. Aeroplanes really did come falling down around us and the station did get very damaged.

"The women's huts were about half a mile away from the main operating station, on the cliff edge. Because we were so secret, even the top brass wasn't allowed to come and visit us. We got shot up quite a lot and had bullet holes in our beds."

Yvonne Axon's radar station at Dover was attacked on multiple occasions during the Battle of Britain. © UK MoD Crown Copyright 2015

> "We got shot up quite a lot and had bullet holes in our beds."
> Yvonne Axon, radar operator

Yvonne Axon in January 2015.
Cpl Neil Bryden © UK MoD Crown Copyright 2015

SUBSCRIBERS CALL FOR YOUR SPECIALS DISCOUNT

£5.99 INC FREE P&P*

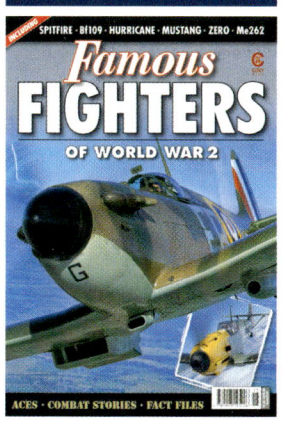

FAMOUS FIGHTERS WW2
'Famous Fighters of World War 2' is timed to celebrate the 70th anniversary of VE Day.

100 PAGES

£4.99 INC FREE P&P*

AIRSHOW 2015
An indispensable guide to the event season, with a rundown of all the airshows from around the world.

84 PAGES

£6.99 INC FREE P&P*

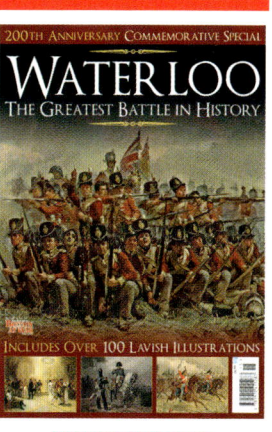

WATERLOO
The Allied nations agreed to combine against Napoleon and in June 1815 they began to mass on France's frontiers.

100 PAGES

£5.99 INC FREE P&P*

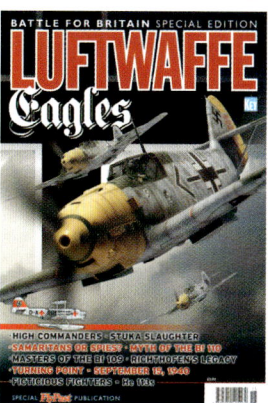

LUFTWAFFE EAGLES
Battle for Britain special edition - featuring all of the major combat types including colour schemes, markings & unit heraldry.

100 PAGES

£5.99 INC FREE P&P*

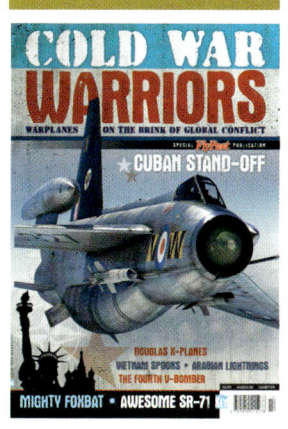

COLD WAR WARRIORS
Warplanes on the brink of global conflict

100 PAGES

£5.99 INC FREE P&P*

FAMOUS FIGHTERS
100th anniversary tribute to the top fighter of World War 1.

100 PAGES

£6.99 INC FREE P&P*

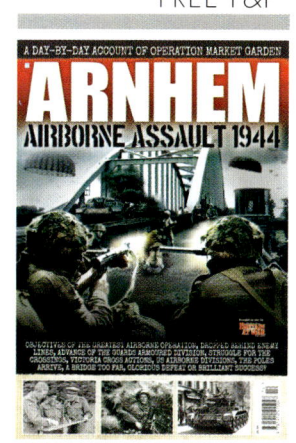

ARNHEM
A day-by-day account of Operation Market Garden year of the Great War.

132 PAGES

£5.99 INC FREE P&P*

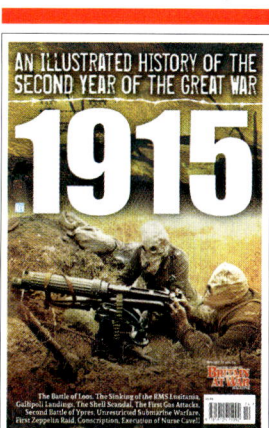

1915
An illustrated history of the second year of the Great War.

100 PAGES

AVIATION SPECIALS
ESSENTIAL reading from the teams behind your FAVOURITE magazines

HOW TO ORDER

VISIT
www.keypublishing.com/shop

OR

PHONE
UK: 01780 480404
ROW: (+44)1780 480404

*Prices correct at time of going to press. Subscriber discount valid on full price items only. Free 2nd class P&P on all UK & BFPO orders. Overseas charges apply. Postage charges vary depending on total order value.

NEW FREE Aviation Specials App 
Simply download to purchase digital versions of your favourite aviation specials in one handy place! Once you have the app, you will be able to download new, out of print or archive specials for less than the cover price!

IN APP ISSUES £3.99

558/15

PEOPLE

The World of the Few

Only those who were there can have a full understanding of what it felt like to take part in the Battle of Britain. Geoff Simpson, a trustee of the Battle of Britain Memorial Trust, takes a look at the men and machines on Fighter Command's frontline

Spitfire Mk I X4474, wearing the 'QV' codes of 19 Sqn and individual code letter 'I', was about to depart for a patrol from its Fowlmere base on September 21, 1940. Battle of Britain pilots operated under conditions of extreme stress, the exhilaration and terror of combat mixing on a daily basis with the relaxation of a 'pint at their local'. RAF (AHB)/© UK MoD Crown Copyright 2015

Spend any time at all on an RAF squadron today and it quickly becomes obvious that nicknames are an important component of Service culture. The same was true during the Battle of Britain, when many felt that receiving a nickname marked their moment of acceptance. It was, perhaps, similar to receiving school colours or a county cap at cricket.

Many names were obvious or traditional – 'Bunny' Currant, 'Sticky' Glew and 'Robin' Hood for example. Others needed some explanation. 'Dimsie' Stones had been caught with the children's book *Dimsie Goes to School*; 'Grumpy' Unwin had been so named by Douglas Bader after expressing discontent at the noise of Bader banging a new tin leg to make it more comfortable; 'Social Type' Jeff was always immaculate.

There can be no doubt that in many regards, Fighter Command was a most British institution, but the war in Europe brought an influx of displaced personnel to join volunteers from the Commonwealth and beyond, all united to fight the Nazi threat. We still do not know how many Allied airmen took part in the Battle of Britain. Exact figures are quoted, but most are likely to prove too low as research continues, new names are found and, occasionally, a name is deleted. The number of men who qualified for the 'immediate' award of the 1939-45 Star with Battle of Britain Clasp for operational service in Fighter Command between July 10 and October 31, 1940 is at least 2,940 and probably approaching 2,950.

Cosmopolitan Command
Fighter Command in the Battle of Britain was certainly a cosmopolitan organisation in which airmen from the Dominions and Empire, the countries of occupied Europe and neutral nations came together with those from the United

PEOPLE

Kingdom to deny the Luftwaffe air superiority over the nation. Their actions were at the forefront of first delaying and then ending the threat of invasion. Approximately 20% of the pilots and other aircrew who flew in the Battle were from outside the UK.

Countries represented in Fighter Command in 1940 included Australia, Belgium, Canada, Czechoslovakia, France, Ireland, Newfoundland, New Zealand, Poland, the Rhodesias, South Africa and the United States. The Poles were certainly the largest non-UK group, with perhaps 145 participants, followed by New Zealand (127), Canada (112) and Czechoslovakia (88).

The number of Canadians was boosted by the fact that 1 Squadron, Royal Canadian Air Force was based in Britain and flew Hurricanes into action, though there were also Canadians serving in the RAF, a significant number of them with 242 Squadron, based at Coltishall and Duxford during the Battle.

One man who earned the Battle of Britain Clasp, Pilot Officer Alfred Lammer, was officially stateless. Born Alfred Ritter von Lammer in Austria in 1909, he joined an anti-Nazi group and then came to London to work for the Austrian Travel Bureau. When the Germans took over his country, von Lammer refused German citizenship. In the Battle he flew as an air gunner in the Defiants of 141 Squadron. He was granted British citizenship in 1941.

Awarded the DFC and bar in 1943, Alfred Lammer survived the war and became a well known photographer, providing images for Royal Mail stamps and becoming an Honorary Fellow of the Royal College of Art. He died in 2000.

Young men from the Commonwealth countries had been joining the RAF in the years before the war, often on short service commissions, as various schemes developed to increase the number of pilots, expanding in the process the backgrounds from which they came.

For most of the Poles and Czechs the route into the RAF was rather different. Many of the Poles, for example, had flown in action as members of the Polish Air Force, resisting the German invasion of their country in September 1939. Then they had escaped by various routes to France, joined the French Air Force, fought another German invasion and then reached Britain.

»

Above: Pilot Officers Jan Zumbach (left) and Feric, Poles with 303 Sqn, at Northolt in October 1940. Zumbach later led '303', before taking a senior position for the invasion of Europe. RAF (AHB)/© UK MoD Crown Copyright 2015

Above: Flight Lieutenant Percival S Turner, a Canadian pilot serving with 242 (Canadian) Squadron at Coltishall, Norfolk, in September 1940. Turner is credited with shooting down ten aircraft during the Battle of Britain. RAF (AHB)/© UK MoD Crown Copyright 2015

PEOPLE

Thought to be from 504 Sqn, these Hurricane pilots were relaxing at The White Hart Inn at Brasted, Kent. RAF (AHB)/© UK MoD Crown Copyright 2015

Three 303 (Polish) Squadron pilots pose with a Hurricane at Northolt in October 1940. From left to right they are Fg Off Zdislaw Henneberg (Polish), Flt Lt John Alexander Kent (the Canadian squadron commander) and Fg Off M Pisarek (Polish). RAF (AHB)/© UK MoD Crown Copyright 2015

Flying Officer Francis Noel Brinsden was a New Zealander flying with 19 Squadron. RAF (AHB)/© UK MoD Crown Copyright 2015

The German takeover of Czechoslovakia was relatively peaceful, but thousands of service personnel were demobilised immediately, starting another series of journeys that ended in Britain.

Two specially created Polish squadrons (302 and 303) flew in the Battle of Britain, as did two Czech squadrons, 310 and 312. Squadron Leader Alfred Hess, who led 310 Squadron into action, was a member of a very select band of the 'Few' born in Queen Victoria's reign. He was 42 years old when, on September 15, 1940, now Battle of Britain Day, he was shot down over the Thames Estuary in combat with enemy fighters. Hess steered his burning Hurricane clear of houses in Essex, before baling out at 400ft (120m). He survived with bruises.

Lists of scores for aircraft shot down by individual pilots in the Battle are unreliable, but many historians now accept that the highest scoring Allied pilot was Sergeant Josef Frantisek, DFM, a Czech flying with the Polish 303 Squadron. He is often credited with 17 enemy aircraft destroyed, but died in a flying accident on October 8, 1940.

Some of the French pilots serving with the RAF flew under sentence of death as 'deserters' in their own country. Most had escaped to Britain via North Africa and Gibraltar.

In 2013 the RAF HQ building in Gibraltar was re-named in honour of one of their number, René Mouchotte. The charismatic Mouchotte failed to return from a sortie escorting bombers to attack a V-2 rocket launch site near St Omer on August 27, 1943. He is also remembered in the name of a Paris street.

When Colonel Henry Lafont, the last surviving French pilot from the Battle of Britain, died in 2011 he was given a national funeral at Les Invalides in Paris. Honorary Brigadier General Tadeusz Sawicz, the last Polish Clasp holder, died that same year in Canada and members of the Queen's Colour Squadron escorted his ashes to Warsaw, where he was accorded a state funeral service.

Both men had played their part 71 years earlier in a partnership of nations that ensured Britain stayed in World War Two and Nazism would be defeated.

Squadron Life

Flying combat from UK stations, there was a strange contrast for the Few between fighting for their lives during the day and spending the evenings in country pubs or London clubs. Many learned that a whiff of oxygen as they were about to take-off for the first sortie of the day was a good cure for a hangover!

For pilots waiting at dispersal, the ringing of a telephone could herald the excitement and terror of a 'Scramble', or an anti-climax as mundane as "NAAFI wagon coming". Many of the Few, even in old age at home, did not enjoy memories brought back by the sound of the phone.

First sight of the enemy could also be a never forgotten moment. 'Sammy' Hall of 152 Sqn remembered being mesmerised and almost colliding with a German bomber. Many others were less fortunate.

Flying Officer Arthur Rose-Price arrived at Gravesend to join 501 Sqn and was killed later the same day, his luggage still unpacked in his car. Sergeant Reg Isaac was a bank worker and member of the RAFVR before the war. He was lost on his first sortie with 64 Sqn.

Sergeant Geoffrey Pearson's operational career with 501 lasted ten days. More than 70 years later, Sqn Ldr Tony Pickering, also a Sergeant Pilot in 1940, stood at Geoffrey Pearson's grave in the churchyard at Lympne, Kent and remembered playing cards with him in the brief time they had known each other. In such circumstances some men determined to make no more friends.

Eric Bann of 238 Sqn wrote in fury to his parents after he had watched fellow sergeant Leslie Pidd killed under his parachute by a German fighter. Less than two weeks later Bann died when his parachute failed to open over the Isle of Wight. A police inspector who had been at the scene wrote an emotional letter to Bann's mother in which he referred to "these gallant men" who were performing, "a most marvellous feat against overwhelming odds and have earned the gratitude of all the civilised world and such is the spirit of the British RAF that their names will live forever as the saviours of our country…"

Meeting Stuffy
Some aircrew were taken aback at the upsurge of hero worship they experienced during the Battle, when their deeds were often witnessed from the ground, in great contrast to the unfair criticism the RAF had received from the Army at the time of Dunkirk. At their head, Air Chief Marshal Dowding remained, unsurprisingly, a remote figure to most.

One Battle of Britain pilot who did come into contact with him was Pilot Officer (later Wing Commander) John Beazley of 249 Sqn, who was recovering from wounds in hospital at Halton when the AOC-in-C visited the ward. Writing in 2003, Beazley recalled: "First one has to understand that 'Stuffy' Dowding could easily have been mistaken for an elderly and rather austere university professor and was certainly blessed with the necessary intellectual gifts. But we were all deeply in awe of him. He inspired our absolute loyalty, trust and respectful admiration.

"Stuffy stopped at each bed in turn and chatted to its occupant. When he came to me he asked me what had happened and I said that at the end of September I had been put out of action by a (Messerschmitt) 110. Stuffy said, 'A 110! Aren't you rather ashamed of yourself? Nobody gets shot down or worsted by a 110.'

"He then asked me if I had suffered any previous adversity, or words to that effect. I said that at the beginning of September I had had to bale out. He asked me what had caused my downfall that time and I said a 110.

"Stuffy said, 'Another 110, you really should be ashamed of yourself!' By way of mitigation, I said that there had been a lot »

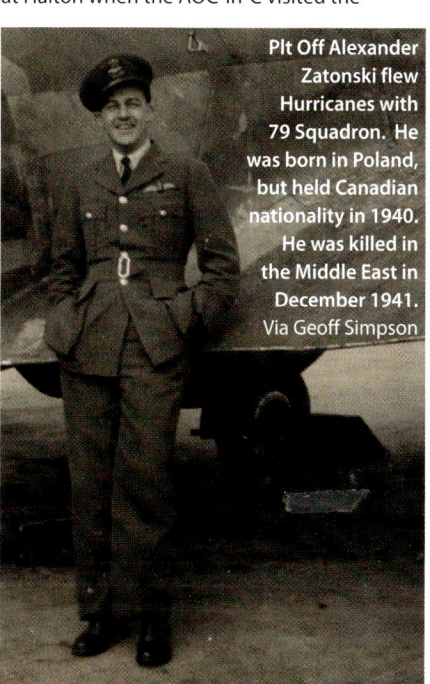

The Polish War memorial, close to RAF Northolt, is dedicated to the personnel lost in the service of the RAF's Polish squadrons, including those involved in the Battle of Britain.
Wing Commander Andy Simpson

> "…such is the spirit of the British RAF that their names will live forever as the saviours of our country…"
> **Isle of Wight police inspector in a letter to a downed airman's mother**

Plt Off Alexander Zatonski flew Hurricanes with 79 Squadron. He was born in Poland, but held Canadian nationality in 1940. He was killed in the Middle East in December 1941.
Via Geoff Simpson

Sitting in the cockpit of his Spitfire on October 1, 1940, Plt Off Phillip H Leckrone was an American flying with 616 Squadron from Kirton-in-Lindsey. He was killed on a training flight while serving with one of the 'Eagle' Squadrons, No. 71, on January 5, 1941. RAF (AHB)/© UK MoD Crown Copyright 2015

PEOPLE

Antennas above and below the port wing indicate that this Blenheim IF has AI radar installed. A Blenheim scored the RAF's first nocturnal AI success, in July 1940. RAF (AHB)/© UK MoD Crown Copyright 2015

of them around at the time. He allowed that this could have been a factor and wished me a full recovery, and I felt that I had been at least partly forgiven."

Turrets and AI
Seventy-one squadrons and other units were finally established as being 'accredited' in terms of the award of the Battle of Britain Clasp, including two from the Fleet Air Arm (FAA) and a number from Coastal Command that were attached to Fighter Command for at least part of the Battle. The Hurricane and Spitfire were, of course, the key aircraft types operated by RAF Fighter Command in the Battle of Britain, but they were far from being the only aircraft flown by the Few.

Two squadrons, for example, were equipped with the Defiant two-man turret fighter, which was hopelessly vulnerable in daylight once the Luftwaffe had worked out its weaknesses. The fighter version of the Blenheim was flown by a number of squadrons, in the night-fighter role, on convoy patrols, escorting bombers, and escorting other aircraft arriving in the UK.

From September 1940, some Blenheim squadrons began receiving the hastily designed, yet highly successful, two-seat Beaufighter which, using airborne interception (AI) radar, became much more effective in countering the night blitz than the Blenheim.

The airborne radar system was being developed as quickly as possible during the Battle of Britain. A pioneering success came at night on July 23, 1940 when, using AI, a Blenheim of the Fighter Interception Unit, flying from Tangmere, intercepted a Dornier Do 17 and shot it down into the Channel south of Bognor Regis. The crew that played a part in this piece of RAF history was Flg Off Ashfield, Plt Off Morris and Sgt Leyland. Credit also went to the Poling Chain Home station, which had detected the presence of the enemy aircraft.

Day Fighters
Although the heyday of the biplane had long since passed, 247 Squadron qualified as a Battle of Britain unit while equipped with Gloster Gladiators, based at Roborough to defend Plymouth and its docks, while one of the accredited Naval Air Squadrons flew Sea Gladiators. Another FAA unit patrolled the naval base at Scapa Flow, Orkney, with Fairey Fulmars. Normally flown by a two-man crew in naval service, under Fighter Command the Fulmar was flown solo, there being no need for complicated navigation.

In the frontline of the fighter battle Hurricanes and Spitfires faced the Luftwaffe's Bf 109 and Bf 110 fighters. The pilots who flew the British aircraft often retained loyal feelings towards the type they happened

Among these 249 Squadron Hurricane pilots at North Weald in September 1940 are: Plt Off Percy Burton (extreme left), killed in action on September 27 (having been promoted to Flying Officer the day before); Plt Off Tom Neil (fifth from left); Plt Off John Beazley (sixth from left), who met a less than impressed Dowding while recuperating in hospital; Sqn Ldr John Grandy (seventh from left), the CO and later CAS; and George Barclay (second from right). Via Geoff Simpson

72 | ROYAL AIR FORCE SALUTE 2015

PEOPLE

Naval thinking required an extra crewman to ease the complex task of overwater navigation for FAA fighter pilots. The Fairey Fulmar adhered to this requirement, emerging as a slow, unwieldy machine, albeit with the latest eight-gun armament. RAF (AHB)/© UK MoD Crown Copyright 2015

Interwar strategists believed that bomber formations would penetrate enemy airspace unescorted, relying on their defensive weapons and speed to get through. The Defiant was designed to counter such attacks, flying alongside the bomber stream while its turret gunner engaged. The resulting aircraft had little combat worth against Luftwaffe fighters. RAF (AHB)/© UK MoD Crown Copyright 2015

to be allocated for years afterwards. Wing Commander Bob Foster, DFC, AE summed this up. As a pilot officer he flew Hurricanes with 605 (County of Warwick) Sqn, based at Croydon, from September 7, 1940.

When quizzed on which was the superior aircraft, Foster commented, "I've been asked this question many times, and we always dodge it, or I do, because they were both very good aeroplanes, they both did their job excellently. I suppose, in a way, that the Spitfire was not easier to fly, but I suppose lighter to fly, for want of a better word. I regarded the Hurricane as a wonderful aeroplane because it was the first one (of the two) I flew. It was a good solid old aircraft and, of course, it was an older design than the Spitfire." The Hurricane did not have the speed or altitude capability of the Spitfire, but could turn more tightly. Many pilots also felt that the Hurricane could take much more punishment, while damaged aircraft were often repaired on the station whereas a Spitfire might have to go to a maintenance unit.

However, the design and construction of the Hurricane made it more likely to inflict severe burns on its pilot if it was hit. Pilot Officer Geoffrey Page of 56 Sqn experienced that situation, baling out into the sea from a burning Hurricane on August 12, 1940. He became a founding committee member of the Guinea Pig Club at the Queen Victoria Hospital, East Grinstead, consisting of RAF aircrew treated by the team lead by the brilliant plastic surgeon Archie (later Sir Archibald) McIndoe.

Geoffrey Page returned to operations, earned the DSO, DFC and bar, was injured again and found himself back at East Grinstead. Many years later he established the Battle of Britain Memorial Trust, which created the National Memorial to The Few, at Capel-le-Ferne, Kent.

In his book *Shot Down in Flames*, Wing Commander Page who, like Bob Foster, flew both types in action, wrote, "Whereas the Spitfire had all the speed and grace of a greyhound in its sleek appearance, the Hurricane portrayed the excellent qualities of the bulldog, being slower but much more solidly built. To the Spitfire pilot there will only be one machine and similarly to the man who flew the Hurricane. To the fortunate one who often took to the skies in both types there will be an everlasting love for both that borders on sweet-sadness that these aircraft, like human beings, last but a little while and then are gone."

The Beaufighter proved a far more effective fighter than the Blenheim. Developed early on as a night-fighter, the Beaufighter matured as an excellent attack aircraft. These 'Beaus' belonged to 25 Sqn. RAF (AHB)/© UK MoD Crown Copyright 2015

Squadrons Then and Now

Number	Established	Initial aircraft	Aircraft in 1940	2015 role	Aircraft
56	June 8, 1916	S.E.5	Hurricane	ISTAR	None
501	June 14, 1929	DH.9A	Hurricane	Logistics	None
504	March 26, 1928	Horsley	Hurricane	Logistics	None
605	October 15, 1926	DH.9A	Hurricane	Logistics	None

ROYAL AIR FORCE SALUTE 2015 | 73

HERITAGE

Spitfire Mk IIA P7350 currently flies as 'EB-G', representing 41 Sqn Mk IA N3162, flown by Plt Off Eric Lock to score three kills in one sortie on September 5, 1940.
Photo © John Dibbs

HERITAGE

A Very Special Spitfire

Royal Air Force Battle of Britain Memorial Flight Spitfire Mk IIA P7350 is the sole surviving Spitfire from the Battle of Britain remaining in airworthy condition. Squadron Leader Clive Rowley MBE RAF (Retd) tells the aircraft's historic tale

HERITAGE

P7350 was the 14th of 11,939 Spitfires eventually built at the Castle Bromwich 'Shadow' factory, although it was not, in fact, the 14th delivered to the RAF. First flown by famous test pilot Alex Henshaw in August 1940, it was taken on charge on the 13th and delivered, by Henshaw, to No. 6 Maintenance Unit (MU) at Brize Norton four days later, for the fitting of operational equipment.

Battle of Britain
The Spitfire was allocated to No. 266 Squadron at Wittering on September 6, where it was given the code letters 'UO-T'. The unit subsequently moved to Martlesham Heath and then Collyweston, taking P7350 with it. On October 17, P7350 was one of 13 Mk IIA Spitfires transferred to 603 (City of Edinburgh) Squadron at Hornchurch. Its code letters were changed for the 'XT' of 603 Squadron and its individual letter is thought to have become 'W'.

On October 25, while being flown as part of a squadron scramble by Polish pilot Ludwik Martel, P7350 was shot down by machine-gun and cannon fire from a Bf 109. A cannon shell punched a large hole in the port wing and shrapnel wounded Martel in the left side of his body and legs. Despite his injuries, Martel managed to fly the aircraft down through 16,000ft of thick cloud, before force-landing in a field near Hastings.

P7350 was dispatched to No. 1 Civilian Repair Unit at Cowley on October 31, where it was repaired and ready for collection on December 7, when it was flown to No. 37 MU at Burtonwood for service preparation and storage.

Fighter Sweeps
The Spitfire's next operational unit was No. 616 (County of South Yorkshire) Squadron, based at Tangmere, to which it was issued on March 18, 1941. On April 10 it was transferred to 64 Squadron at Hornchurch. With these units P7350 flew fighter sweeps over occupied Europe as Fighter Command continued its offensive through 1941. Having seemingly incurred damage from an unknown incident,

Eric Lock as a Flight Lieutenant, in the cockpit of a 611 Sqn Spitfire Mk VB.

On the ground the Spitfire's long nose obscures the view forwards and pilots taxi with the hood open, weaving from side to side and alternately looking left and right from the cockpit. Cpl Paul Robertshaw/© UK MoD Crown Copyright 2015

HERITAGE

P7350 in October 2009 as 'QJ-K', representing a Spitfire flown by Geoffrey Wellum with 92 Sqn. Photo © Jim Dooley

possibly a landing accident, P7350 was with Scottish Aviation Ltd at Prestwick on August 5 for overhaul and repair. It was flown to No. 37 MU again on January 29, 1942.

Training Duties

With higher-performance, better-armed versions of the Spitfire now available, the time had come to withdraw the Mk IIAs from operational flying and, on April 27, 1942, P7350 was issued to the Central Gunnery School at Sutton Bridge, near Kings Lynn in Norfolk. Here it spent the next 10 months, suffering another Category B accident (beyond repair on site) on February 4, 1943 and being transferred to Air Services Training Ltd at Hamble for repairs. These were completed by March 20 and, after passing through 6 MU at Brize Norton again, P7350 was issued to No. 57 Operational Training Unit (OTU) at Eshott, Northumberland.

The next 12 months of its use as a training machine were uneventful, but on April 22, 1944 another Spitfire taxied into it, causing further Category B damage, which once again saw P7350 at Air Services Training Ltd for repairs. Fixed again, the aircraft was placed in storage with No. 39 MU at Colerne.

Scrapped, Almost

Having survived its wartime adventures, P7350 was declared surplus to Air Ministry requirement in 1947 and in 1948 it was sold as scrap to Messrs John Dale and Sons Ltd for £25. On realising the historical importance of the venerable aircraft, the company generously presented it to RAF Colerne as a museum piece, where it remained until 1967.

The making of the movie *Battle of Britain* saw Spitfire P7350 emerge from 20 years of dormancy when it was selected to fly in the film. The aircraft was delivered to No. 71 MU at Henlow on March 3, 1967 to be overhauled to airworthy standard and on May 20, 1968 it was flown to Duxford for use in aerial sequences for the film.

»

The Mk II and Mk VB are similar in appearance and handling qualities, but quite different to BBMF's other Spitfires – a Mk IX, XVI and two Mk XIXs. Pilots new to the Flight gain hours first on the Hurricane, then the Spitfire IX or XVI, with their larger rudders and slightly more benign ground handling. SAC Graham Taylor/© UK MoD Crown Copyright 2015

Royal Air Force Salute 2015 | 27

HERITAGE

The Flight's aircraft are finished as accurately as possible, right down to their detail markings. The red patches on the wing leading edge are pieces of canvas covering the machine gun muzzles. Photo © Jim Dooley

A Personal View

Squadron Leader Dunc Mason is in his final year as Officer Commanding BBMF and, by his own admission, could talk all day, every day about flying Spitfires. This is his personal view of P7350.

"For those of us lucky enough to be allowed to fly the Spitfires of the BBMF, it is always a wonderful thing to fly P7350, the Flight's very special 'baby' Mk II Spitfire.

"Walking out to the aircraft, I am always struck by the beauty of it. Approaching from behind, the elliptical wing, the cockpit nestled behind the long nose that points skyward, there is no doubt that this aircraft is a masterpiece. There is a poignancy and reverence about taking it into the air. Maybe this is because she is the sole airworthy survivor of the world's greatest ever air battle; perhaps it is because she has an airborne elegance that belies her ferocious nature?

"Whatever the reason, the expectation is always palpable. The feeling is very difficult to describe; excitement like that of a young boy who has been given the most amazing aircraft to wheel around the sky, mixed with a great sense of responsibility to keep her safe at all costs. After all, if anything happened to this irreplaceable artefact of the nation's aviation heritage, even if it was not the pilot's fault, he would probably never be forgiven!

"In the air she is different from other Spitfires. She is lighter and more 'twitchy' if you are not steady handed with her and she purrs more than making the harsh growl of the later-engine Spitfires. She accelerates faster and, especially on the ground, with her small rudder, she is more skittish and requires more attention than her weightier younger sisters with their bigger rudders.

"Safely back on the ground, as I walk away, I have to turn and have one last look at this beautiful aircraft – the Spitfire of all Spitfires – with which I'm completely enchanted."

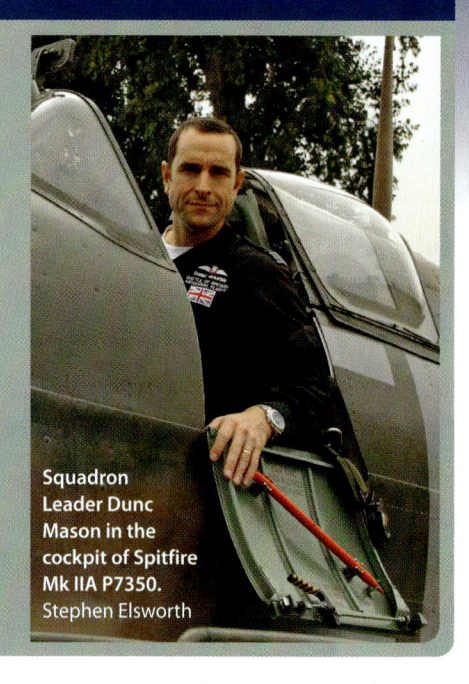

Squadron Leader Dunc Mason in the cockpit of Spitfire Mk IIA P7350. Stephen Elsworth

In company with several Spitfires of various marks, P7350 (nearest the camera) awaits scrapping in 1948.

HERITAGE

"I have to turn and have one last look at this beautiful aircraft – the Spitfire of all Spitfires – with which I'm completely enchanted."
Squadron Leader
Dunc Mason, OC BBMF

The yellow 'diamond' on P7350's port wing replicates the 'gas patch' frequently carried by aircraft during the early war period. It changed colour on exposure to toxic gas, warning ground crew if an aircraft had passed through such material, or pilots if their airfield had been attacked with chemical weapons. Photo © John Dibbs

HERITAGE

P7350 back in the scheme it wore with 603 Sqn during the Battle of Britain. Photo © John Dibbs

Marked as 92 Sqn's 'QJ-K', P7350 flies with BBMF's Hurricane IIC LF363 in April 2010. The Hurricane is painted as 17 Sqn's P3878/YB-W, based at North Weald in September 1940. SAC Neil Chapman/© UK MoD Crown Copyright 2015

BBMF

In October 1968, after filming for the movie was complete, P7350 was allocated to the Battle of Britain Flight at Coltishall, being flown there by Sqn Ldr Tim Mills on November 5. It has served with the BBMF ever since, as a much admired survivor and precious artefact of British aviation history and the RAF's wartime heritage.

Although much of the aircraft's structure remains original, components have been replaced when necessary to maintain it in airworthy condition. P7350's last major overhaul was completed at Duxford between September 2008 and September 2009, when it received new spars for both wings and skin sections were renewed.

HERITAGE

Commemorating Eric Lock

P7350 is currently presented as Spitfire Mk IA N3162/EB-G of No. 41 Squadron, the aircraft flown by Pilot Officer Eric Lock (later DSO DFC and Bar), on September 5, 1940, when he achieved three confirmed kills in a single sortie. During the aerial fighting that day, 41 Squadron's commanding officer and one of the flight commanders were killed, three pilots were wounded (including Eric Lock), three of the squadron's aircraft were destroyed and four were damaged (one of them seriously). However, 41's pilots claimed nine enemy aircraft destroyed, five probably destroyed and five more damaged.

Modern research credits Lock with a total of 21 kills during the Battle of Britain period, plus eight 'probables'. This makes him the highest scoring RAF pilot of the Battle by some margin. Eric was himself shot down and badly wounded in November 1940 and spent the next six months in hospital. Sadly, not long after he returned to flying duties, he was killed in action on August 3, 1941, near Calais. His aircraft (Spitfire Mk VB W3257) and his body have never been found, despite extensive searches, and he has no known grave. Eric Lock's name is carved on the Runnymede Memorial in Surrey, along with those of 20,400 other British and Commonwealth airmen who vanished without trace in World War Two.

Although Eric Lock's war was relatively short – in the one-year period from his first encounter with the enemy, he was on 'ops' for less than four months – his final score of 26½ enemy aircraft destroyed makes him one of the RAF's top ten aces of the conflict. Even in this exalted company he was something special; his 'strike rate' was extraordinary and his aggression, fighting spirit and shooting ability were exceptional. All but three of his remarkable tally of victories was achieved with 41 Squadron in just a few weeks of fighting and most (18 kills) were against Bf 109 fighters.

> This story is adapted from an article that first appeared in the *Official RAF Memorial Flight Club Year Book 2015*. The website address for joining the BBMF Club is: www.memorialflightclub.com

ROYAL AIR FORCE SALUTE 2015 | 81

PEOPLE

The Many Behind the Few

Luftwaffe attacks against RAF airfields and other installations kept Fighter Command's ground personnel on the frontline through most of the Battle of Britain. As Stuart Hadaway of the Air Historical Branch (RAF) explains, they performed with exceptional valour

"On-the-spot repairs of damaged aircraft were carried out by our own ground crews, who were magnificent. All night long, lights burned in the shuttered hangars as the fitters, electricians, armourers and riggers worked unceasingly to put the maximum number on the line for the next day's operations. All day too they worked, not even ceasing when the airfield was threatened with attack. A grand body of men about whom too little has been written but without whose efforts victory would not have been possible."

In these words Flying Officer (later Air Commodore) Al Deere summed up his admiration for the thousands of men and women who risked their lives daily to keep the 'Few' flying. So often overlooked, ground crews and ground staff across the RAF toiled ceaselessly to keep the frontline squadrons operational. Whether repairing damaged aircraft, keeping the pilots supplied with tea and sandwiches from dawn to dusk, or processing the paperwork that kept fuel, ammunition and spare parts flowing, these men and women played a vital role in winning the Battle.

It was dangerous work, too. Airfields and other RAF installations, including radar stations, were regularly attacked, mostly in the south of England, but also elsewhere across the country. On August 13, 1940 the German high command launched a three-week long concerted effort to destroy the RAF on the ground.

That day the RAF suffered 81 aircrew casualties, including 15 fighter pilots lost in action and 52 bomber crewmen. On the ground, 96 men and women were killed or wounded in air raids, with RAF Detling and RAF Eastchurch particularly badly hit. A few days later, on August 18 (later dubbed 'The Hardest Day' owing to the severity of the air fighting), RAF Fighter Command lost 28 pilots killed or wounded in action. Meanwhile, 36 men and women were killed or wounded on the ground. At Biggin Hill, 39 men were killed on August 30 when an air raid shelter took a direct hit.

Airfield Attacks

Leading Aircraftsman Maurice Haffenden was an engine fitter with 43 Squadron at RAF Tangmere when it was raided: "At 1pm the loudspeaker, with a greater urgency than »

82 | ROYAL AIR FORCE SALUTE 2015

PEOPLE

Riggers from 264 Sqn examine a Defiant's elevators at RAF Duxford, just before the Battle of Britain. All RAF (AHB)/© UK MoD Crown Copyright 2015

Ground crew rearm a 19 Sqn Spitfire at RAF Fowlmere in September 1940. Ammunition was fed in through hatches under the wings.

Rearming continues at Fowlmere as Spitfire IA P9368/QV-K receives attention. This aircraft was often flown by 19 Squadron's CO, Sqn Ldr 'Sandy' Lane and was also the preferred mount of 'A' Flight Commander, Flt Lt 'Farmer' Lawson.

Refuelling fighters out in the open was a dangerous operation if the airfield was under attack.

Al Deere, here as a wing commander in 1944, was among the pilots who sang the praises of his ground crew during the Battle.

Ground crew perform more extensive work on a 601 Sqn Hurricane. As well as repairing aircraft, ground crews had to keep up with routine maintenance to keep their aircraft flying.

ROYAL AIR FORCE SALUTE 2015 | 83

PEOPLE

Squadrons Then and Now

Number	Established	Initial aircraft	Aircraft in 1940	2015 role	Aircraft
54	May 15, 1916	Pup	Spitfire	ISTAR	None

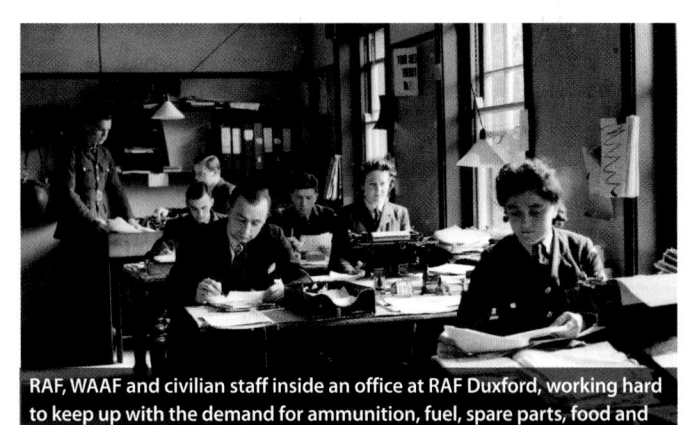

RAF, WAAF and civilian staff inside an office at RAF Duxford, working hard to keep up with the demand for ammunition, fuel, spare parts, food and other supplies that the station needed to maintain high tempo operations.

Inside the Sector 'G' Operations Room at RAF Duxford. These rooms were part of a system that was crucial in allowing RAF Fighter Command use its limited resources to best effect.

before, suddenly appealed, 'Take cover! Take cover!' Within three minutes of that warning I saw the first of the Junkers coming straight down on the 'drome in a vertical dive… I went headfirst down a manhole as the first bomb landed on the cookhouse. For seven minutes their thousand pounders were scoring direct hits and everything was swept away by machine-gun bullets. I never believed such desolation and destruction to be possible. Everything is wrecked – the hangars, the stores, the hospital, the armoury, the cookhouses, the canteen – well, everything."

Several stations were severally damaged, and casualties could be high. So bad was the bombing that some pilots considered themselves safer in the air. Sergeant Iain Hutchinson flew with 54 Squadron from RAF Hornchurch, and had to land during a raid to refuel and rearm: "The airfield was under attack and chunks of shrapnel were raining down. When I taxied towards the dispersal no one was to be seen; they were all in the air raid shelters taking cover.

"Before I rolled to a halt and cut the engine, 'B' Flight ground crew, under their flight sergeant, were swarming around my Spitfire; the bowser was racing out to refuel the aircraft, while the armament men, laden with ammunition, were reloading the guns. The noise from the explosions going on around us was terrifying, but not one of those magnificent men faltered for a moment in their tasks. I was frankly relieved to be taking off again."

Calmly Carrying On

Many men performed acts of great courage while carrying out their duties. Refuelling and rearming an aircraft, with a bowser full of volatile fuel and piles of ammunition right next to them while bombs rained down, was tremendously dangerous.

Notably during the Battle of Britain, many members of the Women's Auxiliary Air Force also carried out their duties with distinction. It was the first time that a British female military force had served on what was effectively the frontline. At airfields they worked beside the men to keep stations operational. In radar stations and operations rooms, WAAFs continued to calmly plot and report on the movements of enemy formations, even when those formations were aimed at attacking and destroying the very installations they were working in.

At RAF Biggin Hill three members of the WAAF were decorated with the Military Medal for bravery under fire, the first time such an award had been made to women. On August 18, Sergeant Elizabeth Mortimer had stayed at her post in the station armoury during a raid, coordinating communications between the airfield defence posts. She then joined the efforts to help returning pilots land safely by marking the many craters and unexploded bombs that littered the runway, despite being ordered to take cover. Two weeks later, on August 31, Sergeant Helen Turner and Corporal Elspeth Henderson refused to leave their places in the operations room even as bombs fell around them, and then onto the ops room itself. They were among the first to prove that women could conduct support operations in frontline areas beside their male counterparts.

Even after the main focus of the German attacks shifted to London and other cities, smaller raids continued on airfields and other installations. In hundreds of roles at scores of stations, the ground crew struggled around the clock to keep Fighter Command flying. Without their dedication and bravery, the Battle of Britain could not have been won. ⊙

Sgt Mortimer, Cpl Henderson and Sgt Turner (left to right) all received the Military Medal for gallantry under fire.

An RAF sergeant instructs Czech ground crew on a 310 Sqn Hurricane at RAF Duxford.

Czech armourers prepare ammunition in October 1940.

84 | ROYAL AIR FORCE SALUTE 2015

HERITAGE

Spitfire Down!

The Royal Air Force Battle of Britain Memorial Flight's remarkable Spitfire IIA was in the thick of the fighting as the Battle of Britain drew to a close, but on October 25 its luck ran out. Sqn Ldr Clive Rowley MBE RAF (Retd) tells the story

During 2006, P7350 was marked as it appeared when it was shot down in 603 Sqn service on October 25, 1940. Photo © John Dibbs

ROYAL AIR FORCE SALUTE 2015 | 85

HERITAGE

Towards the end of October 1940 the Battle of Britain was almost won, but it was not quite over and the Royal Air Force was still fighting for the nation's very survival. The RAF BBMF's Spitfire Mk IIA P7350 was, at this time, on the strength of No. 603 (City of Edinburgh) Squadron, based at RAF Hornchurch, Essex. It had been delivered on October 17 as one of 13 Mk IIA Spitfires transferred to 603 Squadron as Mk I replacements. Shortly after arrival the aircraft was painted with the squadron's 'XT' code letters and the individual letter 'W'.

Pilot Officer Ludwik Martel, a 21-year old Pole, was flying P7350 on Friday, October 25. Born in Piotrkow, central Poland in 1919, Ludwik grew up yearning to fly. He took a gliding course and in 1937 enlisted in the Polish Air Force. Still a cadet pilot when Germany invaded Poland on September 1, 1939, Martel was ordered to make for neutral Romania, where he was interned, but he escaped on September 29 and travelled via the Balkans to France.

Arriving in England in early 1940, Martel was commissioned into the RAF in May and then transferred to the re-formed Polish Air Force in August. He joined No. 54 Squadron, which was equipped with Spitfires, on August 10, at the height of the Battle of Britain, and transferred to 603 Squadron in October. On October 5 he claimed a Bf 109 destroyed over the English Channel.

Messerschmitt Bounce
On the morning of October 25, 603 Squadron was scrambled with 12 Spitfires, including Ludwik Martel in P7350, to engage Luftwaffe aircraft intent on attacking London. It was an overcast day and the squadron was forced to climb through thick, dark cloud, flying in tight formation. As they climbed, the Spitfire pilots heard the controller on the radio informing them, from the air picture provided to him by the radar system and his plotters, that there were enemy aircraft in the area.

Then there was a second warning that enemy aircraft were very close, almost on top of them. As the squadron burst out of cloud into clear blue sky at 20,000ft, all the pilots trying to adjust their eyes to the bright sunlight, they were unceremoniously 'bounced' by a group of Bf 109 fighters. The Messerschmitts roared down on them from above, flashing past with their cannon and machine guns spitting destruction.

It was every man for himself, as the squadron broke apart. Some fought to survive; others gave chase. Three Spitfires were hit, two of the pilots forced to bale out immediately over Sussex. Pilot Officer Peter Olver was wounded and Pilot Officer John Soden badly injured his leg when he landed by parachute near Chartham, Kent. Both had probably fallen victim to the famous German fighter ace Werner Mölders.

The third aircraft hit was P7350 with Ludwik Martel at the controls – a gaping hole appeared in 'P7's' left wing, there were banging noises behind him and Ludwik felt a sharp pain in the left side of his body and leg. He immediately put his aircraft back into the cloud where he would not be seen and could not be shot at any more. Little blood was visible, but Ludwik's leather flying jacket was torn and he knew he had been hit by shrapnel and wounded in the left leg. Aside from the shock of being hit, he was also less than impressed

> This story is adapted from an article that first appeared in the Autumn 2013 issue of the *Official RAF Memorial Flight Club Magazine*. The website address for joining the BBMF Club is: www.memorialflightclub.com

Spitfire Mk IIA P7350, resplendent in its wartime markings as 'XT-W'. Photo © John Dibbs

86 ROYAL AIR FORCE SALUTE 2015

HERITAGE

that he would now have to descend through the same thick cloud he had just penetrated on the way up.

It was much harder work on the way back down with the aircraft shot up; it was difficult to ignore the pain and concentrate on the instruments, as he had to, in order to nurse the Spitfire towards the ground. He could feel himself slipping into unconsciousness, but managed to break through the cloud at 4,000ft.

It is not a good idea to lower the undercarriage on a Spitfire for a landing on an unprepared surface, since this risks the aircraft somersaulting and coming to rest upside down with the pilot trapped in the cockpit. So Ludwik force landed the machine wheels-up, in a grassy field near Hastings.

Lucky Pilot, Lucky Spitfire

Ludwik Martel and P7350 had survived this brush with death and destruction and, by the time they were both repaired and able to re-join the fray, the Battle of Britain was officially over, the planned Nazi invasion of Britain postponed indefinitely.

It was December 6 before Ludwik was able to fly again. He went on to join the Polish No. 317 (City of Wilno) Squadron, flying offensive fighter sweeps over occupied France.

In March 1942 he was one of the Polish pilots who formed the famous 'Skalski's Circus', officially 'The Polish Fighting Team'. The unit operated in the Western Desert and in a few weeks destroyed 30 enemy aircraft. Martel downed a Bf 109 and damaged another, to add to his Bf 109 destroyed and one damaged during the Battle of Britain; he also destroyed an Italian Macchi MC.200.

He returned to 317 Squadron, then spent time as a flying instructor, before returning again to 317 as a flight commander, flying ground-attack sorties in support of the D-Day operations. In September 1944 his operational flying came to an end when he was posted to the Polish Air Force HQ. Martel survived the war and afterwards settled in England. He died in April 2010, aged 91.

Spitfire P7350 was sent to the Cowley Motor Works, Oxford for repairs and it was 1941 before it returned to the air. Against all odds P7350 survived the war, but in 1948 faced a threat even greater than enemy gunfire, when it was sold for scrap for just £25.

The aircraft would have been melted down were it not for the generosity and far-sightedness of the scrap merchant, John Dale & Sons, which recognised the Spitfire's pedigree and presented it to the RAF Museum. After 20 years on the ground, 'P7' was made airworthy in 1968 for the epic film *Battle of Britain*. When filming was completed in November 1968, it was presented to the BBMF.

It is easy to become blasé about the historic aircraft operated by the RAF BBMF, so it does no harm to be reminded that this marvellous and truly historic Spitfire, which is the pride of the Flight, was almost lost to the enemy in October 1940 and almost lost to the 'scrap man' in 1948. But it is still here and still flying, 75 years after it first saw action in the Battle of Britain!

The badge of 603 Sqn.
RAF (AHB)/© UK MoD
Crown Copyright 2015

Ludwik Martel.

ROYAL AIR FORCE SALUTE 2015 | 87

HERITAGE

1 (Fighter) Squadron:
First In All Things

Among the RAF units that fought the Battle of Britain, Number 1 (Fighter) Squadron is one of the few that continues in the same role. Today equipped with the Eurofighter Typhoon, the squadron is stationed at RAF Lossiemouth, Moray. Paul E Eden recounts its history

"It is a great privilege to serve on 1(F) Squadron. We are the oldest military flying squadron in existence, and every member of the team is proud of our heritage and history, and determined to maintain the high standards and finest traditions of those who have gone before.

"This is a particularly poignant year, since it marks not only the 75th anniversary of the Battle of Britain, but also the centenary of 1(F) Squadron's first operational deployment during World War One (as a Royal Flying Corps' squadron). Between March and June 1915 we flew hundreds of combat sorties over the Western Front, conducting bombing, reconnaissance, and air combat (dogfighting), so while we think of today's multi-role capability as being a new concept, in fact it has been at the heart of Combat Air since its very inception," says Wing Commander Mike 'Sooty' Sutton, who took over as Officer Commanding 1(F) Squadron in October 2014.

On May 13, 1912 the Royal Flying Corps (RFC) had come into being and No. 1 Company, Air Battalion, Royal Engineers was redesignated as 1 Squadron, RFC. Its first equipment – three airships – arrived in the autumn and the squadron continued as a lighter-than-air unit until May 1, 1914. After a period of working up, it deployed to France with RAF B.E.8 and Avro 504 aircraft in February 1915.

Reconnaissance was the primary mission, continuing when the squadron re-equipped with Moranes from December. In March 1916 it took its first fighters, Nieuport 17 C.1 biplanes, with which to defend its Moranes. Thus began the unit's tenure as a fighter squadron, emphasised in January 1917 when it relinquished the reconnaissance role altogether. Air fighting was now the primary concern, although enemy trenches were machine-gunned and bombed during the Battle of Messines that summer. By the end of the year, with improved Nieuport 27s on strength, 1 Sqn's scoreboard for aerial victories stood at 200.

Paveway IV has introduced a precision laser/GPS-guided weapon to the Typhoon's armoury. No. 1(F) Sqn has taken a key role in introducing the capability. © UK MoD Crown Copyright 2015

88 ROYAL AIR FORCE SALUTE 2015

HERITAGE

The squadron began flying Nieuport 27 fighters in 1917. RAF (AHB)/© UK MoD Crown Copyright 2015

This formation of 1 Sqn Snipes was up near Baghdad in 1926. RAF (AHB)/© UK MoD Crown Copyright 2015

From January 1918 No. 1 began receiving the excellent RAF S.E.5A to replace its Nieuports. With the new aircraft it fought savagely to the Armistice, when the S.E.5As were returned to the UK and destroyed, the squadron finally disbanding in January 1920.

Inter-war Action

A resurgent No. 1 Sqn simultaneously stood up at Risalpur, India, moving to Bangalore to train on the Sopwith Snipe and, briefly, the Nieuport Nighthawk, then, in April 1921, on to Hinaidi, Iraq. In spring 1925 the squadron, now officially 1(F), flew strafing attacks as it assisted in settling tribal unrest, continuing in action until disbanded on November 1, 1926.

The following February saw it reform at Tangmere, Sussex on the Armstrong Whitworth Siskin IIIA, an aircraft it retained until February 1932, when the Hawker Fury I took over. Capable of more than 200mph (322km/h), the Fury also provided No. 1(F) with a spectacular aerobatic mount. The squadron formed a display team and flew it at the 1932 Hendon Display, as well as becoming the first RAF squadron to visit North America, when the team toured Canada in 1934.

Back at home war clouds had begun to gather and the Furys lost their silver finish and bright unit markings in favour of green and brown camouflage. Their time in warpaint was limited, however, since the first 1(F) Sqn Hurricane arrived at Tangmere in February 1939. Assigned to the Allied Air Striking Force, the squadron deployed to France on the outbreak of war.

> "…every member of the team is proud of our heritage and history, and determined to maintain the high standards and finest traditions of those who have gone before."
> **Wing Commander Mike 'Sooty' Sutton, OC 1(F) Sqn**

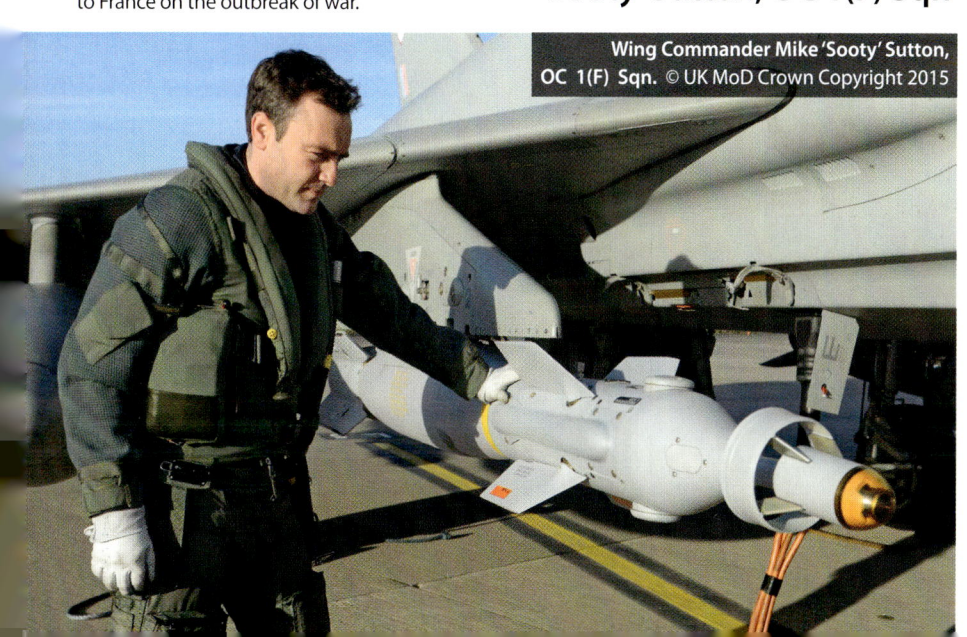

Wing Commander Mike 'Sooty' Sutton, OC 1(F) Sqn. © UK MoD Crown Copyright 2015

World War Two

On October 31, 1939 a Dornier Do 17 fell to the guns of Plt Off Mould's 1 Sqn Hurricane and once again the unit was in combat. The fighting was fierce, especially after May 10, 1940, when German troops marched into France. As the Allies were forced back towards the Channel, so 1 Sqn staged between bases in a fighting retreat. Initially involved in escorting Fairey Battles in their epic but ultimately wasted attempts to slow the advance, the squadron remained on the Continent until June 17, when its surviving Hurricanes flew back to Tangmere.

There was barely time to catch breath before No. 1 was operational again on July 3, engaging Luftwaffe aircraft over the Channel as operations built up ahead of the battle to come. The squadron engaged completely during the Battle of Britain, pilots typically flying two sorties every day and the CO totalling 66 in August alone.

Today's No. 1(F) is taking care to look back at that difficult period with pride in this anniversary year, as Wg Cdr Sutton explained when he spoke to *Salute* in April: "The RAF is marking the 75th anniversary of the Battle of Britain with events throughout the year. We're looking forward to flying over Buckingham Palace in June to mark the anniversary, and we'll be attending ceremonies and services in the coming months to celebrate the occasion and remember the terrible loss and sacrifice made by so many of our brave airmen all those years ago."

Turning to the offensive in 1941, No. 1 Sqn (the 'F' had been dropped in May 1939) soon re-equipped with the Hurricane II, especially appreciating the Mk IIC and its four-cannon armament. This proved particularly effective as the new CO, Sqn Ldr J Maclachan worked with Sgt Kuttelwascher, a Czech pilot, on developing night tactics. The squadron then specialised in night intruder work, until re-equipping again, this time with the Hawker Typhoon.

Typhoon work-up began in July 1942 and in September the squadron claimed its first kills with the type – two Messerschmitt Me 210s. Subsequent Typhoon operations included chasing down fast-flying, low-level Focke-Wulf Fw 190 fighter-bombers delivering 'tip-and-run' attacks along the south coast and, into 1944, escorting the Typhoons of fighter-bomber squadrons as they attacked targets in France. »

HERITAGE

Right: In May 1952 the squadron marked its 50th anniversary with this '1'-shaped formation of Meteor F8s. RAF (AHB)/© UK MoD Crown Copyright 2015

With the Fury the RAF had a fighter that for the first time could exceed 200mph. These aircraft have the red and white squadron markings worn today in slightly smaller form on 1(F)'s Typhoons. RAF (AHB)/© UK MoD Crown Copyright 2015

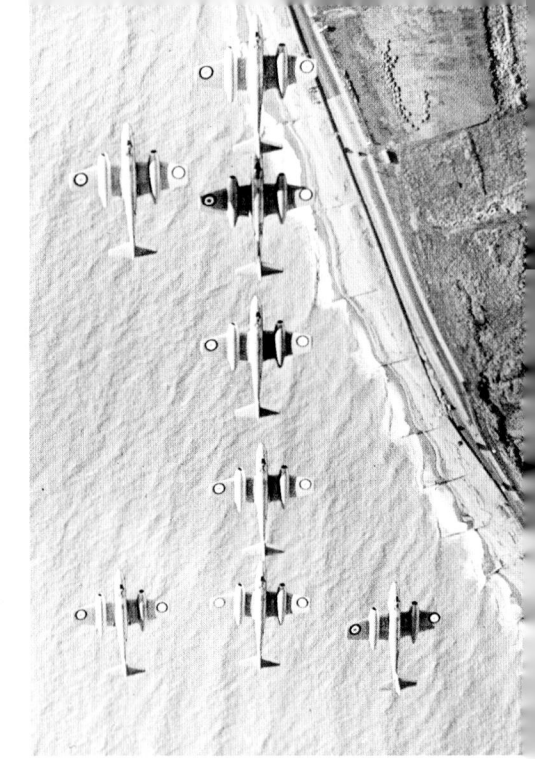

The build-up to D-Day was progressing rapidly when 1 Sqn stood down in March to take on the Supermarine Spitfire Mk IX. Briefly flying as a pure fighter unit, No. 1 was soon back attacking targets in France, dropping bombs from its Spitfires and working over and around the beachhead.

Germany had begun striking back at Britain with its V-1 flying bombs and 1 Sqn was also tasked with anti V-1 'diver' patrols. It flew them from late June until the end of August, accounting for 47 missiles. The remainder of the war was spent on fighter escort duties.

Post-War Changes

In May 1945 the Spitfire Mk IX gave way to the altogether more powerful Mk 21, but these served for little more than a year, because No. 1 Sqn became a jet unit from October 1946. Its initial Gloster Meteor F.Mk 3 equipment was briefly replaced by Harvards and Airspeed Oxfords as the squadron spent an uncharacteristic eight months on training duties, but it was back as a fighter squadron with Meteor F.Mk 4s in May 1948. It replaced them with Mk 8s from 1950.

The graceful Hawker Hunter F.Mk 5 followed from 1955 and 1 Sqn took these to Cyprus in 1956 for its part in the Suez Crisis. It returned home to Tangmere in December and business continued as usual until June 23, 1958, when Tangmere closed and 1 Sqn disbanded.

It stood up again simultaneously at Stradishall, as Hunter F.Mk 6-equipped 263 Sqn renumbered, maintaining its fighter role until January 1960, when Hunter FGA.Mk 9 ground-attack jets began to arrive. These remained No. 1's equipment until January 1970, when the squadron lived up to its 'First In All Things' motto by becoming the world's first Hawker Siddeley Harrier unit.

Number 1(F)'s association with the Harrier lasted longer than its time with any other type. It took successive marks of the aircraft, including the GR.Mk 3 with which it went to war in the Falkland Islands in 1982, flying off Royal Navy carrier decks and providing air defence cover for the islands in the immediate aftermath of the conflict. The GR.Mk 5, first of the second generation Harriers, arrived on November 23, 1988 and in 1992 the unit converted onto the GR.Mk 7, equipped for night attack and with which it returned to carrier operations.

The squadron took its GR7s into action over northern Iraq and the Balkans in the 1990s and back to Iraq for Operation Telic in 2003, as part of a wider RAF Harrier force involved in the action. In 2004 it made its first deployment to Afghanistan under Operation Herrick, gradually re-equipping with upgraded GR.Mk 9 and 9A jets, and taking its turn on rotation back into Afghanistan until the Herrick mission passed to the Tornado Force in 2009. The Harrier was then rapidly withdrawn from service as a result of the *2010 Strategic Defence and Security Review*, and 1(F) Sqn disbanded.

Typhoon… Again!

Reformed at RAF Leuchars on September 12, 2012, No. 1 (Fighter) Squadron became the RAF's fourth frontline Typhoon unit. It remained at the Fife station for almost two years, before moving across to RAF Lossiemouth, which was transitioning from a long history of maritime and attack flying.

According to 'Sooty' Sutton, the move has worked out well: "The Squadron is absolutely thriving at Lossiemouth. We have a superb team who set themselves extremely high standards, and are constantly striving to innovate and improve what we do. In recent months 1(F) Squadron has led the introduction of a major capability enhancement on the Typhoon (which has given us a significantly improved precision strike capability) and we have recently returned from Exercise Red Flag.

"We flew swing-role sorties involving air-air missions while simultaneously releasing high explosive laser/GPS-guided weapons

Plt Off Arthur 'Taffy' Clowes with his 1 Sqn Hurricane in October 1940. He claimed ten kills and a probable in the Battle of Britain. RAF (AHB)/© UK MoD Crown Copyright 2015

No. 1 was barely operational on the Hurricane when it deployed to France. This aircraft was being serviced at Vassincourt during April 1940. RAF (AHB)/© UK MoD Crown Copyright 2015

Hunter Mk 5s replaced the Meteors. This formation was flying from Tangmere on April 26, 1956. RAF (AHB)/© UK MoD Crown Copyright 2015

against challenging targets, and integrating with USAF stealth platforms. This involved the co-ordination of more than 80 combat aircraft, by day and night and in all weathers, fighting against very realistic surface and air threats, and provided us with exceptional training. The Squadron put in a superb performance and I am extremely proud of what everyone achieved."

Looking forward to the remainder of 2015 and beyond, he says: "We're currently training a number of new pilots and engineers, and conducting large exercises based in the UK, including Joint Warrior, which saw us integrate with a host of other units, including Turkish F-16s, and Royal Navy destroyers. We're also enhancing our tactical reconnaissance capability and planning is well underway for a deployment to Spain for a NATO training exercise later in the year. The Squadron continues to conduct QRA on a daily basis, and we retain our core swing-role skill sets so that we can deploy around the globe at a moment's notice should we need to.

"We talk a lot about technology and capability in the RAF, and the Typhoon is a superb fast jet to operate. We deploy across the world on operations and for training, and every day the pilots put an exceptional fighter through its paces, striving to improve and hone our tactics, which is both a challenge and extremely rewarding. But unquestionably, our true capability lies in the efforts, vision and dedication of our people.

"I value the culture as the most important aspect of what we do on 1(F) Squadron. Ethos, teamwork, understanding and the right mindset are critical to success, and if you get this right, then you truly have a battle-winning capability."

The squadron regularly flew its Harrier GR7s off carrier decks, here operating alongside Sea Harriers aboard HMS *Illustrious*. LA (Phot) Billy Bunting/© UK MoD Crown Copyright 2015

PEOPLE

Reserves on the Frontline

At a time when Reserve strength is again becoming of critical importance to regular RAF operations, a look back at Royal Air Force Volunteer Reserve and Auxiliary Air Force involvement in the Battle of Britain is particularly illuminating. Trustee of the Battle of Britain Memorial Trust Geoff Simpson investigates the Reserve effort

Sergeant George William Brimble joined the RAFVR in March 1939 and flew Hurricanes with 242 Sqn in the Battle of France and the Battle of Britain. Via Geoff Simpson

Examine the figures and the contribution of the Reserves to victory in the Battle of Britain becomes very clear. Among the pilots, almost 800 had the Royal Air Force Volunteer Reserve (RAFVR, or simply VR) as their 'portal of entry' to the Service, while a little fewer than 200 had been pre-war weekend fliers with the Auxiliary Air Force (AAF), or had been AAF ground crew selected for pilot training. The Reserve of Air Force Officers contributed 11 men, and slightly less than 100 personnel had served in the Oxford, Cambridge and London University Air Squadrons.

Volunteer Reserve
The RAFVR had been founded in 1936 and was particularly important among the schemes to broaden the scope of recruitment of RAF pilots. As Group Captain Alex Dickson, historian of the RAFVR has written: "Young men, who did not have to give up their jobs, could learn to fly and to fight on week nights, Saturdays and Sundays, and at summer camps. This was to be a citizen's army of the air, part of our national insurance policy, training just in case."

Many of those young men probably saw their membership of the VR as a rather glamorous hobby and a cheap means of learning to fly. The awful reality became apparent to a large number in the summer and autumn of 1940, when many of the replacement pilots arriving on fighter squadrons were VRs, often with little or no experience of flying the aircraft they were now expected to take into combat.

Royal Air Force Volunteer Reserve and Auxiliary Air Force squadrons involved in the Battle of Britain. The VR units had 5xx numbers, the AAF 6xx.

501 (County of Gloucester) Squadron
504 (County of Nottingham) Squadron
600 (City of London) Squadron
601 (County of London) Squadron
602 (City of Glasgow) Squadron
603 (City of Edinburgh) Squadron
604 (County of Middlesex) Squadron
605 (County of Warwick) Squadron
607 (County of Durham) Squadron
609 (West Riding) Squadron
610 (County of Chester) Squadron
611 (West Lancashire) Squadron
615 (County of Surrey 'Churchill's Own') Squadron
616 (South Yorkshire) Squadron

Pilots of 601 (County of London) Squadron with one of the unit's Hurricanes at Exeter, in November 1940. RAF (AHB)/© UK MoD Crown Copyright 2015

PEOPLE

These 504 Sqn pilots were awaiting their next mission at Filton, in September 1940. RAF (AHB)/© UK MoD Crown Copyright 2015

Pilot Officer Cecil Young flew Hurricanes with 607 Squadron. He was at Tangmere in September 1940. RAF (AHB)/© UK MoD Crown Copyright 2015

This liaison telephonist has the VR badge on his sleeve. RAF (AHB)/© UK MoD Crown Copyright 2015

Pilot Officers David Crook (left) and Geoffrey Gaunt flew Spitfires with 609 Sqn. Gaunt, a cousin of actor James Mason, was killed over London on September 15. RAF (AHB)/© UK MoD Crown Copyright 2015

Squadrons Then and Now

Number	Established	Initial aircraft	Aircraft in 1940	2015 role	Aircraft
600	October 14, 1925	DH.9A	Blenheim IF	Joint Force Air Command support	None
602	September 15, 1925	DH.9A	Spitfire	ABM and ISTAR	None
603	October 14, 1925	DH.9A	Spitfire	Force Protection	None
607	March 17, 1930	Wapiti (from 1933)	Hurricane	Operations	None
609	February 10, 1936	Hart	Spitfire	Force Protection	None
611	February 10, 1936	Hart	Spitfire	Operations	None

The list of RAF squadrons and other units 'accredited' with having participated in the Battle of Britain changed on various occasions between 1945 and 1961. The figure eventually arrived at was 71, of which 14 were pre-war AAF squadrons, some of which accumulated very high scores in the Battle.

Auxiliary Air Force

When the development of the AAF began in 1925, Sir Hugh (later Viscount) Trenchard, Chief of the Air Staff, envisaged, according to Viscount Templewood (former Foreign and Home Secretary Sir Samuel Hoare), "…a Corps d'elite, composed of the kind of young men who earlier would have been interested in horses, but who now wished to serve their country in machines. Esprit de corps was to be the dominating force in the squadrons and each, therefore, was to have

"This was to be a citizen's army of the air, part of our national insurance policy, training just in case."
Group Captain Alex Dickson, RAFVR historian

a well equipped headquarters, mess, and distinctive life of its own."

In the Battle of Britain, high achieving AAF members from before the war included acting Squadron Leader Archie McKellar, who had originally served with 602 (City of Glasgow) Squadron, but commanded 605 (County of Warwick) Squadron, and Flying Officer John Dundas of 609 (West Riding) Squadron. McKellar was killed on November 1, 1940 and Dundas on November 27. His brother, Flying Officer Hugh 'Cocky' Dundas, flew with 616 (South Yorkshire) Squadron.

A commanding officer's time as boss was sometimes measured only in days, or in at least one case, less than that, but on the outstanding 603 (City of Edinburgh) Squadron, Sqn Ldr 'Uncle George' Denholm remained in command throughout the Battle. He survived the war and lived to be 88. ⊙

CAPABILITY

A Hart Trainer of 10 SFTS. RAF (AHB) via author

The Battle of Britain has often been described as a 'close run thing'. One of the most significant reasons for this was the availability of pilots in its early phases. Air Cdre (Retd) Graham Pitchfork gives the background to this crucial issue, while Wg Cdr Chris Cartmell, OC 72(R) Sqn describes RAF flying training today

A Magister I of 8 EFTS, with a student under the hood on an instrument flying training sortie. RAF (AHB) via author

In the period leading up to the outbreak of World War Two, the requirement for RAF pilots increased dramatically. For many years, RAF pilot strength comprised:

- Officers on a permanent commission, the majority trained at the RAF College Cranwell
- Officers on a five-year short service commission with a reserve commitment on completion of service
- Selected airmen who flew for five years as senior non-commissioned officer (SNCO) pilots before returning to their trade
- Auxiliary Air Force pilots who trained and flew at weekends and manned 21 squadrons at the outbreak of war

With a deteriorating international political situation in the early 1930s, the RAF embarked on a series of 'Expansion Schemes', the first in 1934. This called for, among other things, a huge increase in the need for aircrew, particularly pilots. As part of a major reorganisation of the RAF in 1936, a Royal Air Force Volunteer Reserve (RAFVR) was instituted with a need for 800 reserve pilots a year in each of the three years to 1938 and a similar number of observers and wireless operators.

This demand led to a substantial increase in the need for training aircraft, airfields and flying instructors. To provide elementary flying training, civilian flying training schools were used as Elementary Flying Training Schools (EFTSs). The most common aircraft in use was the de Havilland Tiger Moth biplane, with the Miles Magister coming into service in increasing numbers.

As the Expansion Schemes were reviewed each year, the annual need for pilots soon rose to 1,200 and this increased further as war loomed. By 1939 the requirement for pilots had reached 2,500 per year. In addition to the training of new pilots, those who had qualified as reserve pilots needed to remain current by flying at weekends and during annual summer camps. This created the need for even more facilities.

An important development was the introduction of 51 Link Trainers by December 1937 and in view of their immediate success, the order of another 150. This lessened the gravity of the lack of suitable modern aircraft.

A device for teaching and practicing instrument flying and blind landing procedures, the Link Trainer was designed to reproduce natural flying manoeuvres under relatively realistic conditions. It was fitted with full blind

ROYAL AIR FORCE SALUTE 2015

CAPABILITY

Training to Fly, Then... And Now

flying equipment and worked in conjunction with an instrument that graphically recorded the manoeuvres carried out. The official Air Historical Branch *Narrative on Flying Training* commented, "Its importance in making the transition from flying by the senses to precise instrument flying cannot be exaggerated."

Scheme L
The German annexation of parts of Czechoslovakia in 1938 caused an acceleration in flying training plans, although the Munich Agreement of September 1938 bought Britain time. The next updated Expansion Scheme (Scheme L) gave priority to a considerable increase in reserve numbers, accelerated re-equipment with modern aircraft and a concentration on building up fighter strength, among other measures.

The Scheme identified that there would be a deficiency of 500 pilots on regular engagements, so it was decided to retain all pilots due to pass to the Reserve or to their basic trades, to accelerate the opening of three Flying Training Schools (FTSs) and to increase the output from the existing 15 FTSs.

With this rapidly expanding requirement for regular and reserve aircrew, and many ground trades, the load became too great to be handled by Training Command, and Reserve Command was established on February 1, 1939.

Owing to the time needed to create all the necessary flying schools, provide aircraft and instructors and recruit candidates, it is not surprising that the training programme always lagged the increasing requirement. To limit any shortfalls, overseas training was considered, and this would become a reality soon after the outbreak of war. Some training aircraft were obtained from overseas, most notably the North American Harvard, and the Reserve Organisation was further expanded. By the beginning of the war it stood at:

- 46 Elementary and Reserve (Civil) Flying Training Schools, training between 100 and 200 pupils each
- Three University Air Squadrons
- 20 Auxiliary Air Force Squadrons
- 61 Flying Clubs operating with the Civil Air Guard and training 7,500 men and women to Civil 'A' licence standard

On August 24, 1939 Readiness State 'C' and general mobilisation were declared, placing the RAF on a war footing; all Auxiliary and »

CAPABILITY

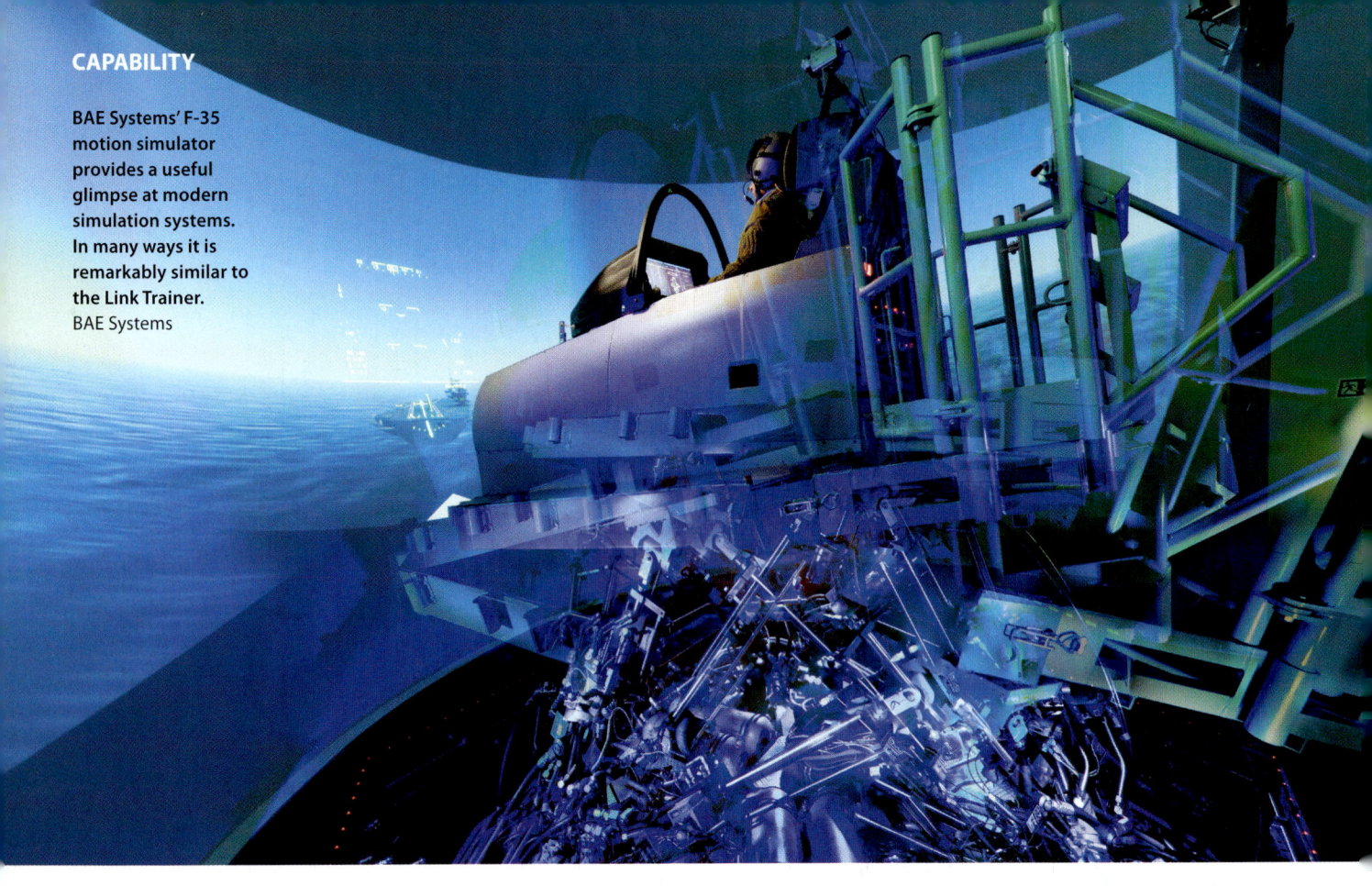

BAE Systems' F-35 motion simulator provides a useful glimpse at modern simulation systems. In many ways it is remarkably similar to the Link Trainer.
BAE Systems

RAFVR personnel were ordered to report to their mobilisation centres. Needless to say, this created a serious glut of pilots trained to elementary standard and waiting to pass through to the next phase of training at the Service Flying Training Schools (SFTSs).

Service Training Shortage
The lack of sufficient SFTSs created the main obstacle to expanding the pilot training programme. For this reason the EFTSs retained the ten-week course instead of the planned wartime eight-week course. There were so many elementary reserve pilots in the early stage of training that a number of them returned to civilian life after mobilisation to wait until the training capacity became available.

An early Link Trainer, with painted scenery. RAF (AHB) via author

War entrants also had to wait until the volunteer Reservists had passed into schools.

Thus, although there were sufficient volunteers and reserve aircrew, the limitations of the training organisation could not produce the required numbers for the frontline, which was also expanding with the formation of many new squadrons. The problem of providing the huge increase in aircrew to meet the flying training plans was further exacerbated once casualties began to occur, placing additional demands to provide replacements.

As the loss of fighters, and many of their pilots in France mounted, a Training Progress Meeting was held on May 21, 1940 when it was decided to reduce the course for single-engine pilots to 12 weeks by cutting out most of the applied elements from the SFTS syllabus. Secondly, it was decided to start 'pre-fighter' training for certain pilots at two of the EFTSs. The provision of aircraft to meet these commitments proved difficult and instead of the required number of 144 each to provide every student with 100 hours of flying, the SFTSs had to operate with 108 aircraft apiece.

Training Pipeline
By April 1940 the supply of pilots to the RAF came from 19 EFTSs, which served 12 SFTSs, each dealing with 160 pupils on 16-week courses, training both Group I (Single Engine) and Group II (Twin Engine) pilots. The output was at the rate of 5,300 per year. Initially Hawker Harts and Hinds were used at the SFTSs, before the Miles Master and Harvard gradually replaced them.

After completing the course at SFTS, and the award of their 'wings', pilots were posted directly to a squadron, where they received 'on-the-job' training, or to a 'pool' awaiting posting.

Fighter Command had resisted the need for Operational Training Units (OTUs), claiming that fighters were too valuable to be used for training. However, by June 1940, with the imminent threat of the collapse of France, the Command accepted that there had to be a dedicated course to convert new pilots to the fighter role. A four-week course was devised but, as losses mounted and the need for replacements accelerated, this had to be cut to just two weeks. The Master and early marks of Hurricane and Spitfire were used, with some of the pilots who had flown during the Battle for France becoming instructors.

Losses over France had exposed the limitations of the rapidly expanding training organisation and replacement pilots were in short supply and, of course, they were less

CAPABILITY

This Master belonged to 14 SFTS at Cranfield. The aircraft behind N7576's tail is a Harvard. RAF (AHB) via author

experienced than those they replaced. These issues were partly offset by seeking volunteers from army co-operation squadrons, using a number of pilots from the Fleet Air Arm and the arrival of recruits from overseas, some already trained as fighter pilots, including Poles and Czechs. By August 1940 the availability of pilots had improved and this allowed the OTU course to be restored to four weeks.

The Battle of Britain provided many lessons for the training of pilots and, within months, many new and innovative measures were introduced, not least the amazingly successful British Commonwealth Air Training Plan. The wartime flying training programme expanded rapidly once more resources became available and it proved to be a triumph owing, to a large extent, to the foresight of the planning staffs during the period leading up to the declaration of war in September 1939.

… And Now

Basic Fast jet training has come a long way from the flying training that prepared fighter pilots for the Battle of Britain, although in some respects it remains remarkably similar.

'Basic', 'BFJT', or 'Linton', Basic Fast Jet Training is known by many names and exists "to train tomorrow's fast jet pilots"; those are the very words that greet you on the sign as you drive through the gate at RAF Linton-on-Ouse, North Yorkshire. The station is the home of 72 (Reserve) Squadron, whose task is to deliver Basic Fast Jet Training on the Shorts Tucano T1 as part of 1 Flying Training School. Prospective fast jet pilots have been making that slightly nervous first journey through the same gate for almost 50 years, and with the exception of a few new buildings here and there, the initial impression is that little has changed.

The 1 FTS output has indeed changed very little over the years. The aim has always been to train pilots to meet the exacting demands of the next stage of training – today that means the BAE Systems Hawk T2 at RAF Valley for most.

The majority of Linton's trainees will ultimately succeed, but sadly for some, their dream of becoming a fast jet pilot will end here; in the business of fast jet training there are no shortcuts, no byes, no lowering of standards. There is a place available in a frontline fast jet cockpit for every student who starts the course. The prize is there for the taking, but they must achieve the standard required.

Recent years have seen a reduction in the number of frontline fast jet cockpits and therefore the number of students passing through Basic Fast Jet Training has reduced. This stage of training now only takes place at Linton, whereas even in the 1990s both Royal Air Force College Cranwell and RAF Church Fenton shared the task. There may be fewer of them, but are modern day trainee fast jet pilots any different from those of 10, 20 or even 30 years ago?

There is no doubt that the aircraft they aspire to fly, for most the Typhoon or Lightning II, are vastly different from the frontline jets of previous decades, but are the trainees themselves different, in their personalities and character? Are we now even beyond the 'PlayStation generation'? Are we training a selection of carbon copies?

The simple answer is a resounding and emphatic no. The trainees are not robots, not carbon copies. They learn to be individuals yet work as part of a close-knit team – the most successful courses are always those that figure this out from the start. They are all inevitably highly motivated, articulate and determined »

The step between Tucano and Hawk T2 is a large one, the jet offering a wealth of training potential that prepares students better than ever before for their first operational fast jet. The Hawk might be considered the modern day Master or Harvard. Paul Heasman

ROYAL AIR FORCE SALUTE 2015 | 97

CAPABILITY

Today the Tucano represents the intermediate stage between elementary training and a fledgling pilot's first fast jet, the Hawk. It represents a category of training aircraft somewhere between the Magister and Master of 1940. © UK MoD Crown Copyright 2015

to a man or woman to succeed; ultimately they are no different to their predecessors.

Elementary Flying Training

Just like those predecessors, before trainees even get to Linton they will have completed Elementary Flying Training (EFT) on the Grob Tutor. Only when they have successfully completed that course will they be presented to a selection board where they are assessed for suitability for the multi-engine, rotary or fast-jet streams. A combination of factors determines whether they come to Linton, but a good performance on EFT and a strong motivation to fly fast jets are absolute musts.

More recently Linton has seen an increasingly diverse mix of pilots arriving from EFT. The RAF and RN have always shared the fast-jet pipeline, but recently Linton has also had the privilege of training students from the Royal Saudi Air Force and Qatar Emiri Air Force. A mixture of nationalities at BFJT is nothing new and not only does it enhance the already vibrant crew room atmosphere, but on a more serious note it serves to educate and broaden cultural understanding.

Basic Fast Jet Training

The aircraft that the trainees ultimately aspire to fly have inevitably evolved, the technology that is involved in the Lightning II is a far cry from that of the single-seat fast jets of previous generations, but for the current BFJT trainees it is a realistic future aspiration. In the medium term the aircraft used for the 'Basic' element of flying training will also change, but for now the Tucano T1 soldiers on after almost 30 years in service and continues to perform an admirable job.

Nonetheless, the BFJT syllabus has evolved to keep pace with developments further down the 'pipeline', and although many of the basic aspects remain – the first solo still takes place on trip nine – others are unrecognisable compared to 50 years ago. Trainee pilots are now awarded their wings on successful graduation from Basic Fast Jet Training and however they arrived at Linton, they all have the sole aim of passing the course and achieving those wings.

They are pushed hard during the course. Its content means that graduates will have grafted hard to earn the right to wear the highly coveted flying badge. The average BFJT student still completes a 120-hour flying course across a variety of disciplines including aerobatics, navigation, general handling, instrument flying, formation and night flying. The course continues to use the standard flying training 'building block' approach, and students employ a combination of flying hours in the aircraft and the simulator to hone their skills.

Students are put forward for their 'wings ride' at the end of the course, having successfully completed no fewer than six separate flying tests. Unlike in previous years, the wings ride now takes place over two sorties, designed to ensure the student has assimilated all the appropriate flying skill and judgement, and that they are ready for the next stage of training.

The test involves leading a pair of aircraft to an airfield anywhere in the UK, with a variety of 'injects', either simulated or, more often than not, real, that mean the trainee is tested on every aspect of BFJT. But that is only part of the story. On return from the first sortie they will feel drained, but they have to produce the goods once more, since they must be able to function under significant pressure, as they would on a frontline squadron. Only on successful completion of both trips will students be awarded their wings.

The aircraft to which today's trainees aspire have changed significantly and the course itself has evolved, but ultimately they possess the same qualities and motivations as those who have passed through Linton's gates for almost half a century. When it comes to training 'tomorrow's fast jet pilots' there is still only one place to come, regardless of service or nationality, a station that continues to deliver world class training and always holds a special place in the hearts of those who have served there – RAF Linton-on-Ouse.

Pilots moving on to a fighter squadron in 1939 typically went to the Hurricane or Spitfire, the less fortunate to the Defiant. In 2015 they go to 29(R) Sqn to learn the Typhoon – as here – or XV(R) Sqn for the Tornado. © UK MoD Crown Copyright 2015

ROYAL AIR FORCE SALUTE 2015

The Story of
HANUMAN

the 'Monkey' god

by
Rupa Gupta

Hemkunt

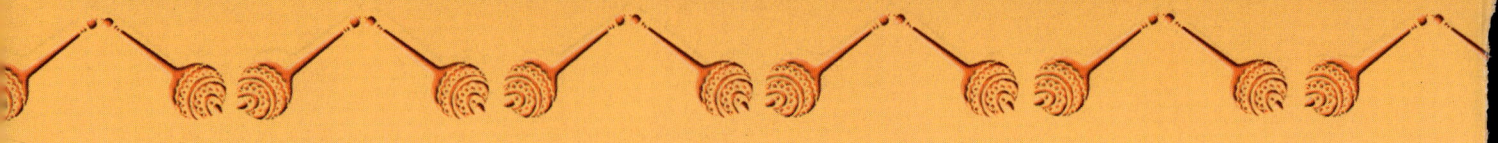

© Hemkunt Press
Fourth Revised Impression 2006

ISBN 81-7010-211-1

Published by:

Hemkunt Press
A-78 Naraina Industrial Area Phase-I, New Delhi-110 028
Ph.: 4141-2083, 2579-5079   Fax: 91-11-4540-4165
E-mail : hemkunt@ndf.vsnl.net.in

www.hemkuntpublishers.com

Books in this Series

- Stories from Panchatantra
- More Stories from Panchatantra
- Stories from the Arabian Nights
- More Stories from the Arabian Nights
- Sindbad the Sailor
- Tales from Arabian Nights
- Fairy Tales from India
- Folk Tales from India
- More Folk Tales from India
- South Indian Folk Tales
- Tales from Eastern India
- Stories of Birbal and Akbar
- Tales of Birbal and Akbar
- More Tales of Birbal and Akbar
- Jatak Tales
- The Story of Ramayan
- The Story of Mahabharata
- The Story of Krishna
- The Story of Guru Nanak
- Life Story of Guru Nanak
- Life Story of Guru Gobind Singh
- Story of Mohammad the Prophet
- The Story of Buddha
- Tales from Indian Classics
- Tales from Indian Mythology
- Story of Hanuman
- Story of Maharaja Ranjit Singh
- Bedtime Stories from Around the World
- The Story of Lord Mahavira
- Stories About Sikh Traditions
- Stories About Ten Sikh Gurus

Library Cataloguing

Gupta, Rupa, The Story of Hanuman, H.B., 2006, Pg 76, Rs. 175
Typeset in 14pt Souvenir

Printed and bound in India by **HEMKUNT TECHNOLOGIES INDIA** Custom Printing & Publishing

Contents

	Introduction	5
1.	A Monkey Named Hanuman	7
2.	On to Kishkinda	12
3.	Meeting with Ram	15
4.	Helps Sugreev	19
5.	How Hanuman Protects Sugreev	23
6.	Path on the Back	26
7.	To the Rescue	30
8.	News About Sita	34
9.	The Mighty Leap	37
10.	Lanka at Last	39
11.	Finding of Sita	42
12.	Sita Consoled	44
13.	Captured	47
14.	Warning to Ravan	50
15.	Lanka on Fire	53
16.	A Proud Moment	56
17.	Bridge to Lanka	59
18.	In the Battle-Field	64
19.	The Saddest Moment	68
20.	Death of Indrajit	72
21.	Reunion of Sita and Ram	75

Introduction

Hanuman was the greatest warrior hero, the extraordinary 'Monkey God'. He is a symbol of strength, valour and devotion. According to folklore, Hanuman held mystic and divine powers. He could fly, expand to gigantic proportions and had legendry strength.

The Story of Hanuman is an epic tale of Hanuman's devotion to Lord Ram and the search for Sita through the battled savagery of Ravan to rescue Sita, wife of Lord Ram.

Hanuman is one of the few Hindu gods who still resides on earth and it is said that he shall live among humans as long as the name of Lord Ram is remembered.

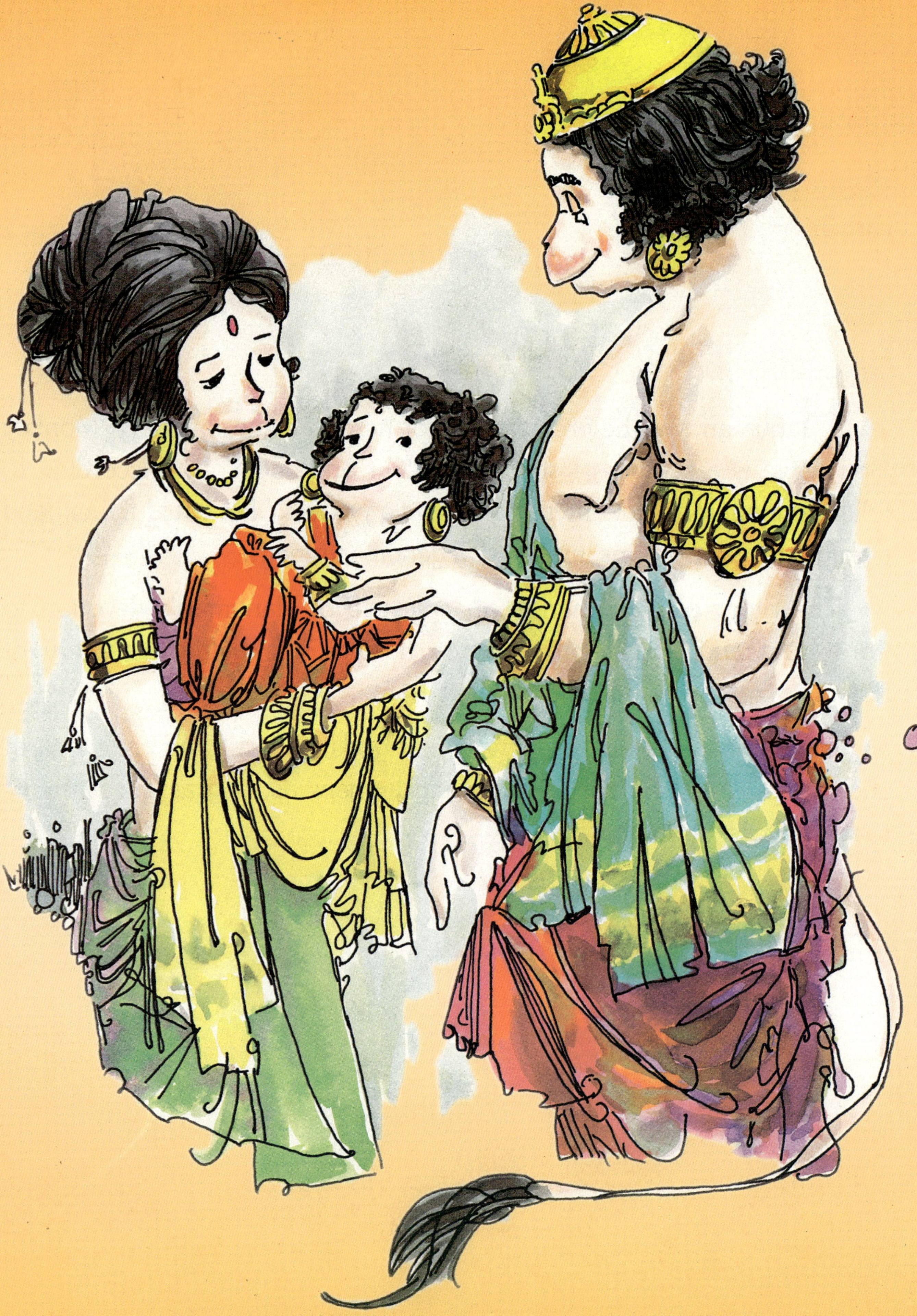

A Monkey Named Hanuman

Kesari, the brave monkey chief bent down to look at his newborn son. His wife Anjana held up the baby, "See the *kundalas* in his ears!" she whispered, "he was born with them."

And Kesari was amazed to see that hanging by his son's tender earlobes were a pair of shining gold danglers studded with precious stones. But just as Anjana began feeding the baby the danglers disappeared.

"What a strange thing to happen," exclaimed Anjana, "I wonder what this means?"

"This only means that our son is no ordinary infant, he will grow up to be someone very special, just mark my words", replied Kesari.

The little baby monkey grew fast.

One fine morning as the little monkey was playing outside his cave he saw the sun rising in the east. He looked wide-eyed at the glowing red object. He had never seen the sun before and thought that it was a big luscious fruit. He leapt up and began to rush straight towards the sun, his mouth open wide ready to gulp down the fascinating fruit.

As he was nearing the sun, he saw another dark object approaching the sun. This was Rahu, the demon without a body. He was the sun's greatest enemy. He spent his life chasing the sun. The monkey took one look at Rahu and thought "Ah, here is a bigger fruit. A big black fruit." He left the sun and rushed greedily towards Rahu.

Seeing the hungry little monkey rushing towards him, the demon was scared and began to scream. Lord Indra, the king of Heaven hurried out to see what all the fuss was about. He was riding on his grand white elephant. But as soon as the baby monkey saw the elephant, he got distracted "Here is a larger fruit" he thought to himself "and white too." And he left Rahu and attacked the elephant.

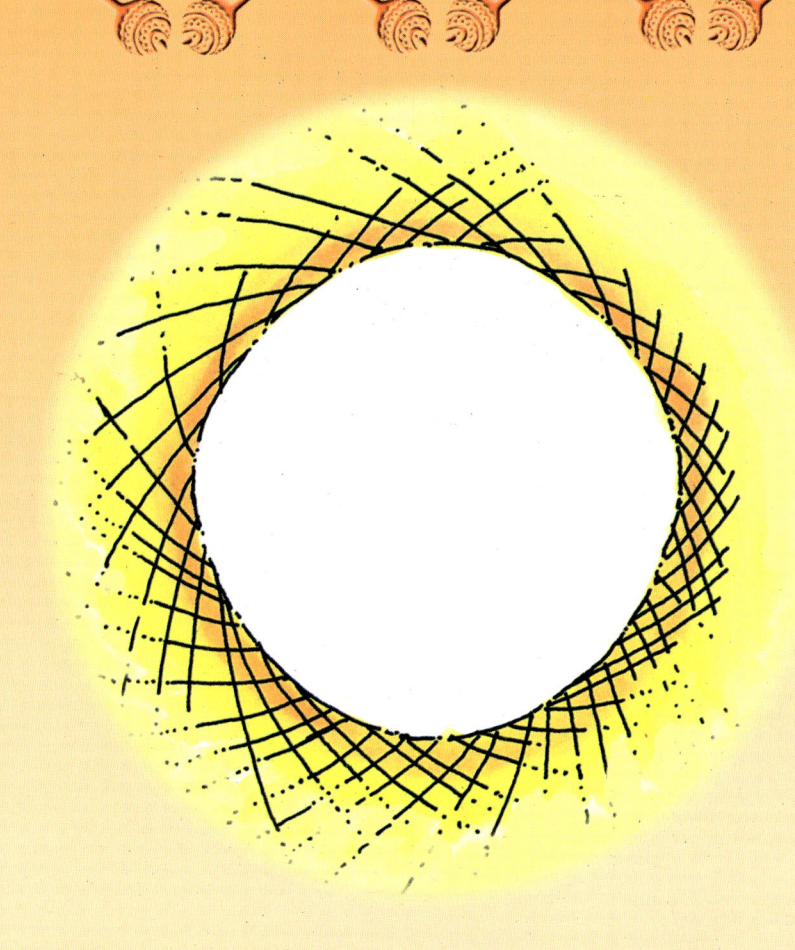

This made the heavenly king very angry and he hurled his special weapon at the child which wounded him. "Ooh Aah" cried the monkey in pain and tumbled down from the sky.

One person was watching all this and that was Pawan Dev — the Wind god. He had taken an immense liking to the spirited little monkey and rushed to catch him as he fell from the sky. He was also angry that Indra had hurt the little fellow.

So Pawan Dev carried the monkey way down to *Patala*, the heart of the earth. There in a cave he looked after the child and nursed him back to health.

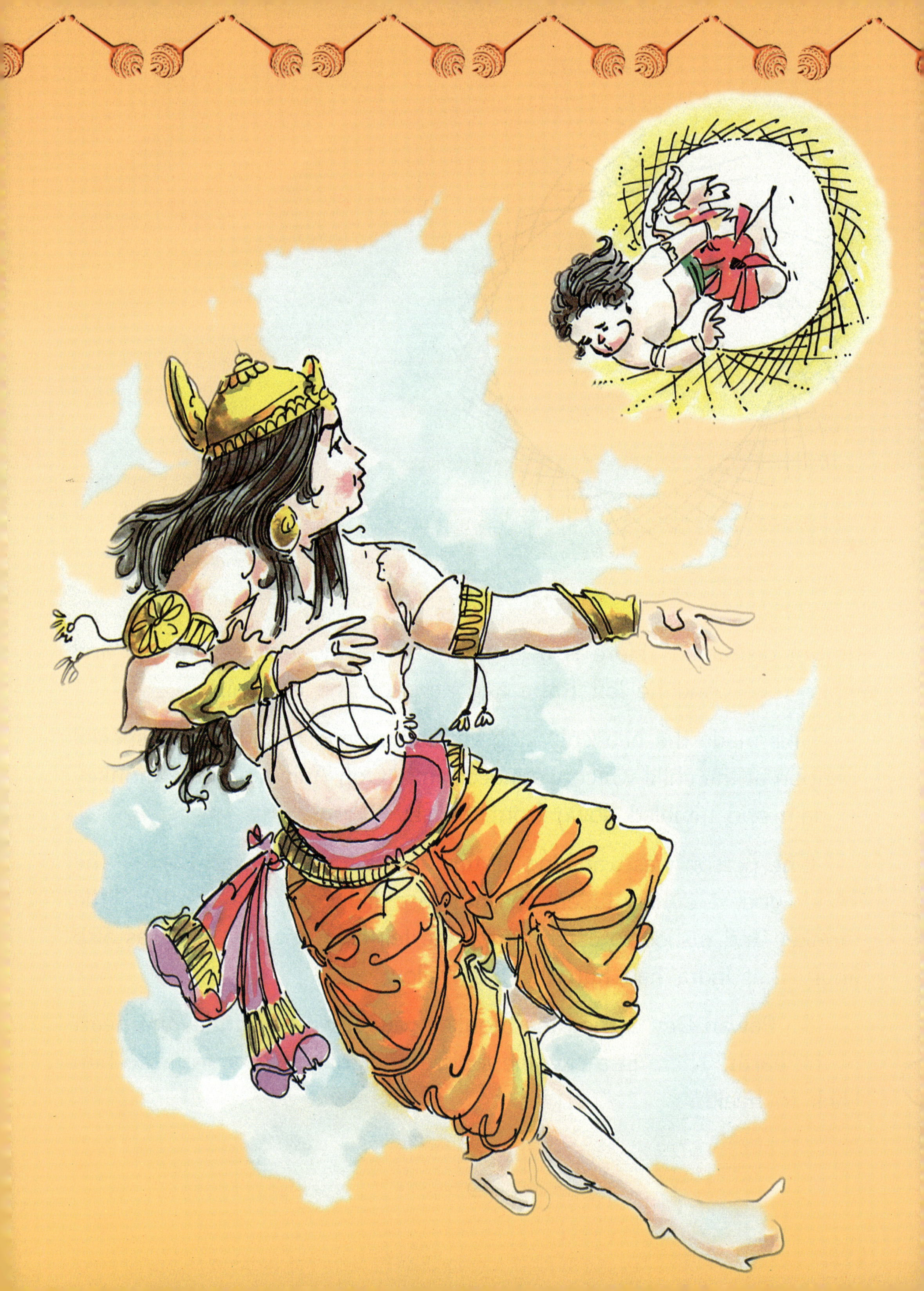

But as soon as the Wind god disappeared into the Patala, the whole world began to suffer. Because there was no air on earth, all living beings became weak. The *Devtas* now realised that unless they went down and pacified the Wind god, everything would be destroyed.

First of all Lord Brahma spoke, "I promise that your ward will never again be hurt by any weapon", he said. Next it was Indra's turn. He felt very ashamed at having so severely punished the little monkey for his mischief. "I bless him that he will never die, until he himself wants to," declared the Lord of the Heaven. Then he looked at the deep cut in the boy's chin which had been made by his weapon and said gently, "From today he will be famous in all three worlds as Hanuman— the one with a cleft chin".

On to Kishkinda

The Wind god carried the little monkey back to earth. But before leaving, granted Hanuman a boon, "I shall give you all my powers", he told Hanuman.

"You will be able to leap as far or as high as you please. You will be able to enter any place, take any shape and be as strong as you wish to be. You will also be able to go without food or water as long as you want to."

After that, the Wind god blessed the little monkey and left. Hanuman stood thinking for a long time... "I am now strong and powerful, but what is the use of all my powers without any knowledge. I shall not be satisfied till I get all the knowledge in the world".

All the knowledge in the world lies in the ancient books called the Vedas. And Vedas are in the care of Surya Dev— the Sun god. So early the next morning Hanuman humbly approached the rising Sun god and folding his hands over his breast bent down and said, "Brilliance unlimited, light up my soul".

Surya Dev was pleased by Hanuman's manners and told him, "You are a good monkey. I would love to teach you, but you can see that I am moving forward constantly. I just don't have time".

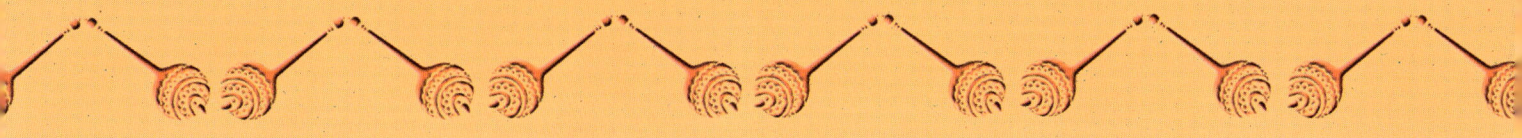

But the clever little monkey had already found a solution to the problem. "That is all right Sir, you can go on moving while you give me lessons. I will take my lessons standing before you and moving backward at the same speed."

Surya Dev laughed out loud when he heard this and began giving lessons straightaway. At last when the lessons were over, the Sun god told Hanuman, "You will now have to give me the teacher's fee — the *gurudakshina*."

"*Gurudakshina*", exclaimed Hanuman, "I do not have anything Sir. What can I offer you?"

Hearing this the Sun god smiled, "Why child, you have yourself. Give yourself to me, by serving my son, Sugreev, the Prince of Kishkinda".

"Yes, Sir" said Hanuman respectfully, falling at his divine teacher's feet. When he got up the sun had set.

Hanuman started for the city of Kishkinda.

His way lay through dense forests. On his way he twisted the tails of animals and screwed their ears. He was thrilled with his great power.

Hanuman's mischief increased as he went on. He picked up a lion and threw it at an elephant. The elephant bolted off in fright and caused other animals to run helter skelter in all directions. The elephant ran madly into an ashram, the place where hermits lived, trampling down the shrubs, grass and fruit trees there.

Meeting with Ram

King Rikshaviraja was a mighty monkey king and was the ruler of Kishkinda country. He had two sons named Bali and Sugreev.

Princes Bali and Sugreev were thrilled when their father brought Hanuman to them and the three soon became inseparable friends. For many years Hanuman had a quiet but happy life in the royal palace of Kishkinda.

After some years, King Rikshaviraja passed away and Bali became the king.

The days that followed were not very happy ones. Bali and Sugreev began to argue and fight about every small matter. One small quarrel led to another. Small quarrels grew into big ones. Before a year went by, the brothers became sworn enemies and it ended with Bali driving Sugreev out of the kingdom. Not satisfied with this, Bali chased his younger brother from place to place, ill-treating him and making his life miserable.

Once Hanuman came to know that there was a place called Malaygiri in Rishyamooka mountain where Bali could not enter. The reason for this was that Bali had once hurt a hermit who lived there and the angry hermit had hurled a curse on him saying that Bali would die of a

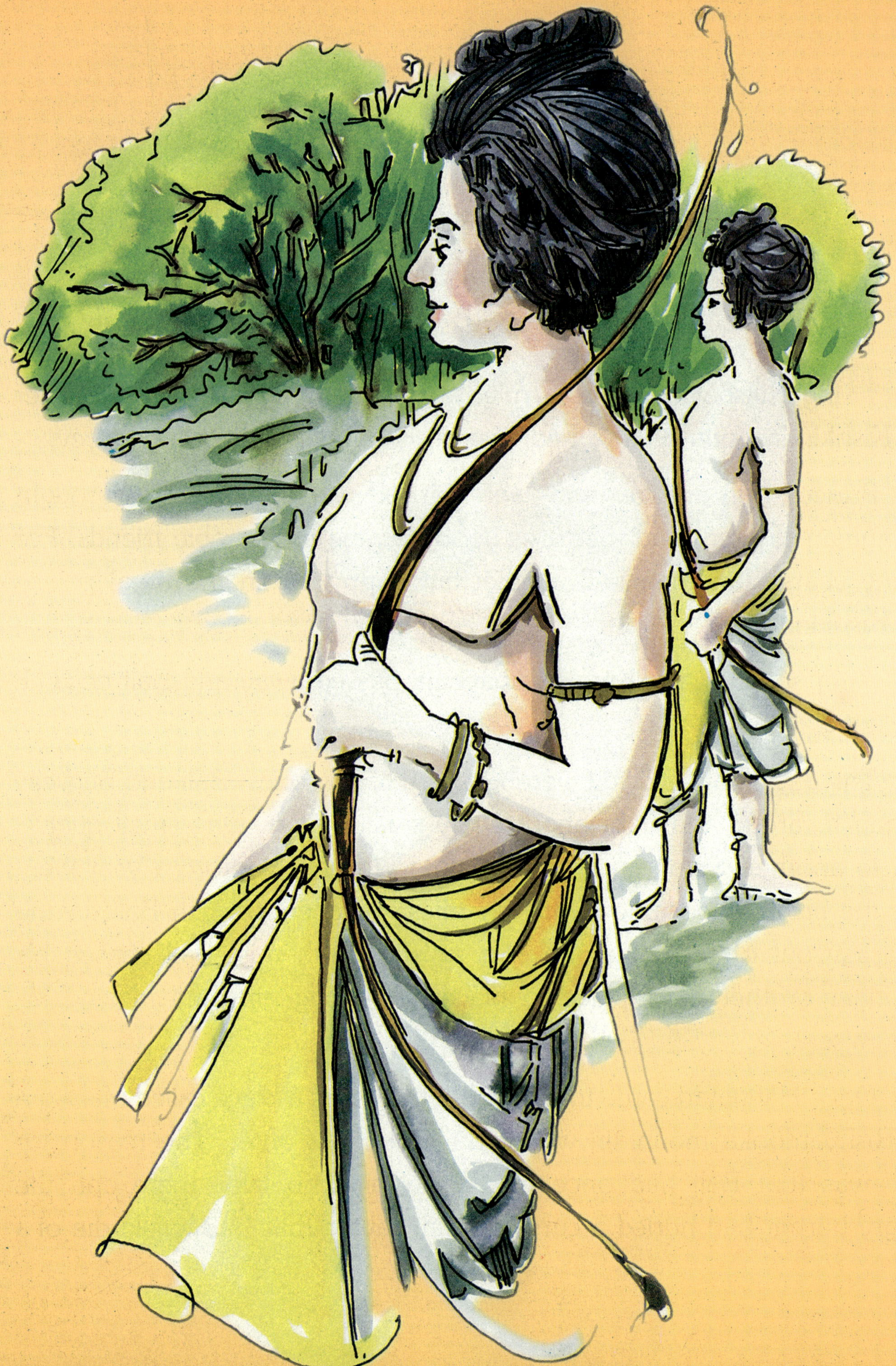

broken skull if ever he dared to enter Malaygiri. Hanuman now decided to take his friend Sugreev to this forest, since this was the only place where his friend would be safe. Along with them went three older and wiser monkeys called Jambavan, Neel and Nal and all five of them began living quietly amongst the hills waiting for better times to come.

One day, Ram and Lakshman, the princes of Ayodhya, passed by Malaygiri in the course of their search for Sita, whom Ravan had stolen away. Though they were simply dressed, they looked like mighty soldiers and held fine bows in their hands. Seeing them Sugreev was alarmed. "Those two must be Bali's spies, disguised as *Rishis* and searching for me", he exclaimed in fear.

Hanuman said to Sugreev, "Don't you know that you are safe from Bali's power in this Malaygiri?"

Hanuman's words soothed Sugreev considerably but still he insisted that Hanuman should go and find out who these strangers were. "It would be good to have friends like those mighty ones", he added, "see if you can persuade them to join us."

Hanuman agreed striaghtaway and went off to see what he could find out, but he disguised himself as a beggar.

At some distance, he saw Ram sitting under a tree talking to Lakshman. They carried fine bows in their hands. "Strange," thought Hanuman, "they are dressed as hermits in coarse simple clothes but they look like mighty warriors."

He looked at Ram's face and saw tremendous strength and a great deal of kindness there. As he went nearer, he got a feeling of strange peace and joy entering him. His heart filled with a surge of love and devotion. Hanuman fell at Ram's feet. As his forehead touched Ram's feet an extraordinary thing happened. Hanuman began to hear a strange sound. He touched his ears and lo! There were a pair of large *kundalas* hanging by his earlobes!

Helps Sugreev

Ram raised Hanuman and looked into his face and then he began to laugh aloud. He turned to Lakshman and said, "Brother here is a beggar wearing *kundalas* of emerald". Hearing this Lakshman also joined in the laughter.

Hanuman addressed Ram humbly, "I am no beggar, glorious one. It was really silly of me to try to fool you. Please pardon me. I was born with these *kundalas;* they disappeared immediately afterwards, and have reappeared just now as I touched your feet. I am a poor monkey named Hanuman, serving Sugreev, younger prince of Kishkinda".

Hanuman then told the princes all about Sugreev and his troubles.

After he finished his story Hanuman looked at Ram and said, "One thing has been puzzling me a good deal. You are dressed as hermits but you look like kings."

Ram and Lakshman told Hanuman everything about themselves. In the end they said, "We wish to have Sugreev's friendship. He alone can help us to find and regain Sita".

"This is indeed a lucky day for Sugreev", said Hanuman happily. "He is in dire need of powerful friends to help him against Bali. Forever now I will be your servant as well as Sugreev's. Let me now carry you to him".

Hanuman strode proudly up the side of Malaygiri with the princes of Ayodhya on his strong broad shoulders.

Sugreev welcomed Ram and Lakshman warmly.

When all of them were seated comfortably, Ram and Sugreev exchanged their tales of sorrow. Hanuman lit a fire over which the princes of Ayodhya and Kishkinda entered into a treaty of eternal friendship.

Before the sun set that day, Ram killed Bali with just one arrow from his formidable bow called *Kodanda*.

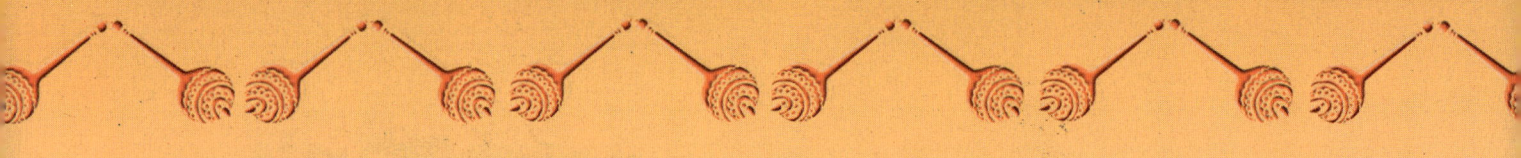

Sugreev said, "Great one, you have proved the value of your friendship. Let me now show my gratitude by finding Sita for you".

Ram was about to speak, when Hanuman asked meekly, "May I utter a few words, please?".

"Certainly," said Ram and Lakshman in one voice.

"First of all, we have to know where Sita is," said Hanuman. "For that, we have to send the monkeys in all directions. The search may take many days, even months. The monsoon is about to begin. The first rains are generally the heaviest. They will make the search extremely difficult; many monkeys may die without achieving anything".

Ram said, "Let the search wait, till the monsoon is over. Sugreev, you go to the palace of Kishkinda. I will not go with you, as I cannot enter any town or city during the period of my exile. Lakshman will go with you and crown you king. During the four rainy months, you must rest and get back your health and spirits. Lakshman and I will stay on one of the hills."

How Hanuman Protects Sugreev

The four months of rain were soon over. But Sugreev was not aware of the change of season. As soon as Lakshman left after installing him on the monkey throne, he had appointed Angad, son of Bali as Prince Royal and Jambavan, Neel, Nal and Hanuman as his ministers. Leaving the four to run the government, he himself retired into the harem and began spending his days in merriment.

Finding that Sugreev had not come out of the harem three days after the last rain of the monsoon, Hanuman got annoyed. He walked into the harem, and said to Sugreev, "You entered into a treaty with Ram, and swore that you would find and restore Sita to him. Ram killed Bali and made you king of Kishkinda on the very day the treaty was made. You have not done anything to fulfil your part of the contract. I cannot allow this. I am going to act on my own."

Hanuman then proceeded to Angad's chamber and got the prince issue a proclamation in the name of the king, calling on all able-bodied monkeys, wherever they were, and in whatsoever duty or pleasure engaged, report to Kishkinda's royal palace within fifteen days.

During the days following the proclamation, monkeys arrived in Kishkinda city from far and near under the command of their local

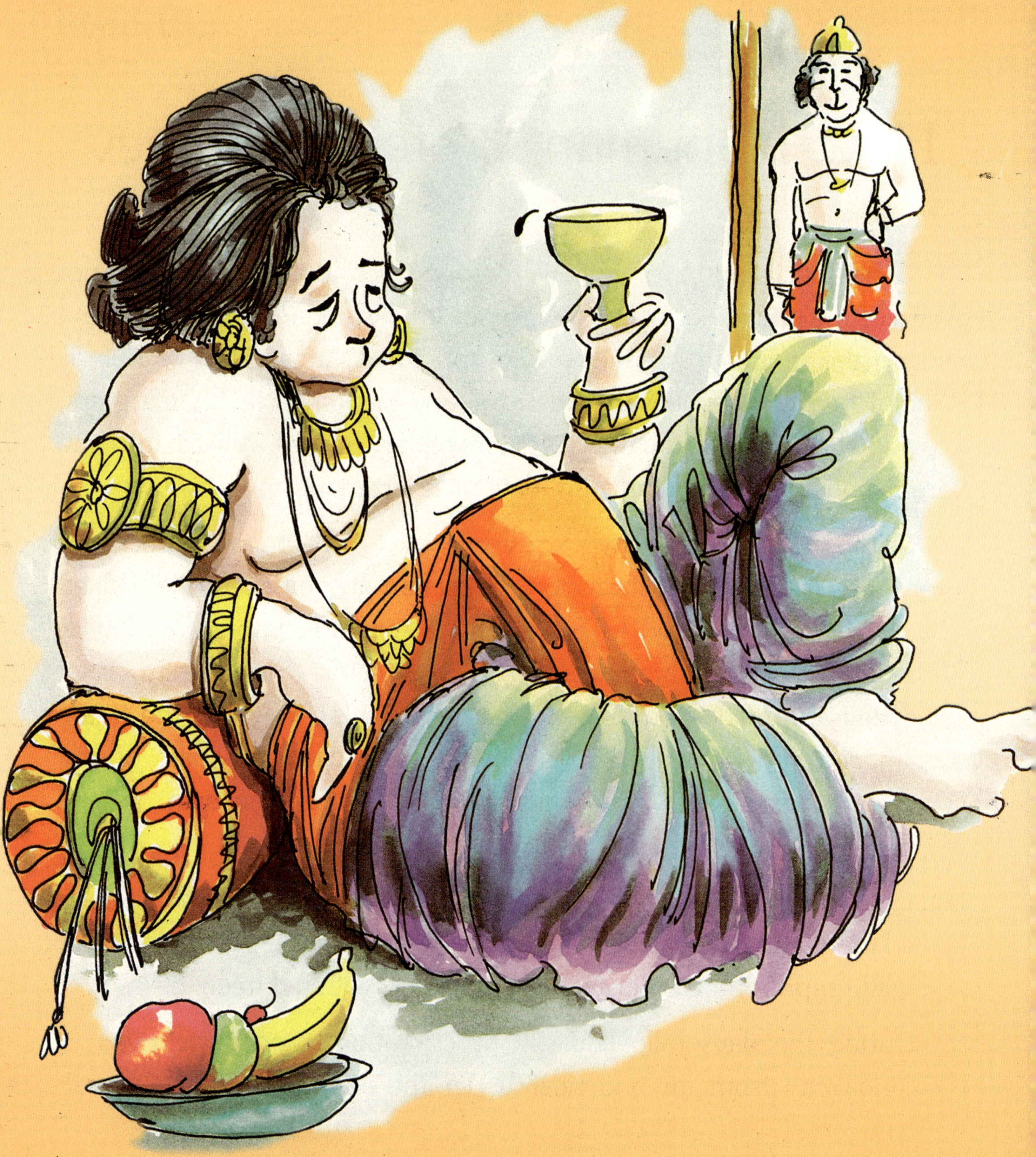

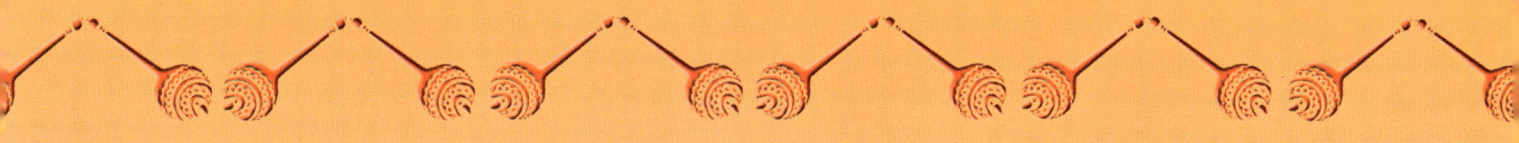

leaders. Monkeys of all shapes, size and colour began to pour in from all parts of the country.

In a week, millions of monkeys had arrived and many more were on the way.

On Prasravana Hill, Ram noticed the setting in of fair weather but was perplexed because no news came from Kishkinda palace even after two weeks. Ram sent Lakshman to see what Sugreev was up to.

When Lakshman reached the city limits, he made a twanging sound with bow strings and Sugreev heard it. He had not heard the din and clamour raised by the monkeys pouring into the city continuously for the last seven days. But he heard that vibration of Lakshman's bow string. It reminded him of the twang Ram had made four months ago before shooting the arrow which killed Bali. Stark fear gripped him. He jumped up and rushed out like mad, his eyes dilated in terror.

When Hanuman heard the twang, he smiled. Then he stroked Angad's tender chin affectionately, and said, "Don't cry child. I will see that no harm befalls any of you. Go in now and bring your mother to the main gate with suitable presents for the younger prince of Ayodhya, for it is he who is twanging his bow-string. I will join you in a few minutes."

Very soon, Sugreev came to where Hanuman was. Hanuman scolded him sternly, "Remember you are a king now. Kings do not leave their palaces by the back door in fright. Come, let us go to meet Lakshman at the front entrance. He cannot kill a coward like you." He took Sugreev's trembling hand into his own.

Pat on the Back

Angad and his mother Tara were waiting at the ornate royal entrance. Hanuman gestured to Tara to go forward with Angad. He followed them with Sugreev. Lakshman looked menacing indeed. No wonder Sugreev tried to hide himself behind Hanuman.

But Lakshman's expression softened when he saw a woman, and that too the recently widowed queen of Kishkinda. He put his bow aside, and greeted Tara.

Tara was a woman of great charm. She fell at Lakshman's feet, along with her weeping son, and said, "Glorious Prince of Ayodhya. Please look on my erring brother-in-law with pity and charity."

Hearing this, Hanuman pulled Sugreev forward and pushed him down to Lakshman's feet. Lakshman raised the king with a smile and said, "Fear not, you will be safe, always; Hanuman will see to that."

Sugreev and Hanuman led Lakshman into the palace. Passing wide halls and long corridors, they came to the rear of the palace. Looking out from there, Lakshman saw the field overflowing with the monkeys. Sugreev said proudly, "Twenty million have arrived, my Commander-in-Chief submits. Eight million more are expected within this week."

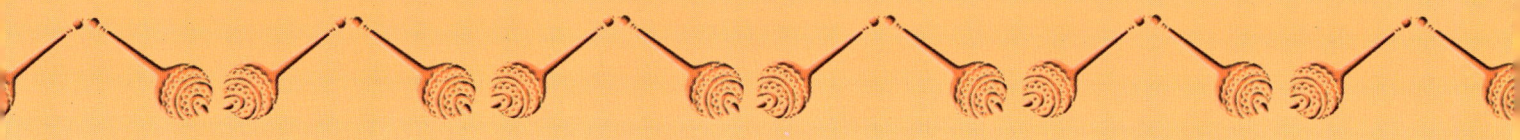

After inspecting the batallions for some time, Sugreev and Lakshman proceeded to the council hall with Hanuman and began planning their future course of action.

After resting for a while, Sugreev said to Hanuman, "Friend, order the chariot which Lord Indra had presented to my brother Bali. We will take Lakshman, the younger prince of Ayodhya to Prasravana Hill and pay our respects to the elder prince—Ram".

So Sugreev, Lakshman and Hanuman reached the cave where Ram was. Sugreev fell at Ram's feet and made a confession how he had neglected duty, and described at great length all that Hanuman had done for him.

When Sugreev ceased speaking, Ram looked at Hanuman approvingly and said, "The moment I first set eyes on this fellow, I knew that you would always do well with a loyal, faithful and sensible friend like him by your side." Hanuman blushed in embarrassment when he heard the lavish praise.

Lakshman told Ram about the vast monkey army Sugreev had in the city and they decided that a few hundred monkeys would be sent in each of the four directions under able leaders. The south deserved special attention; Ram had been told that Ravan had gone south with Sita.

"To the south I shall send the very pick of my leaders. Prince Angad will be in official command. Of course, Hanuman will go with Angad. He has a brilliant brain. He knows no fear. His strength and endurance are unlimited," said Sugreev, proudly.

Hanuman was hiding himself behind Sugreev while the Vanar king

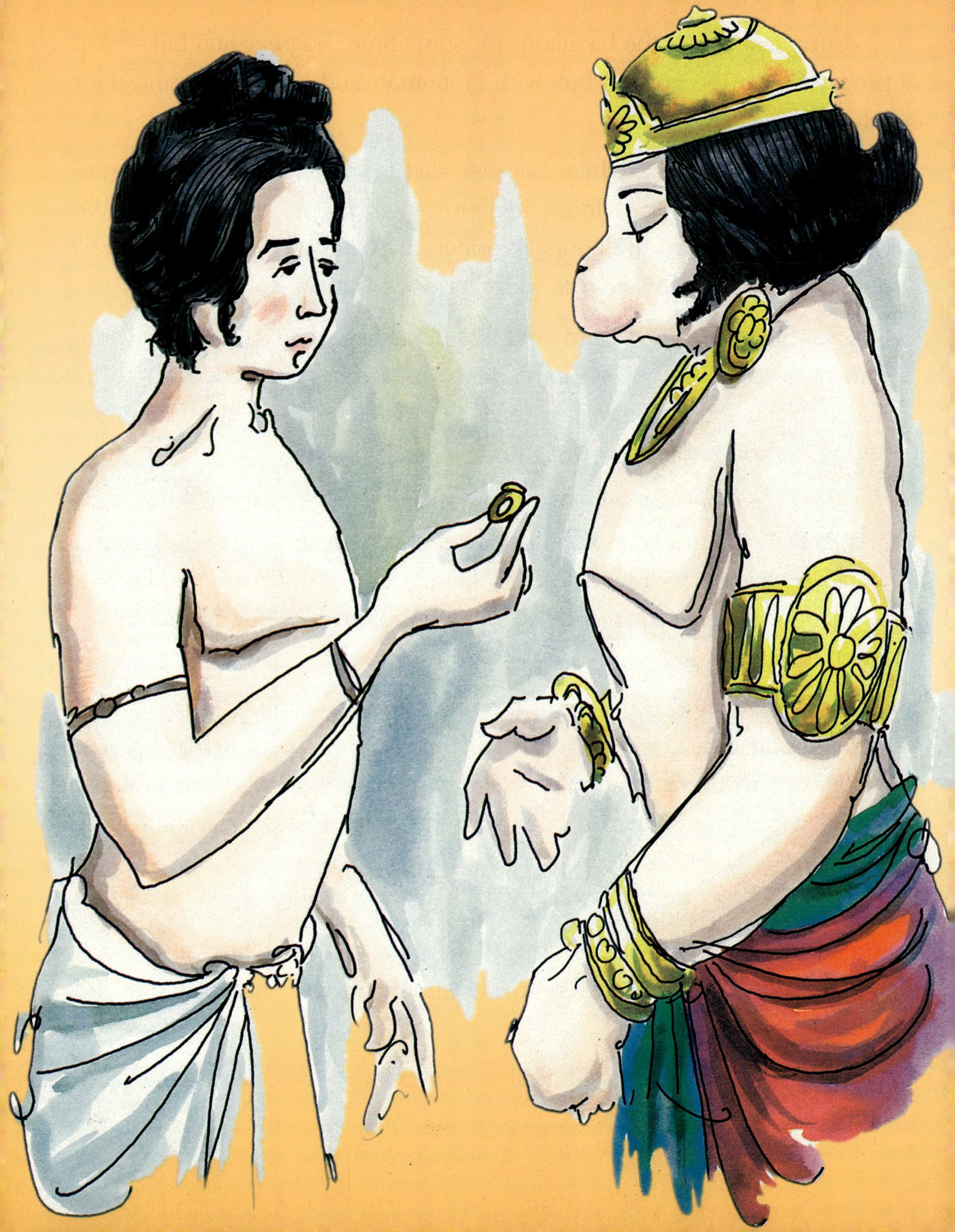

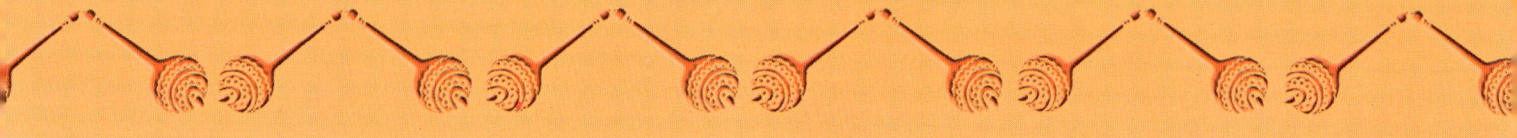

praised him to Ram. He came forward now, very shyly, and placed his forehead to Ram's feet. Raising him up by the chin, and looking into his face with affection and admiration, Ram said: "Something tells me that you are going to find Sita. When you do, show this ring to her, so she may know that you are my messenger. I have no doubt that you know how to console and comfort her." Ram fixed one month for their return.

To the Rescue

When the next day dawned, the search parties had left Kishkinda city.

The South-bound contingent moved fast, examining each locality carefully. Hundreds of miles were covered in a month; but there was no sign of Sita.

The monkeys had suffered much during the month from hunger and fatigue. Now they suffered from thirst too. Not a drop of water was available. "Water, oh God!" they cried in agony. One day Hanuman saw a flock of birds flying off from a hill. As the leader of the flock flew overhead a drop of water fell on his head.

"Comrades; There is water on that hill," cried out Hanuman, and led the excited monkeys up the hill.

But when they reached the top, they did not find any water, instead there was only an empty hole. Obviously, it was the mouth of a shaft. "The bottom must be far, far away," said Angad dolefully. "But there must be a bottom, and there must be water there," said Hanuman, putting his feet into the hole.

At first the others were scared and refused to enter a strange hole but Hanuman told them flatly that if they did not follow him they would in any case die of thirst." Angad, catch my tail", he said firmly "and the others will follow." Chanting Ram's name to give them courage the monkeys led by Hanuman descended into the shaft.

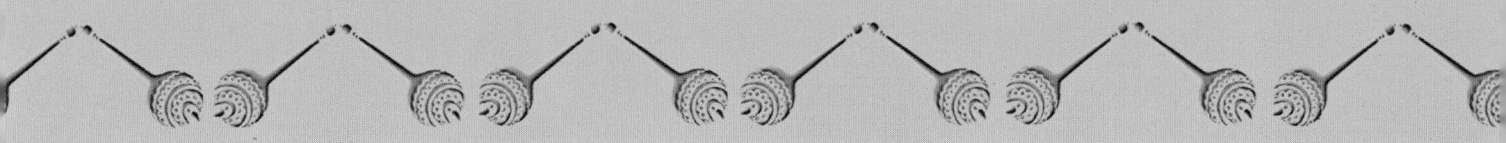

As they proceeded, the shaft became darker and more narrow. Soon, the going became difficult. But Hanuman kept going, and the others followed, somehow. There seemed to be no end to the shaft. They had been going quite a long time. Was it hours or days or weeks? None knew; in that darkness and stillness one could not keep count of time. By and by, the monkeys lost all their senses. But they hung on to Hanuman's tail.

At long last, the light in the shaft increased rapidly, and the air became cooler. Soon, Hanuman saw a large expanse of water, about a mile away. Hanuman held his breath for a moment, closed his eyes, cried out Ram's name and leaped forward and down... down... down they went; and plop; into the water the monkeys fell. Joyously they drunk the cool water, splashed it lustily at one another.

When at last Hanuman came out of the water and sat drying himself in the sun he was startled by the appearance of a woman. Her whole being flittered like a golden statue.

But the angelic being looked distressed. "I hope I have not offended you in any way," said Hanuman. "I am Hanuman, a humble servant of Lord Ram. My mission is to find Sita."

The woman's face lit up when she heard Ram's name. "This is my lucky day; she remarked." She then told Hanuman all about herself.

"I am Swayamprabha, an Apsara, cursed to be born on earth and

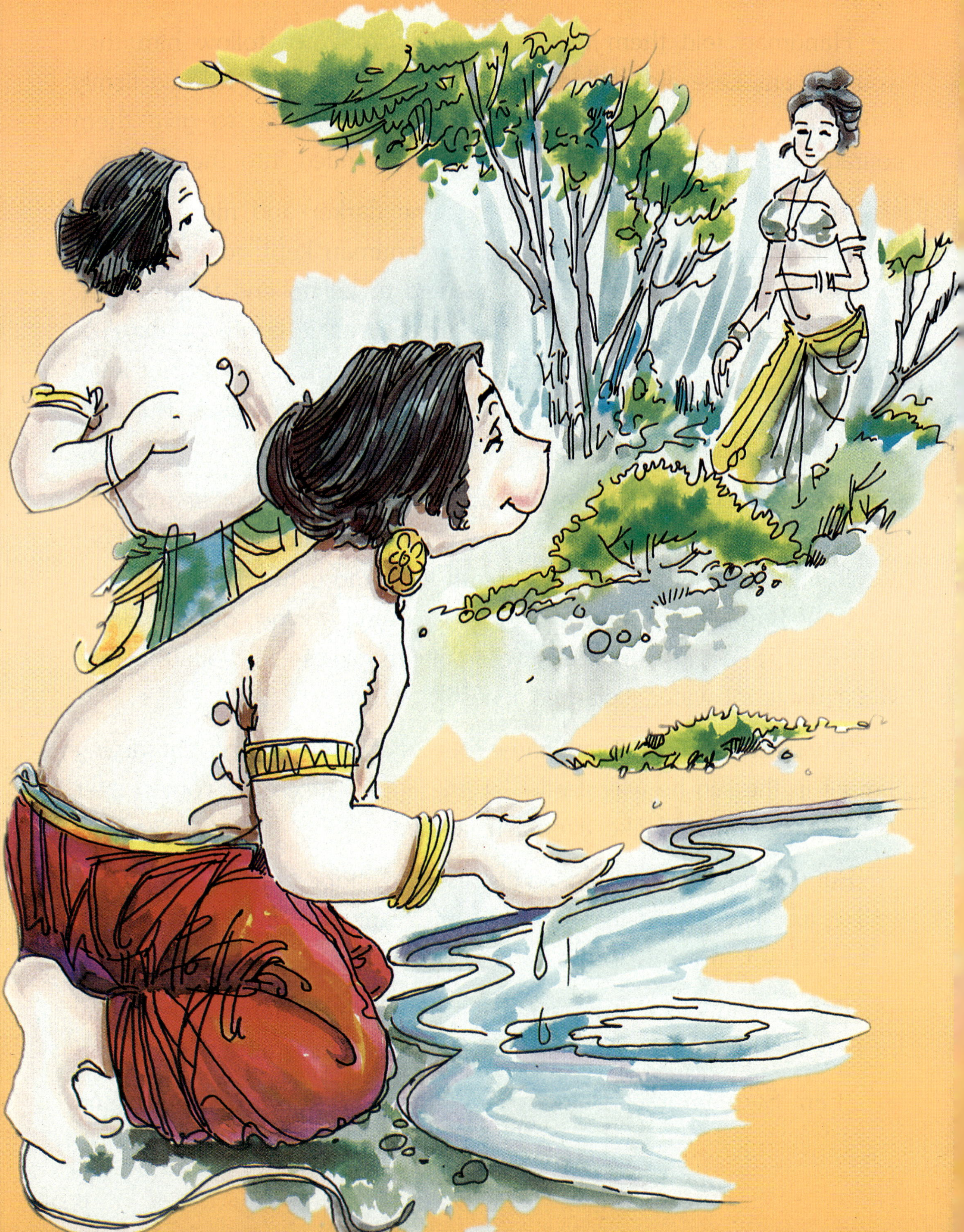

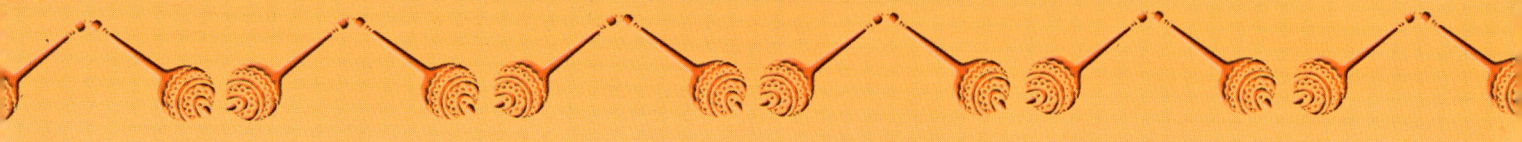

look after this valley till I get a glimpse of Ram. Thank you for telling me where the Lord is. I will go to him immediately. No, no; I must first entertain you and your friends."

Swayamprabha clapped her hands. A hundred lovely maidens came in bearing plates filled with roots, fruits, cooked dishes, honey and *sherbets*.

When her guests were restored to good spirits, Swayamprabha said, "Now, my dears, I must be off to Ram, and you to Sita. You have a very long way still to go. It will take you months to cover it on your feet. I will transport you across the land in a minute. Just close your eyes tight!"

Hanuman and his companions closed their eyes.

News About Sita

Opening their eyes, Hanuman and his comrades looked around in surprise. Blue water lay on one side of them, stretching as far as eye could reach; on the other side was a rocky hill. They were lying on a broad and long strip of sand.

Hanuman then saw a monstrous eagle looking at them through large and ferocious eyes. But Hanuman knew no fear. He stepped up to the creature and asked it, "Who are you? Why do you look at us so cruelly?"

The eagle replied, in a feeble voice: "I am Sampati. I am in great pain. I am dying of hunger and thirst. I cannot fetch food and drink, because I am wingless. My son used to bring me things here. He abandoned me some days ago, and I am suffering. Will you kindly give me a little food and drink?"

Hanuman at once leaped off and disappeared among the trees behind the wall of rocks. He returned within minutes, and placed before the aged bird a leaf with fruits and honey.

Sampati satisfied his hunger and thirst, and then asked, "May I know who has so kindly saved me from a miserable death, and what brings him here?"

Hanuman told the eagle about himself and his mission. Sampati heard him attentively and then said, "It must have been four or five, or even ten months ago. I saw a huge demon going southward flying in a chariot. That must have been Ravan. There was a woman in the chariot, crying aloud, Ram, Ram,". That was Sita, obviously. Without wings, I could not do anything to help Sita. Let me see if I can help you now. Thank God, I have my sight."

Sampati faced south, and looked intently for some minutes. Then he said, "I see the blue waters for five hundred miles. Beyond, lies a city on hills. That must be Lanka. Now I see the royal palace, and Ravan with ten heads and twenty hands is sitting proudly on his throne. And there, under a tree in Ashokavana, is a woman, wearing a soiled *sari* and crying. That must be Sita."

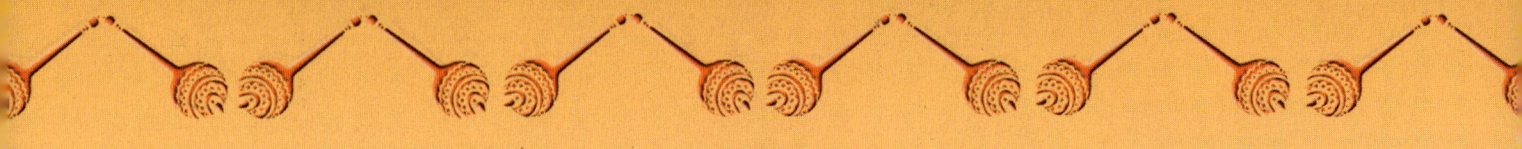

As Sampati spoke, a strange thing happened. Wings grew up gradually on his sides. By the time he concluded, they had become large enough to match his body. Hanuman and his companions were struck with wonder. Sampati became aware of his wings when he stopped speaking. Filled with incredible joy, he cried out; "Glory to Sita; Glory to Ram; Glory to Sita-Ram; Hanuman; I am sure you will go to Lanka and see Sita. Good luck to you and your companions."

The aged bird rose up into the air, and moved northward.

The Mighty Leap

The monkeys were appalled; Sampati had said that Lanka lay five hundred miles away across the sea. Who could even think of going there! They sat mournfully thinking that after all the trouble, they had failed. "What", exclaimed Jambavan, the grand old member of the party suddenly. "Did you not hear what Sampati said last? Hanuman is going to leap off to Lanka, and see Sita." "Of course we cannot take that seriously," exclaimed Hanuman. Now Jambavan decided to remind Hanuman of the tremendous powers he had received as gifts from the gods and how he was made to forget them as a result of a curse.

As Jambavan proceeded with his narration, Hanuman grew in size and splendour. Soon, he stood like a pillar of gold supporting the sky. His face shone like a globe of smokeless fire. He whirled his long bright tail around, and roared mightily, "I am the son of the Wind god; I am as powerful as my divine Father; I am Lord Ram's humblest servant; I can do anything in his service; I will cross the sea and visit Sita in Lanka, and return in perfect safety."

Hanuman roared once more, beat the air with his long and powerful arms, and leaped on to Mount Mahendra near the coast. He stood still on the crest for a moment, closed his eyes and meditated on Ram.

Then he pushed at the mountain side with his legs, stretched his arms and swept forth into the bright morning air.

Mount Mahendra shook to its foundation. The trees on it trembled for a long time, and scattered their fruits and flowers far and wide. The beasts and birds fled helter-skelter filling the air with fearful cries.

Jambavan, Angad and the other monkeys stood with eyes and mouths wide open in wonder, watching Hanuman's glorious take-off.

Lanka at Last

When Hanuman had travelled about two hundred miles, there stood Surasa, a gigantic she-demon with her cave-like mouth wide open. "Enter my mouth and satisfy my hunger; come on"; she said.

Hanuman said, sweetly, "I will enter if you open your mouth a bit more, please." The proud woman enlarged her mouth. Hanuman also enlarged his body, and said, "A little more". In this way, Hanuman went on growing bigger and entreating Surasa to open her mouth wider. After a time, when the demoness' mouth was gaping a hundred times larger than its real size, Hanuman suddenly reduced himself and became quite tiny and entered it and came out through her nose. Then bowing most respectfully he flew off, leaving Surasa gaping in wonder.

There was still a couple of hours to sun-set when Hanuman had covered the five hundred miles of water and alighted on Trikoota Hill on Lanka's North coast. From there he had a good view of the city close by. He was impressed by the size, grandeur and beauty of Lanka.

As soon as the sun set, Hanuman left the Hill and walked to the main gate of the city wall. A fully armed she-demon stood guard there. She refused to let him in. Hanuman tapped her chin lightly with his left palm, and she collapsed to the ground, and said, "Lord Brahma told me that one day, Lord Ram's messenger would come here and hit me down and then I was to leave my post and return to heaven." She told Hanuman, "You must be Hanuman. Enter Lanka, brave one, and may you succeed in your mission." So saying she disappeared.

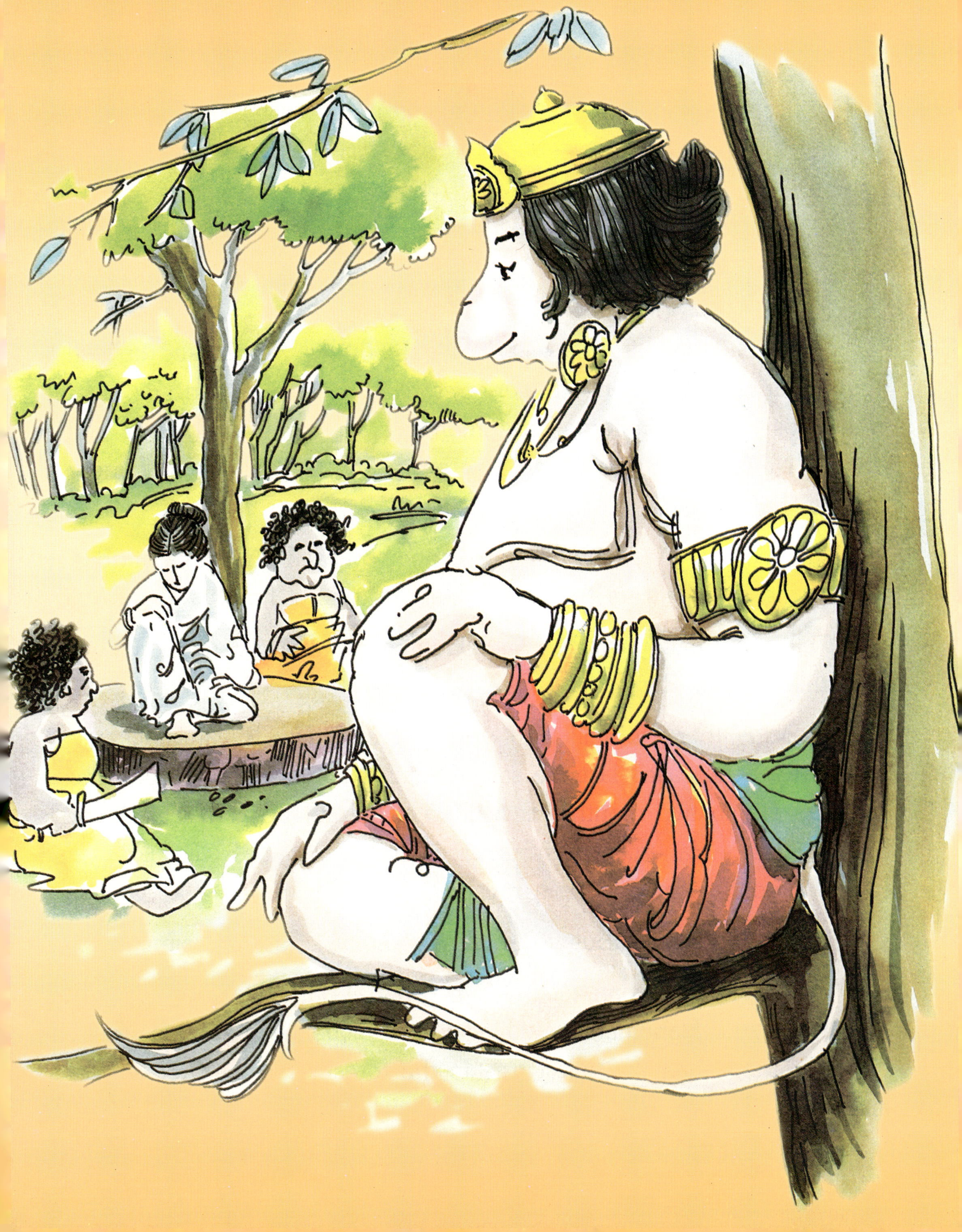

Sita Consoled

Sita looked at the ring with joy and wonder. She picked up and gently placed it to her heart, her eyes filled with tears and she burst with sobs. After sometime, she managed to compose herself and asked, "Now tell me messenger, how he is, and his wonderful younger brother Lakshman".

Hanuman described the miserable condition of the Ayodhya princes, and of the great efforts they were making to find her.

"Tell me about yourself," said Hanuman, after he had told her everything about Ram.

"What is there to tell! You see my condition. Ravan visits me often. When he called last, he said that, if I do not agree to become his wife, within two months, he will have me cut up and cooked for his breakfast". Hanuman was outraged, and declared "I will take you to the Lord, this moment, on my back."

Sita smiled sadly. "But you are quite small". She exclaimed.

"Oh," said Hanuman, "but I can grow as large as the occasion demands." And Hanuman grew bigger, and bigger, and still bigger, till he stood taller than the tallest tree in the forest while Sita looked on amazed.

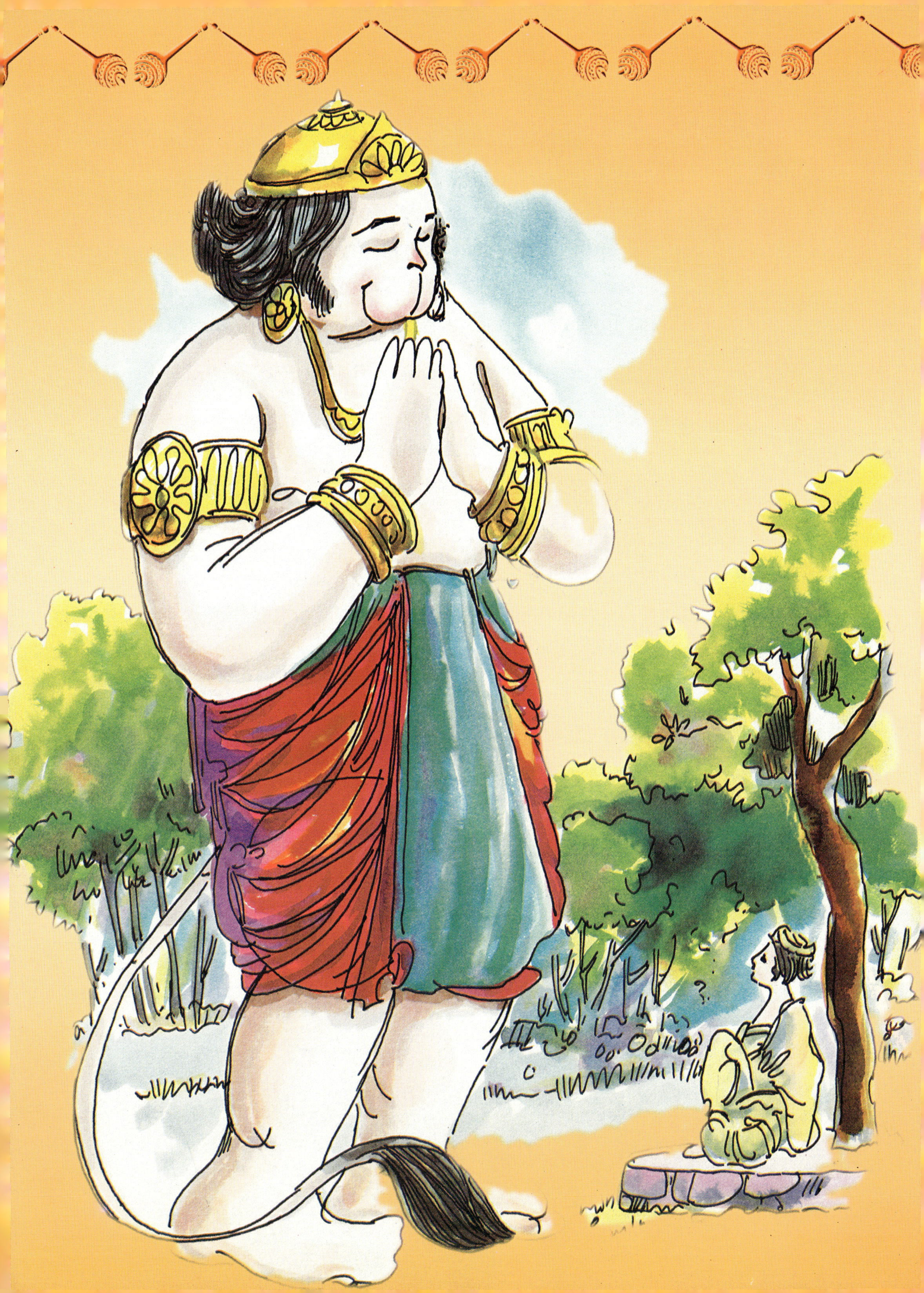

"Stop," she cried out, when Hanuman looked down at her from far above. "I am satisfied about your size but, it will not be proper for me to go to Ram on your back. Ravan took me away from him by cheatery. It is necessary, to let the world know of Ram's might, and his love for me. That can happen only when he himself comes here, chastises Ravan and takes me back openly. Don't you agree with me."

Hanuman had to agree that Sita was right, so he promised instead to rush back and return with Ram and the rest of the monkeys. "He will punish the demon king and take you back," said Hanuman. "Now kindly give me some token of yours to carry to the Lord." Sita gave Hanuman her diamond studded tiara, the only jewel she had with her.

Hanuman touched Sita's feet, and left.

Captured

Hanuman was in a jolly mood. He uprooted the plants and trees in the forest and threw them at the demonesses, scaring them away. The demonesses complained to Ravan. Ravan sent a hundred men to catch the monkey. Hanuman killed all of them with a tree. The demonesses ran to Ravan again.

This time, the demon king ordered five of his army captains to bring the mischievous monkey to him. When they arrived, Hanuman was sitting on a platform in the grove. A colossal iron club lay there, weighing a hundred tons. Ravan lifted it up sometimes with great difficulty, to exercise his limbs. Hanuman kicked up the club as it was a tiny toy, and, whirling it over his head, brought the club down on them with such force that all the five were at once crushed to pulp.

Hearing this Ravan told his younger son Aksha, to drive away the powerful animal. Aksha was a brave and trained warrior. He placed his men around Hanuman, while he shot arrows continuously. Soon, Hanuman was so well covered with darts that he looked like a large porcupine. Aksha and his men thought he was dead, and approached him. Hanuman jerked his body suddenly and violently. The arrows on his coat of hair flew off and hit Aksha's men with such force that they

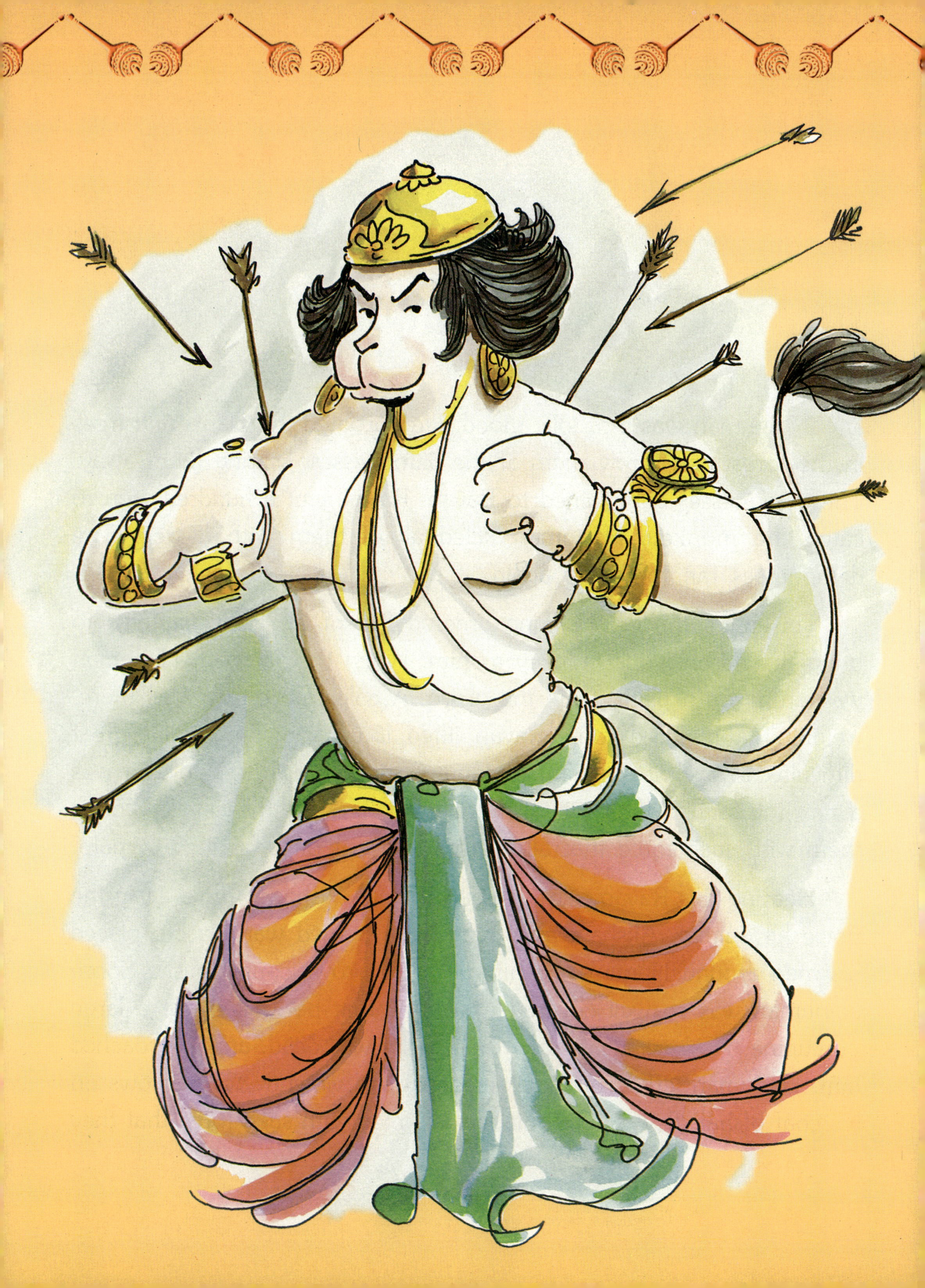

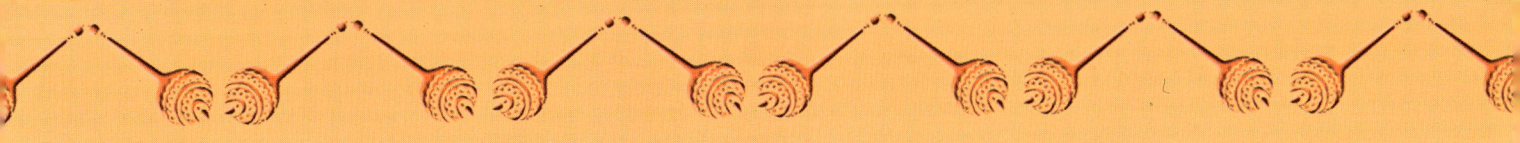

all died immediately. Aksha himself tried to escape, but Hanuman caught him by his legs and beat him against the hard floor of the platform thereby killing the demon prince.

News of Aksha's death saddened Ravan. But, his elder son, Meghnad also called Indrajit, proceeded against Hanuman. Indrajit fought against Hanuman with sword, lance, spear and arrows. All the trees which Hanuman hurled against Indrajit proved useless; Indrajit cut them into bits with arrows. Hanuman then began to use his bare arms, leaping on the prince and fisting him mercilessly.

At last, Indrajit discharged the Brahmastra, his most powerful weapon. Lord Brahma had told Hanuman not to show any resistance to this weapon, but submit to it meekly for an hour after which it would leave him unharmed. Hanuman remembered this in time, and let himself be hit and then fell to the ground.

Finding Hanuman motionless, Indrajit had him bound up by his followers and carried in a procession through the main streets of Lanka. And the people crowded the streets jostling each other to see the curious spectacle.

Warning to Ravan

It took an hour for the procession to reach king Ravan's palace and by then the effect of the Brahmastra had worn off; so by the time Hanuman was taken before Ravan's throne he had begun to feel quite cheerful.

The king of Lanka sat on his glittering throne decked in all his royal splendour. He looked awesome when he shook his ten bejewelled heads in anger. His twenty eyes showed anger and disgust as he beheld Hanuman. But the monkey looked unconcerned.

He was busy making a seat for himself by coiling his tail round and round below his bottom. He made his tail grow longer and longer so that his seat grew higher and higher.

By now every one had stopped talking and were watching the monkey in utter amazement.

Hanuman stopped rising only when his seat was a little higher than Ravan's. He then looked at the king and began speaking in a loud clear voice.

"Oh great king you are a direct descendant of Lord Brahma. You have studied the Vedas and all the ancient scriptures, you have meditated

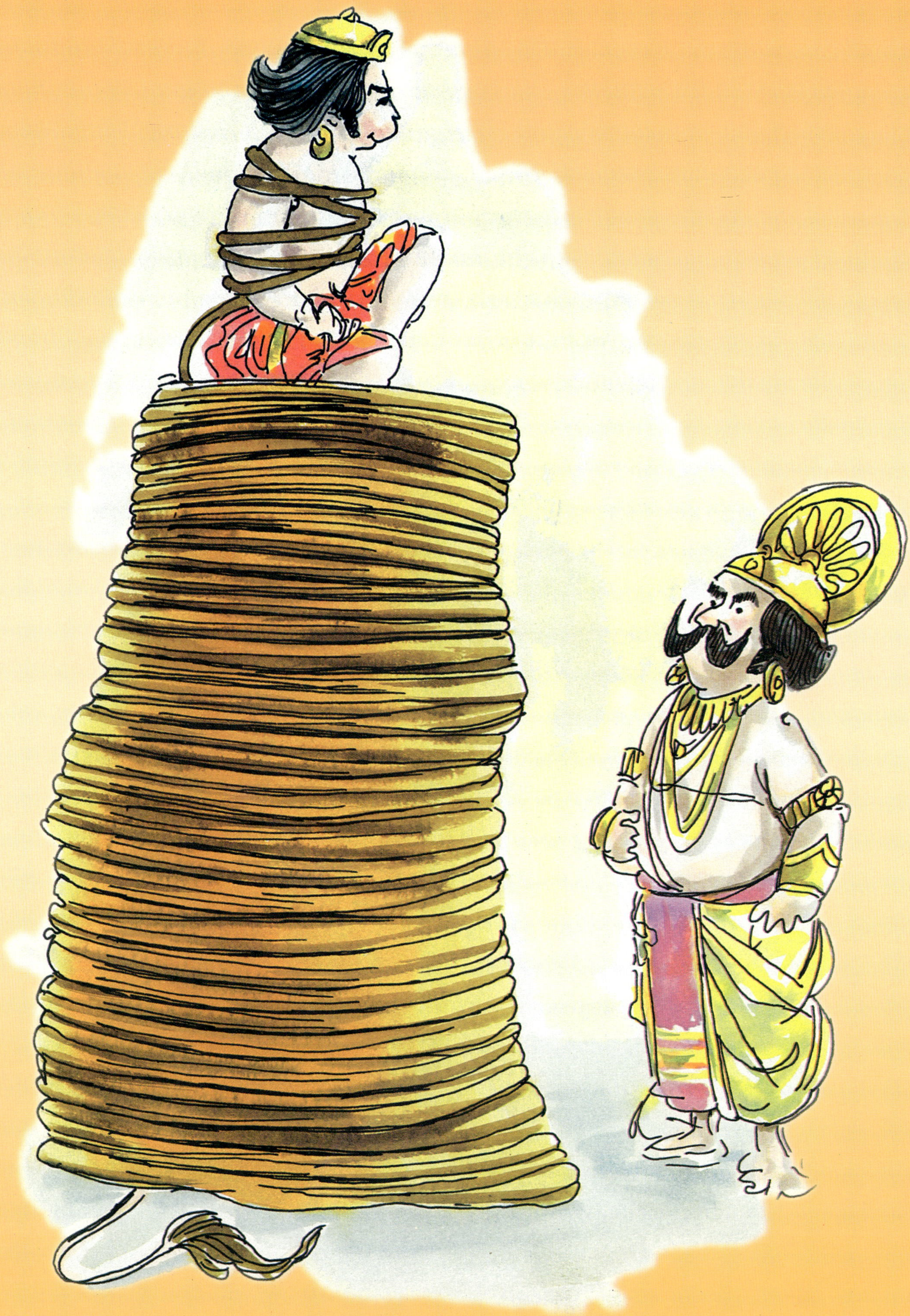

for years. You know what is right and what is wrong, and yet you have committed the unforgiveable sin and crime of stealing another man's wife. You have stolen Sita, the lawfully wedded wife of Ram, the prince of Ayodhya. But so great is my Lord that even now if you return Sita and beg for his mercy he will forgive you, if you don't, the consequences will be terrible. The mighty Ram with his equally powerful brother Lakshman will attack you along with Sugreev and twenty eight million monkeys, then nothing can save you or your kingdom."

Lanka on Fire

Hanuman's speech filled the king of Lanka with fury and he ordered that the monkey's tail should be set on fire to teach him a lesson. The guards saw that a little bit of his tail was stretching out from the bottom of the high coil over which he was sitting. The soldiers brought a piece of cloth and wound it round the tail, but before they could set it on fire, they found the tail had grown a little larger. So they rushed to get some more cloth to cover up the extra bit of tail. But even before they could finish; the tail grew a little more and the soldiers marched off to get more cloth. And every time Ravan's people wrapped up the uncovered bit of tail, it would grow a little more and off they would go to get more cloth.

Ravan who had been growing angrier and angrier as the tail grew longer and longer, at last he cried out, "That's enough; no need to wind any more cloth, just set fire to his tail". Immediately the soldiers set fire to his tail.

Ravan's courtiers laughed and clapped to see Hanuman's tail burn. But their glee was short lived, for Hanuman who had been sitting quietly all this time decided that it was time for some action. He gave one mighty heave and set himself free from the ropes that bound him.

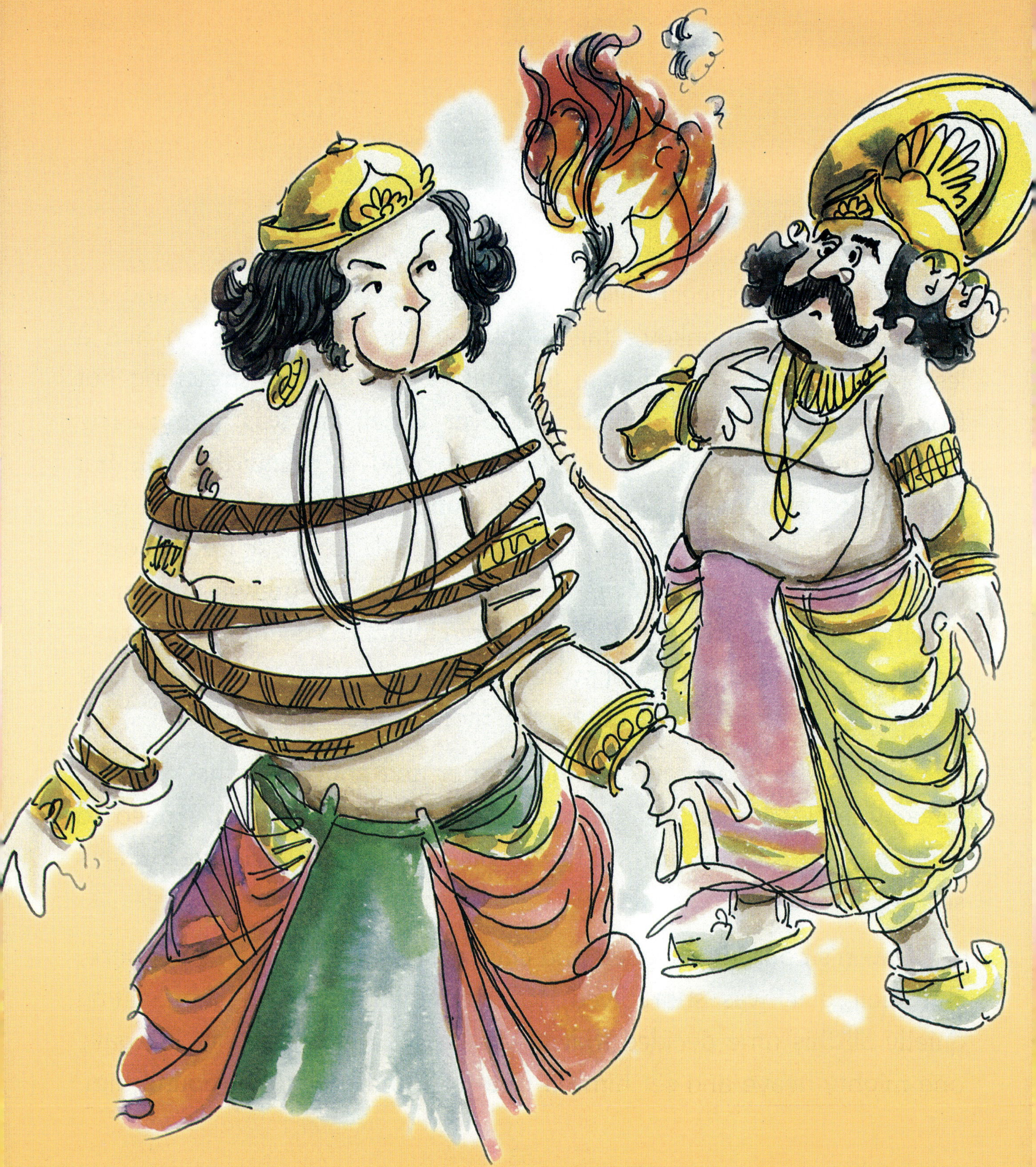

Then he began to grow bigger and bigger till his head almost touched the ceiling. He looked around menacingly and the demons fled in panic. Hanuman waved his tail around the king's face. Ravan was terrifed. He jumped down from his throne and ran for his dear life with his courtiers following him. "Glory to Ram," cried Hanuman and put his tail to the royal umbrella setting it ablaze. He then strolled through the palace, and using his tail as a burning torch, set everything on fire. Soon, the whole palace was burning like a huge bonfire.

Hanuman now jumped from one building to another setting them aflame. Within a short time, the entire city was burning sadly. By morning all that remained of the magnificent Lanka was smouldering fire, charred ruins and heaps of ash.

A Proud Moment

Hanuman looked at the smouldering Lanka and said to himself "My job is done. I must now return to my Lord". But first he had to find out about Sita. A sudden fear gripped his heart. Had she been harmed by the fire? But just then he heard a voice saying, "Put your mind at rest oh worthy messenger of Ram; Sita is safe. The fire has not touched her".

Heaving a sigh of relief Hanuman jumped to the top of the Trikoota Hill. Then with all his might he kicked against it and shot into the air northward, through the golden morning air.

A little later Hanuman landed on Mount Mahendra where his companions were anxiously waiting for him.

Angad, Jambavan and others ran up the side of the mountain to greet him. They carried him back on their shoulders and fed him the best of all the roots, fruits and honey they had collected.

While he ate, Hanuman told the others of his adventures in Lanka. After resting a while the party set off on their return journey.

When Hanuman and his party arrived on Prasravana Hill, they found Ram, Lakshman and Sugreev looking out for them eagerly.

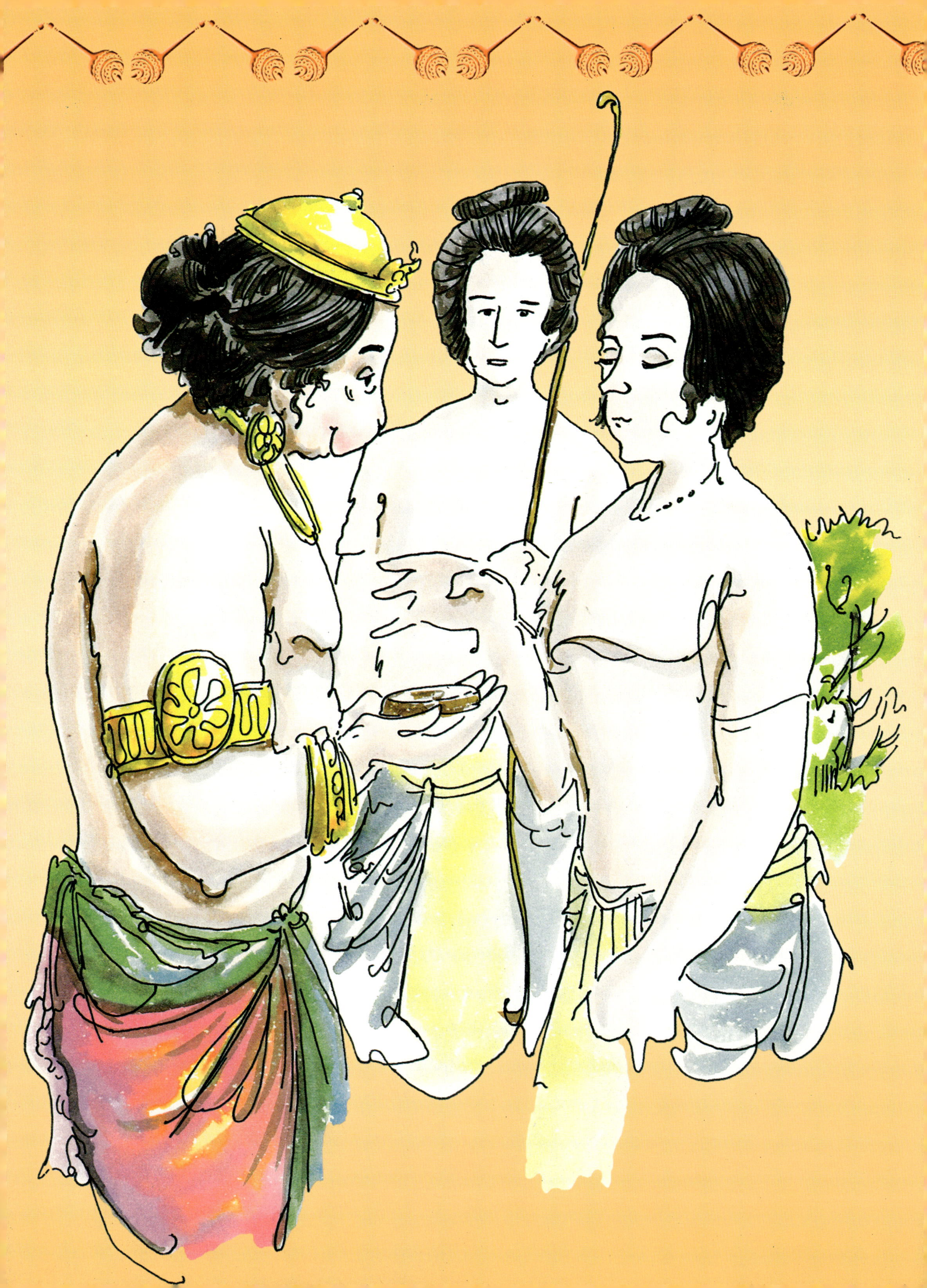

Hanuman hastened to untie Sita's *choodamani* from his crown, and placed it at Ram's feet.

Ram touched the jewel to his eyes and then secured it to his own crown, and heaved a deep sigh. He looked into Hanuman's red eyes. His own blue ones brimming with love and tenderness.

Then, Ram put his hand around Hanuman and embraced him like a long lost brother, he held the loyal monkey to his broad and noble breast. It was the proudest moment in Hanuman's life.

Bridge to Lanka

Angad, assisted by Jambavan, narrated all that Hanuman had done since they left the capital. Hanuman himself sat modestly behind Sugreev, and put his face forward only to say, "Yes, Lord," or "No, Lord" when Ram questioned him on some particular point.

After hearing his report and thinking for a few moments, Ram said to Sugreev: "Please arrange for our leaving for Lanka before the sun sets".

Sugreev arranged accordingly.

Sunset saw Ram, Lakshman, Sugreev and the monkey army marching out of Kishkinda, southward. The monkeys were eager to reach Lanka quickly. But it took them nearly a month to arrive at Dhanushkodi on the south coast.

All the enthusiasm with which the monkeys had marched for a whole month died when they reached the sea coast and saw the mighty ocean with its mountain-high waves. The poor creatures looked at one another in fear and dismay.

Ram, Lakshman and Sugreev were discussing what to do, when they heard a voice from above: "Glorious Prince of Ayodhya; I am

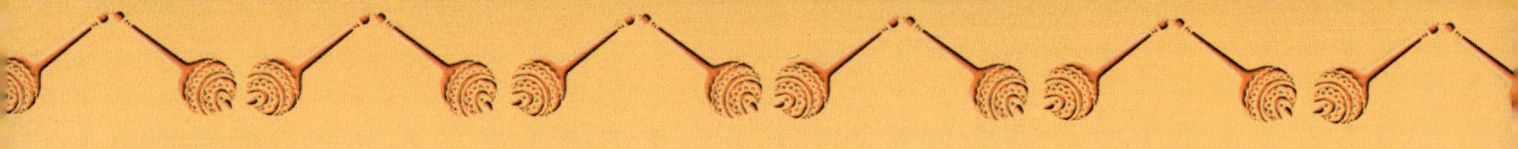

Vibhishan, Ravan's younger brother. Because I dared advise him to surrender Sita to you, Ravan kicked me away from Lanka. I have come seeking your protection". Looking up, they saw five figures in the air.

Ram asked the monkey leaders their opinion about his protecting Vibhishan. All were of the view that it would be wise to kill the five demons immediately.

When all of them had spoken, Hanuman asked meekly, "Am I allowed to speak, please?" Ram smiled and said, "Certainly, poor fellow; I suppose you are one of the leaders here".

Hanuman said, in a humble voice, "I saw Vibhishan in Ravan's court. From the talks among the ministers there I gathered that Vibhishan had always disapproved of Ravan's stealing Sita. When Ravan ordered that I be killed, Vibhishan told him not to do so. From all this, it seems to me that Vibhishan has come to you with good intentions. It will be right and good if you accept him as a friend."

On hearing Hanuman, Ram at once said, "Yes, friends, Hanuman is right, as always; I accept Hanuman's opinion and Vibhishan's friendship."

Vibhishan came down, and met Ram. Very soon, he endeared himself to the princes of Ayodhya, Sugreev and others.

On Vibhishan's advice, Ram prayed to Varuna, God of the seas. Varuna agreed to quieten the waters to Lanka to enable the monkeys construct a bridge over them. Nal undertook to build the bridge.

Sugreev ordered the monkeys to bring the stones, boulders, tree-trunks, leaves and other things required. The monkeys went to work,

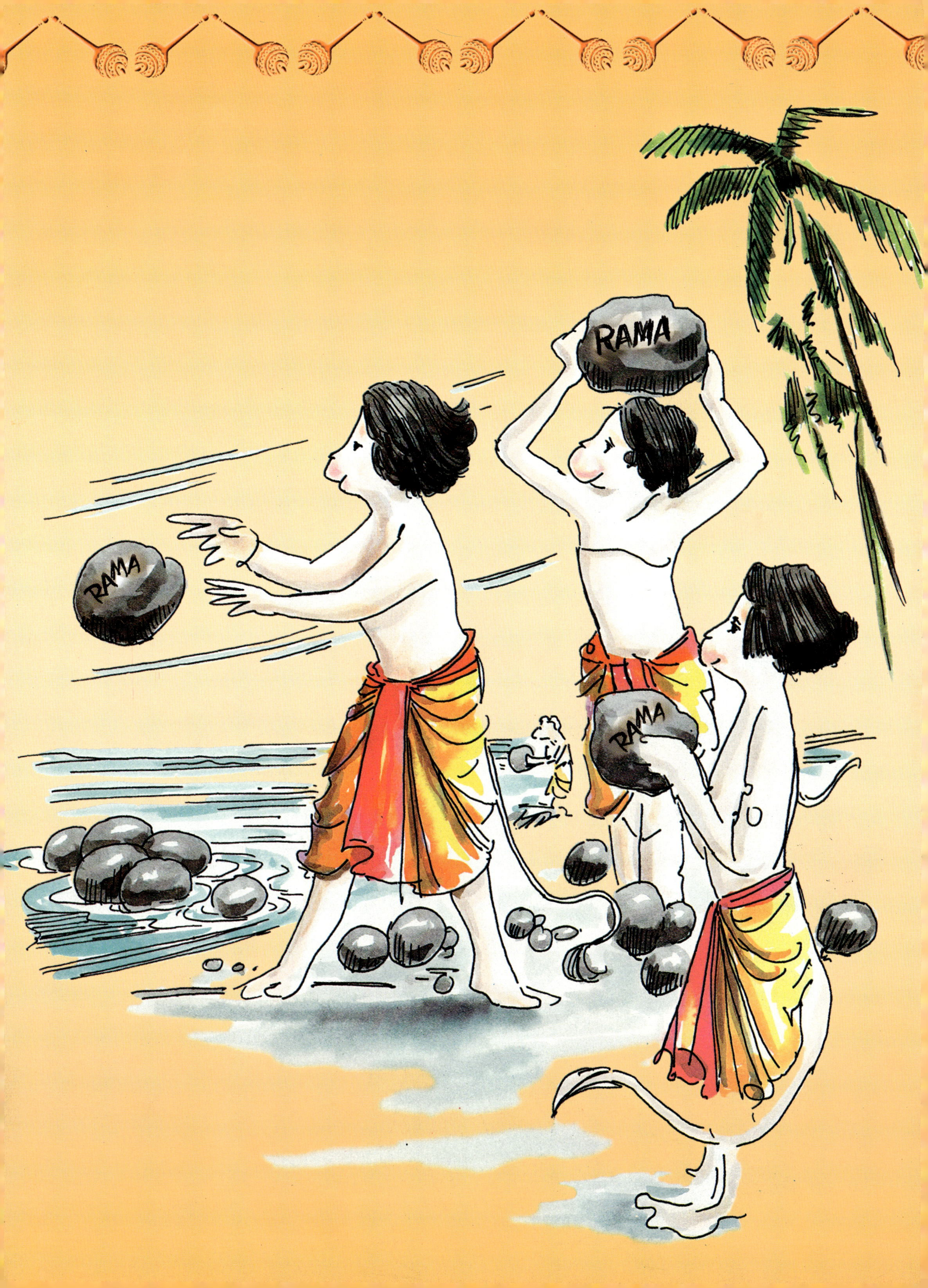
RAMA
RAMA
RAMA

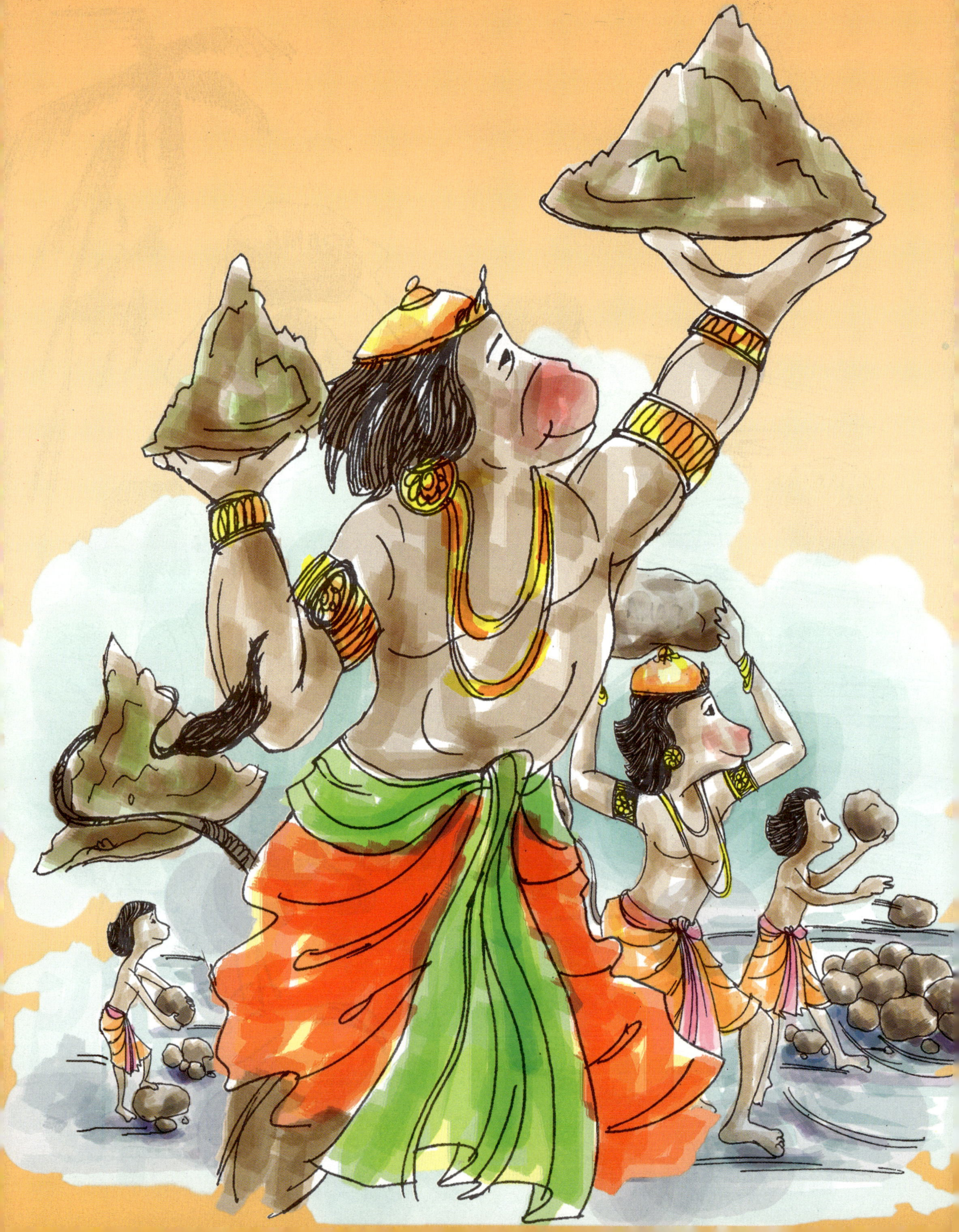

with great enthusiasm. Knowing no fatigue, Hanuman was able to transport more material than all the others put together. Ram's eyes filled with tears of love and admiration as he watched the Wind god's worthy son coming with a huge mountain dragged by his tail, three mountains played between his two hands and many mountains piled one upon another over his shoulders.

In the Battle-Field

The bridge was completed in five days.

Sugreev and his army marched over the bridge, behind Ram sitting over Hanuman's shoulders and Lakshman over Angad's, filling the air above the waters with shouts of "Glory to Ram". "Glory to Sita", and "Glory to Sita-Ram". After another five days, they arrived on Mount Subela on Lanka's North coast, sloping towards the city.

Ram's army started the attack on Lanka at dawn next day.

The proud and brave demons of Lanka, armed with all kinds of weapons and mounted on horses, elephants and chariots, defended the city very well indeed.

The monkeys were no less valorous. They could shoot themselves through the air, and had strong, sharp teeth and nails. They performed great deeds of valour and killed demons in hundreds and thousands.

Hanuman had plenty to do, and he did it well.

Jambumali, a great demon leader, struck him with a whip. Enraged, Hanuman leaped up to the demon's chariot and smashed it to bits with his bare fists. Dheemraksha, one of the important commanders in Ravan's army, destroyed many monkeys and gave much trouble to the

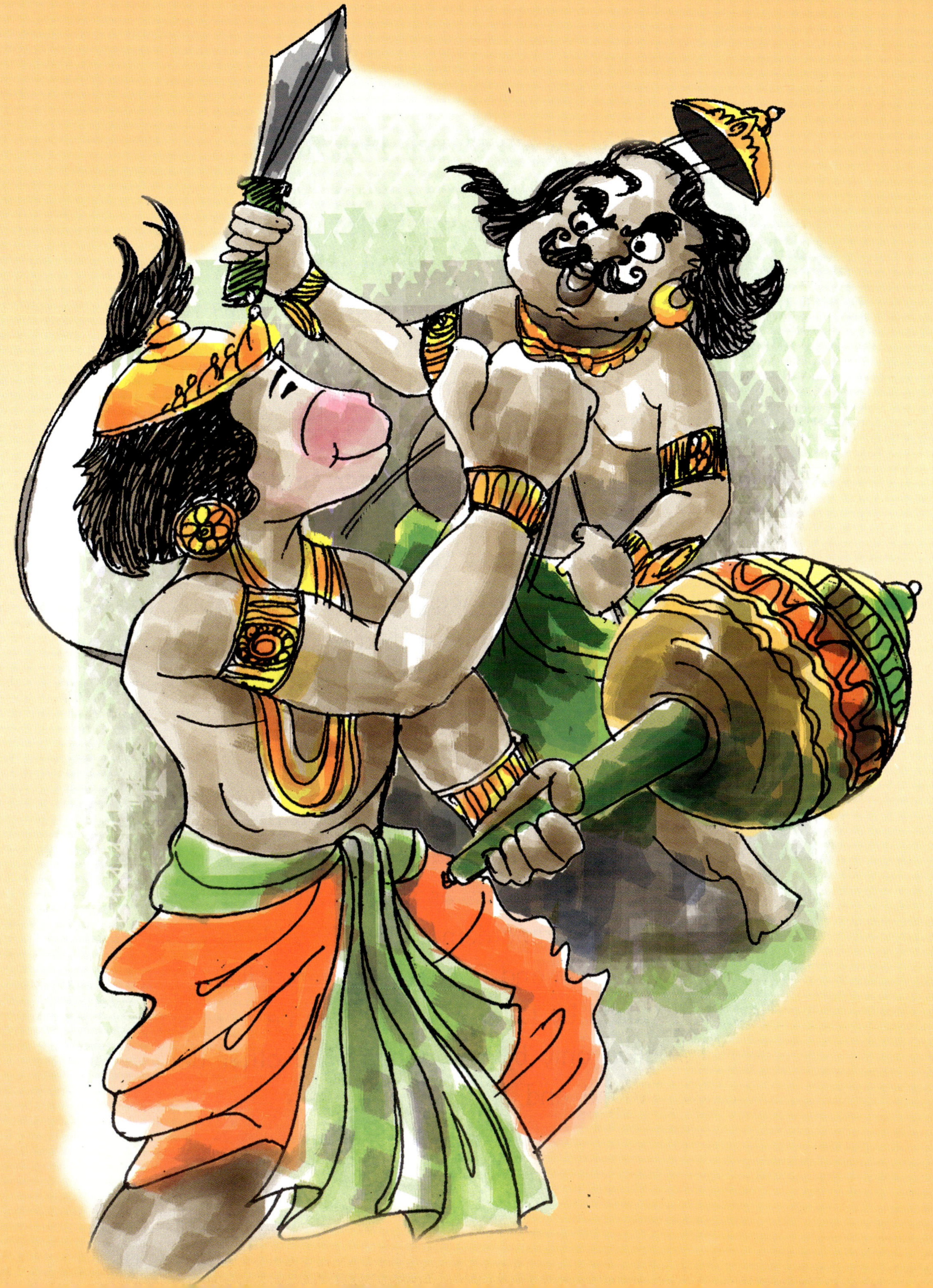

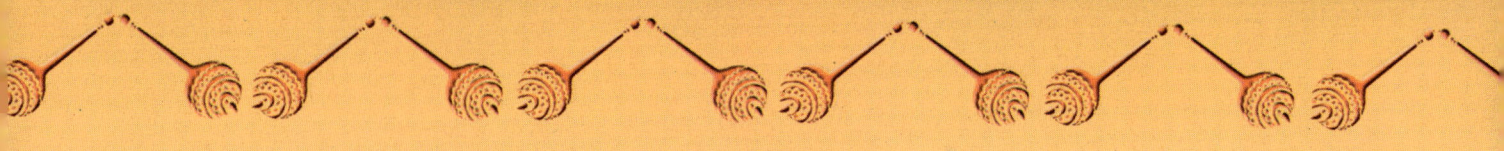

monkey leaders for a long time. It was Hanuman who killed him finally, with a huge tree.

On the second day, Ravan himself took the field in his chariot. Lakshman fought against him bravely for a long time. Finding the Prince of Ayodhya a tough one, Ravan hurled the *Shakti* given to him by Lord Brahma. Lakshman reeled at the hit and fell down unconscious. Hanuman was enraged and hit at Ravan's chin with his right fist. The demon king fainted off and was removed from the field of battle by his loyal charioteer. Hanuman carried unconscious Lakshman to a sheltered place.

Kumbhakarn, Ravan's colossal younger brother, came against the monkeys then. He swallowed thousands of monkeys and hurt double that number. When he saw Sugreev, he threw at the monkey king the *Shoola,* a huge iron pike weighing a hundred tons, presented to him by Brahma. Sugreev would have died on the spot if the weapon hit him. Hanuman leaped forward in time, caught the *Shoola,* and broke it into two over his knee-cap like a twig. After some time, Kumbhakarn himself was destroyed by Ram.

Thrishira, another great demon general, took the field next, along with Ravan's three sons, Devanthaka, Naranthaka and Atikaya, who were attended by five commanders as well as all Ravan's cousins and veterans in warfare. All the nine demons fought with some success for a time. Ultimately, Thrishira and Devanthaka were killed by Hanuman. Athikaya had to be killed by Lakshman, because he possessed a boon that he would be killed only by the prince. The other demons were killed by Sugreev, Angad and Neel.

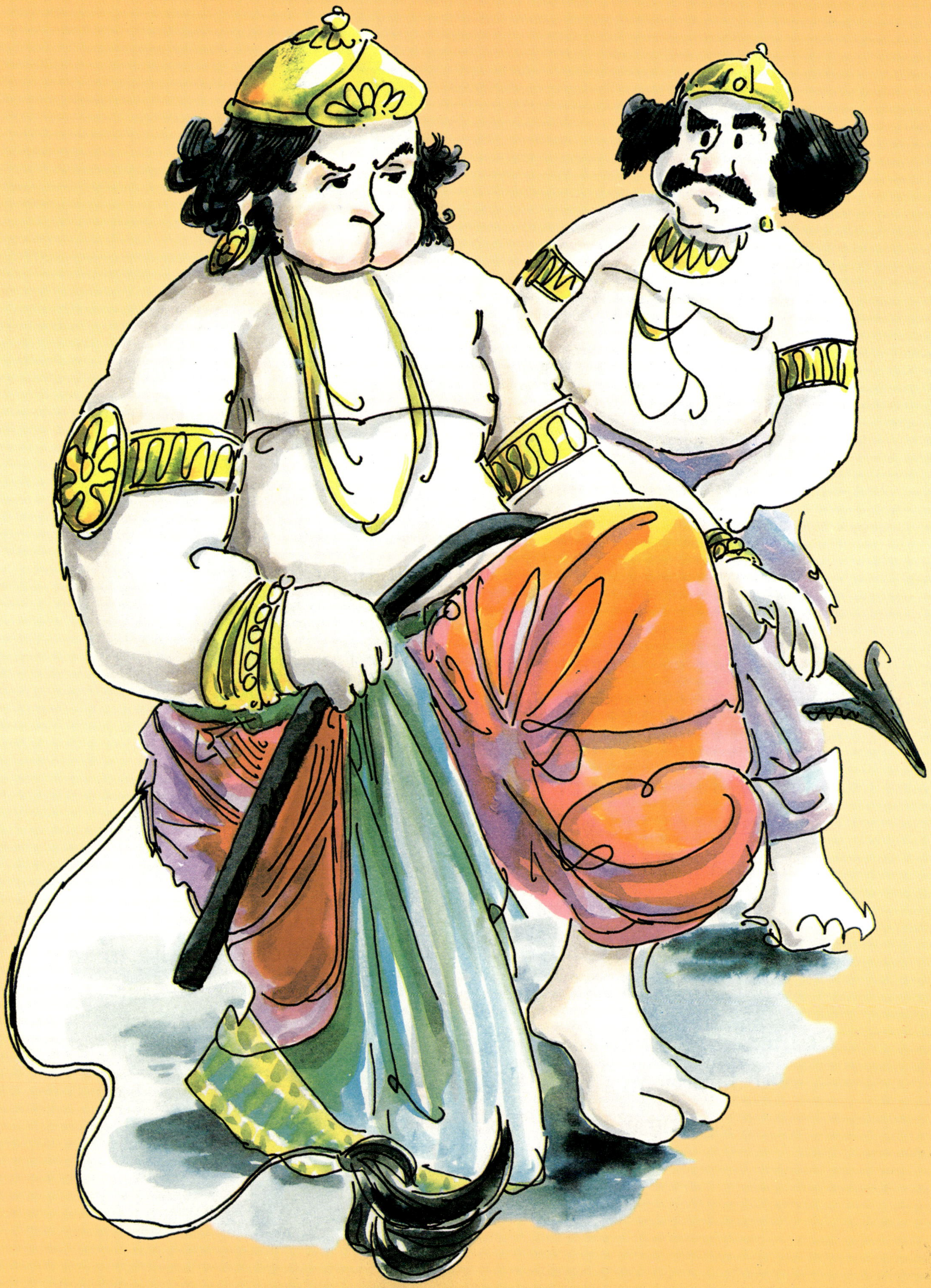

The Saddest Moment

The third day brought Indrajit who had the power to make himself invisible in the battle-field. He was able to do tremendous harm to the monkeys. He soon sent the entire army and the princes of Ayodhya into a deep swoon. Vibhishan, Jambavan and Hanuman were the only three to escape the demon prince's black magic. But they were in different parts of the field and each thought he was the only one to feel so.

Moving in sorrow with a torch in his hand, Vibhishan found Jambavan moaning in pain. Seeing the demon prince, the old monkey asked, "Is Hanuman safe?" Vibhishan asked Jambavan, "How is it that you don't enquire about the welfare of Ram, Lakshman, Sugreev, Angad or any of the others? Why are you so anxious about Hanuman?" "Friend," replied Jambavan, quietly, "I have a good reason. So long as Hanuman is alive and well, the princes of Ayodhya and the monkeys of Kishkinda are safe from death. All our hopes of life and well-being lie in that wonderful fellow Hanuman".

Just then, Hanuman himself came to the two from the darkness, and touched Jambavan's feet. "Come, come, my dear boy," said the aged monkey, sighing in relief, "You will please save the Ikswaku princes

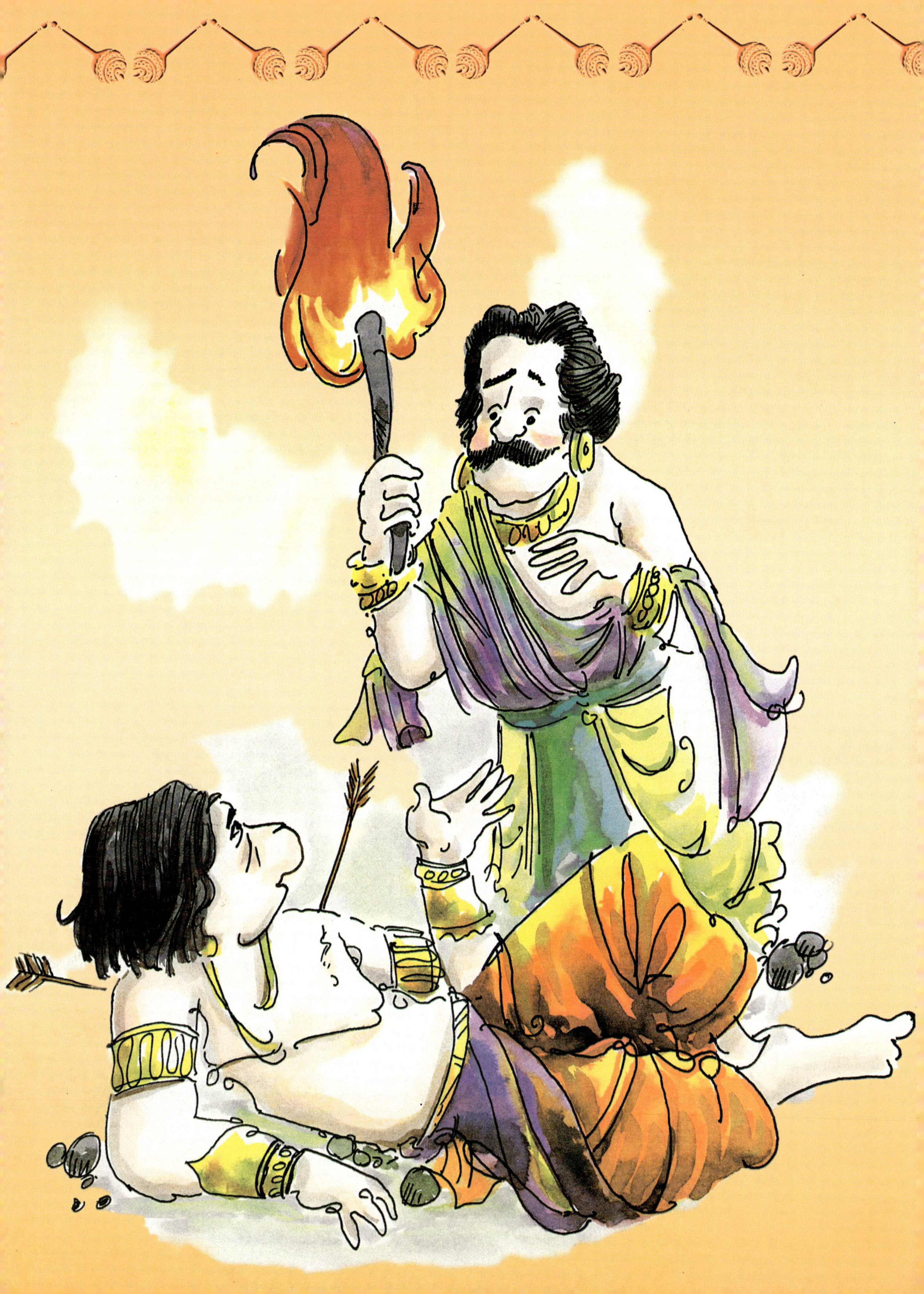

and the monkeys. You alone can do it. Kindly fly to the Himalayas. There, you will find Oshadhiprastha, a peak shining like beaten gold. Four herbs, Mritsanjeevini, Vishalyakarani, Savaranyakarani and Sandhanakarani, grow on it. Bring them to restore all to consciousness and good health."

No sooner had Jambavan finished speaking, than Hanuman was off through the air shouting, "Glory to Sita-Ram". Hanuman's shout and the tremors which his kick-off gave to Lanka city sent the demons into a miserable fright.

Passing over thousands of miles of varying scenery, Hanuman reached Oshadhiprastha in an hour. He saw no herb on it. Annoyed, he fisted the mountain with his right hand until it broke off its foundation and fell into his left palm. Holding Oshadhiprastha in the left palm, he beat the air with the right and flew back to Lanka. The four potent herbs mentioned by Jambavan appeared on the mountain crest as Hanuman neared the field of battle, and the princes of Ayodhya and the monkeys regained consciousness and became well.

Kumbh and Nikumbh, sons of the dead Kumbhakarn, came with a large force to resist the monkeys who now poured into the city with renewed vigour. Hanuman killed Nikumbh; Sugreev, Neel and Nal disposed of the others.

Indrajit now entered the field again. He had with him an image of Sita, made up so cleverly that everyone thought it was the princess in flesh and blood. Indrajit caught the fake Sita by her hair and cut off her head.

Hanuman gasped at the horrible sight. Then he fell down, closed his eyes and wept bitterly.

It was the saddest moment in Hanuman's life.

Death of Indrajit

After a while, Hanuman's grief turned into terrible wrath. He dilated himself into a colossal size with horrible features. Running like one possessed, he hurled at Indrajit rocks, boulders, dead bodies of monkeys and demons, dead and living horses and elephants, whatever came to his hands. The demons around Indrajit fell down dead and maimed in heaps. Hanuman then ran in a mad fury through the demon army, destroying everything which stood in his way.

Meantime, Indrajit had left the battle-field stealthily and gone to Nikumbhila, a hall in Lanka, where he had made preparations for performing a special *yajna* which would enable him to overcome all enemies and remain unharmed by them.

Vibhishan heard the clamour caused by Hanuman, and went to him with Ram and Lakshman. When Hanuman told them about Indrajit's killing Sita, Ram was horrified when he heard this, but Vibhishan assured him and his younger brother that the killing was only a magic performance to make the princes and the monkey leaders idle in sorrow and gain time to perform the *yajna*. He took Lakshman and a pick of monkey commanders with him and proceeded to Nikumbhila. Hanuman was at the head of the force.

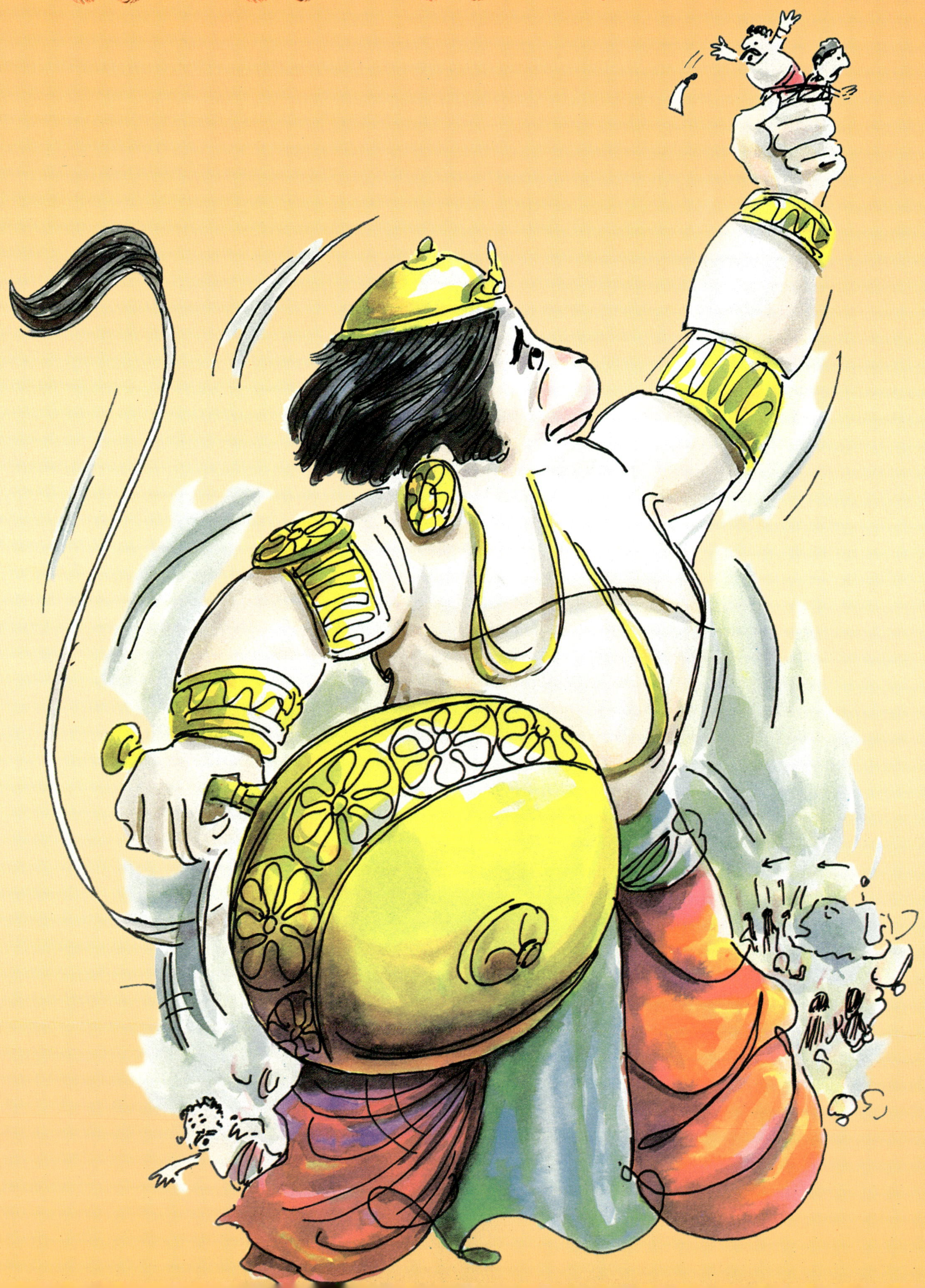

At Nikumbhila, Hanuman continued his work of destruction, and despatched Indrajit's assistants to their deaths in thousands. He also threw away the articles collected for the *yajna*. Indrajit had to give up the *mantra* recitation in which he was engaged, when his followers cried out in pain on being hurt by Hanuman. The prince of Lanka came against Hanuman, Vibhishn advised Lakshman to get on to Hanuman's shoulders and shoot his arrows at Indrajit. Lakshman took the advice. He killed Indrajit after a terrible battle.

Reunion of Sita and Ram

Ravan had to take field again. Anger and sorrow had made him determined to destroy Ram and Lakshman. He went straight towards the princes. He was able to hit Lakshman into unconsciousness with his *Shakti*. Hanuman had to leave for Oshdhiprastha again to bring the potent herbs.

This time the four herbs stood out on its crest and Hanuman had picked them and carried them to Lanka.

Lakshman and the monkey leaders were now more angry than ever before, and sacked Lanka mercilessly from all sides. Ravan had lost all his sons, brothers, cousins and most of his army commanders. For thousands of years he had always been victorious against all his opponents; now, in four days, he had met with so much sorrow and disappointment. He was naturally very sad. Still, he fought bravely and Ram had to exert his utmost against him. It was only after a long time of intense battle that he was able to kill the demon king.

Ram told Vibhishan to console the bereaved. When the religious ceremonies were over, he sent Lakshman to Lanka's royal palace and crowned Vibhishan as king of the demons.

Taking King Vibhishan's permission, Ram told Hanuman to bring

Sita to him. Hanuman did so, with immense pleasure. The union of Ram and Sita was another great moment in the loyal Hanuman's life.

Ram, Sita and Lakshman returned to Ayodhya with Vibhishan, Sugreev and all the monkeys, in the new demon king's air chariot. Ram was crowned king. There was a grand and sumptuous feast and other magnificent celebrations for many, many days.